Touching the Unreachable

MICHIGAN MONOGRAPH SERIES IN JAPANESE STUDIES

NUMBER 91

CENTER FOR JAPANESE STUDIES
UNIVERSITY OF MICHIGAN

Touching the Unreachable

Writing, Skinship, Modern Japan

Fusako Innami

University of Michigan Press
Ann Arbor

Copyright © 2021 by Fusako Innami
All rights reserved

For questions or permissions, please contact um.press.perms@umich.edu

Published in the United States of America by the
University of Michigan Press

Manufactured in the United States of America
Printed on acid-free paper

First published August 2021

A CIP catalog record for this book is available from the British Library.

Library of Congress Cataloging-in-Publication data has been applied for.

ISBN 978-0-472-07498-3 (hardcover: alk. paper)
ISBN 978-0-472-05498-5 (paper: alk. paper)
ISBN 978-0-472-12930-0 (e-book)

Contents

Digital materials related to this title can be found on the Fulcrum platform via the following citable URL: https://doi.org/10.3998/mpub.11747440

Acknowledgements

My work on touch arose through my life-long dialogues with practices.

My parents provided the seed for this project through their caring touch from the moment of my birth up to the present, and have never failed to offer support and encouragement for my journey. It was my mother who, as a piano teacher, first made me conscious of listening to things unexpressed through words. My interest in the body and the senses in general came via my early studies in dance and music. I would like to thank Tsumaki Ritsuko and Atsugi Bonjin, who early recommended that I read a range of thinkers to engage with the body, in particular Washida Kiyokazu and Maurice Merleau-Ponty, initiating my exposure to phenomenological thought. Akutsu Sachi also nurtured my awareness of how different kinds of touch with different parts of fingers with different pressures produce subtle differences of sound of piano. This book emerged from the question about touch in everyday life that I started to have when I was little. Now that I am an academic, my question has become the subject of my research.

The Department of Performance Studies at New York University was where I was exposed to performance theories. It was a psychoanalytic-friendly program, but Ann Pellegrini taught me that psychoanalytic theories have fundamentally emerged through practice; one cannot ignore practice to know theory. I am also indebted to Barbara Browning, André Lepecki, José Esteban Muñoz, and Richard Schechner, for their insights on performance theories during my Master's study in the US. I would like to thank the William Alanson White Institute in NYC, where I was first exposed to the clinical aspect of psychoanalytic psychotherapy. I am not settled yet on which school of thought I am willing to be trained in as a practitioner; I am hoping that such a day may come at some point in my life. However, having tried out self-reflexive writing with a focus on air pressure (unsaid pressure sensed through air, involving race, rank, age, gender, appearance, etc.), I am aware of various alternatives that offer the possibility of knowing oneself in relation to others beyond established therapies.

I would like to thank the supervisors of the doctoral study, Linda Flores of the University of Oxford and Patrick ffrench of King's College London, for their guidance, encouragement, and support. Beyond his inspirational expertise in French thought, I very much appreciated Patrick's supervision style to foster students' awareness as independent researchers. I especially enjoyed, while I was a DPhil student, the opportunity during the seminars to try out my ideas on the Japanese texts under analysis and various thoughts, looking at, say, Tanizaki and Barthes in the same breath. Linda is a brilliant teacher and open-minded mentor who allowed and encouraged my experiments. I am also indebted to Sho Konishi of Oxford who was at that time my college's senior tutor. I have always enjoyed chatting with Sho, on academic/career matters and much else. Quite simply, it is heartening to know that such academics exist.

I would also like thank those who have offered me critical insights and comments during the long process of writing this book. These include, during my doctoral study in the UK, Matthew Bell, Martin Crowley, Stephen Dodd, Stephen Horn, Ian Maclachlan, Jo Malt, and Gian-Piero Persiani; Tsuboi Hideto, who was my host or counterpart, as well as participants in Katsura seminars, at the International Research Center for Japanese Studies (Nichibunken) in Kyoto in Summer 2016, through the International Placement Scheme of the Arts and Humanities Research Council (AHRC), UK; Yuiko Asaba, Laurence Mann, Lucy North, Jonathan Service, Douglas Slaymaker, and Kerim Yasar for our conversations on topics on the body and the senses in the Japanese literature, culture, and translation; academic audiences at the University of Zurich, SOAS, Durham, and at the numerous conferences at which I gave related papers; my undergraduate and graduate students at Durham; and my academic friends who supported me especially at Oxford. Of all these wonderful people, Martin Crowley and Stephen Dodd deserve a special mention: their enthusiastic encouragement of my research and their warm "welcome" to academia at the viva voce meant so much to me.

I am indebted to the Iizuka Takeshi Scholarship Foundation, the Sasakawa Foundation, the British Association for Japanese Studies, and AHRC for their generous financial support. My deepest thanks also to my old colleagues at the Japan Foundation New York where I took a gap year. My work experience there outside academia helped me realize how important it was for me to engage with arts and culture, and also the ways in which I wished to do so.

I am also deeply indebted to my colleagues at Durham University where I completed this book. I would like to especially thank Sare Alicanri, Yael Almog, Adam Bronson, Amaleena Damlé, Abbie Garrington, Francisco-J. Hernández Adrián, John O'Brian, Zoë Roth, Marc Schachter, William Schaefer, Don Starr, Janet Stewart, Luke Sunderland, Katrin Wehling-Giorgi, and Thomas Wynn, for reading the drafts I produced, for giving me advice and suggestions, or being receptive interlocutors over a coffee, pint, or a glass of whisky. William and Luke read and reread my writing, with patience, thoughtfulness, and insight, offering constructive feedback. Glenn McGregor and Miyoko Yamashita-McGregor offered conviviality and stimulating company. I am grateful for the financial support that was made available by the School of Modern Languages and Cultures and the Faculty of Arts and Humanities at Durham University, including a year-long, institutional research leave. This was to work on my next project on the body and the senses, but it provided the time to give a final edit to this monograph, and I found it beneficial to have the chance to experience a self-reflexive move back and forth between this project on touch and the next one on the body and the senses.

I thank anonymous readers for their thoughtful feedback and Christopher Dreyer for editorial guidance and colleagues involved in publication process at the University of Michigan Press, and anonymous reviews from journals of *Contemporary Japan, Culture, Theory and Critique*, and *Asian Studies*, on earlier versions of chapters 1 and 4. I would like to acknowledge all the many people who have supported me in various ways in the completion of this book.

Finally, I want to thank my families. My Italian parents and Carlotta have given me longstanding love and support since my days in high school. My uncle Masaki and aunt Yukiko have been like a second Japanese family to me. I am grateful to my brother Takehito, and to my other elder sibling, unborn, who first made me start thinking about my body and life as something "given," not something I alone own. Due to my wanderings across borders, I have ended up having multiple families to all of whom I am close. Without you, I would have never thought about touch this much, still less completed an entire monograph on touch and human communication.

Notes on Citations and Names

For works originally published in Japanese, both the Japanese title and the English translation are provided for the first reference. Thereafter, I employ the translated title in English. Where no published translation is available, translations are my own. For the names of authors, East Asian names follow the East Asian convention (the family name followed by the given name) unless the texts were originally published in English or a European language.

Introduction

Literary Touch to Mediate the Senses

Touch as I conceive of it in this book is a site of an encounter in which one recognizes the fundamental unknowability of the other as well as of the self. This encounter occurs in a self-reflexive manner, thereby constantly renewing one's awareness of being. By "unknowability," I refer to the fact that any act of touch not only involves the direct contact of that moment but also is inevitably mediated by memories of previous experiences of touching, and the accumulation of sensations, all of which create an interstitial space between those in contact. Thus, touch always involves encountering the unreachability and unknowability of the entities involved. The writer who first awakened me to the mediatory properties, and the accumulative nature, of touch, which I had intuited but never verbally registered until then, was Yoshiyuki Junnosuke (1924–1994), whose presence in many ways underlies this book. In his 1969 novel *Anshitsu* [*The Dark Room*], Yoshiyuki has his narrator describe the relationship between the male protagonist, the middle-aged novelist Nakata, and his lover, Natsue, in the following way:

> She did, in fact, have a number of physical habits she'd picked up in her relationships with other men. Those lovers were always there, like a thin membrane [*maku*] between her body and mine. But in a sense, it was this that allowed our affair to continue ... Physically, then, we were linked; but her body alone wasn't enough to tie me to her.

> From around that time, the membrane between our bodies began to fulfill all kinds of functions.[1]

Stimulated by contact with the skin, repetitive touch over time forms a thin imaginary membrane for the protagonist that mediates the touch that occurs between bodies and affects them. By "mediates," I refer to both connecting with and interrupting the relation to the other, with touch as a medium to assemble material elements and practices. The act of touching the other is already and necessarily mediated through material elements, such as skin and objects, as well as immaterial elements, such as layers of previous contacts and memories: an imaginary membrane. It suggests that there may be some interstice that both connects and inhibits truly reaching the other—rendering the intended object as unreachable—and that forms reflexive consciousness of the self.

It was with such questions of mediated touch in mind, a wish to enquire into the role that sense experience plays in the transitive relations between the perceiver and the world, and also how writing may or may not succeed in translating sensory elements that are thought of as irreducible to language, that I started my work on touch, hoping to contribute to discussions around the body, embodiment, and translation. In particular, when touch is thought as a continuous process developed throughout one's life, I wanted to inquire into the ways of rendering the gap between childhood and adulthood experience of touch. Despite the frequently noted bonds between parents and children in Japan, they do not maintain the same sort of skin-based communication throughout life. There is a transitional period between familial touch and romantic touch where intimate friendship comes to the fore: to recognize one's sexuality.

In this book I argue that writing, in its inevitable physical and temporal distance both from the intended object within the story and indeed the reader, shapes a particular aesthetics of touch that involves attempting to touch that which is unreachable, in an endeavour that is essentially an act of translation of the felt experience into the verbalized. Yoshiyuki is a writer

---

1. Yoshiyuki Junnosuke, *The Dark Room*, trans. John Bester (New York: Kōdansha International, 1979), 144; "Anshitsu," in *Yoshiyuki Junnosuke Zenshū* [*The Complete Works of Yoshiyuki Junnosuke*], vol. 7 (Tokyo: Shinchōsha, 1998), 309–310. Hereafter abbreviated as *YJZ*. Originally published in twelve installments in the journal *Gunzō* in 1969, and published as a book *Anshitsu* in 1970 by Kōdansha.

who illuminates the uncertainties of contact through the acute attention that he pays to the materiality and function of surfaces, to perceptions, and to traces of contact from the past, and his attention to the "weight" of the body. This is in contradistinction to two earlier writers, Kawabata Yasunari (1899–1972) and Tanizaki Jun'ichirō (1886–1965), who concentrated more on the delay, or deferral, of touch. All three of these male writers, together with another, a female writer, Matsuura Rieko (1958–) who pays particular attention to the sensuality arising from the skin, will be discussed in the course of this book. My intention is to explore literary touch as a mode of shaping relationships to the other, transcending the distance that separates us—between self, other, and texts. Yoshiyuki depicts subtle physiological changes and the characters' interpretation and verbalization of those experiences, which are then projected onto figures with whom the characters construct a relationality; relationality here is understood as the state of existing through self-other configurations.[2] Touch is a way to invoke others as well as oneself, and in such a way as to expect some response in reaching the other, thinking of another's mind, and imagining another's experience. None of these things is ever entirely reachable, as the self will always remain unlimitedly unknowable.

The dynamic interplay involved in touch as explored by Yoshiyuki demonstrates the incompletely attainable amidst conflicting forces, the desire to possess and the unwillingness to be taken hold of in that space, mediatedness and immediacy, hesitation and the fantasy of touch. Writing about touch necessarily requires further temporal and spatial journeys to be made between feeling sensations through the body and the verbalization of them through language. The written and delayed format of pre-verbal sensations, especially those appearing in literary texts (often involving statements that are not-yet-uttered by characters yet written by authors), always involves an impossibility of reaching the object: touching the other through language without the involvement of actual physical touch. Touch as I examine it in this book comprises a quest for relationship-building, the desire to make contact with the other, a quest that inevitably holds the possibility of disappointment. And the result of the quest is that one's

---

2. That is what, according to Stephen A. Mitchell, purely intrapsychic psychoanalysis has left bracketed for decades. Stephen A. Mitchell, *Relationality: From Attachment to Intersubjectivity* (New York: Psychology Press, 2014), x.

body and self-consciousness is inevitably constructed reflexively, through contact with the world and the consciousness of others.

"Touch," as I use it here, includes its displacement in the body and time. In Maurice Merleau-Ponty's understanding, bodily sensations and movements retained as kinaesthetic residues begin to awaken virtual movements, forming one's intentionality for the next movement.[3] In Yoshiyuki's fiction, things accumulated in the body narrate its experience even without a verbal utterance. The memory of past touch affects current and future touch, and it is through the contact with and relation to others that one becomes aware of oneself. Merleau-Ponty's concept of "flesh," which connects the relationship between the body and the world and which occurs due to encroachment of those inseparable entities, suggests that a body has a mutual relationship with the world, with further proximity between the tangible and the touching and the tangible and the visible.[4] The touch I write about involves a point where the individuals become aware of themselves in relation to the other, momentarily experiencing, potentially, the duality of being both subject and object, and of different sense modalities. At the same time, embodied and lived experiences shape the mind and transform consciousness. Thomas J. Csordas writes of embodiment as "an indeterminate methodological field defined by perceptual experience and mode of presence and engagement in the world."[5] Touch continuously reconstructs one's sense of the self and its relation to the world. Touch challenges one's possibilities for reaching the other and forming a relationality across the bodily frontier.

---

3. Maurice Merleau-Ponty, *Phenomenology of Perception*, trans. Donald A. Landes (Abingdon: Oxon; and New York: Routledge, 2014), 110–111, 113. Originally published as *Phénoménologie de la perception* in 1945 by Éditions Gallimard.
4. Maurice Merleau-Ponty, *The Visible and the Invisible*, trans. Alphonso Lingis (Evanston, IL: Northwestern University Press, 1968, 133–143); Merleau-Ponty, *Signs*, trans. Richard C. McCleary (Evanston, IL: Northwestern University Press, 1964), 170. Originally published in 1964 as *Le Visible et l'invisible* and 1960 as *Signes* by Gallimard.
5. Thomas J. Csordas, "Introduction," in *Embodiment and Experience: The Existential Ground of Culture and Self*, Thomas J. Csordas, ed. (Cambridge: Cambridge University Press 1994), 12. Also, Elizabeth Grosz argues for an embodied subjectivity that deconstructs the dichotomous body/mind opposition from feminist theories. See Elizabeth Grosz, *Volatile Bodies: Toward a Corporeal Feminism* (Bloomington: Indiana University Press, 1994).

The human geographer Mark Paterson differentiates between the haptic (the sense of touch in general), the cutaneous (the skin as a sense organ), and the tactile (the cutaneous sense considered in relation to pressure), and develops the idea of a "felt" phenomenology against the predominant focus in our societies on vision. He writes, "touch is always already mediated through whatever means, haptic sensations arising through interaction and the cutaneous surface of the skin, the organ of touch."[6] How one makes contact, distances, and relates with others comprise essential elements for human beings who have to learn both how to regulate the self and to understand their experiences. Even when one withdraws from actual interpersonal relationships into the self-closed spaces of the virtual,[7] these issues remain important, perhaps especially so when relationality is absent, lost, or dissolved, and there is a consciousness of the need for it to be regenerated.

Is touch necessarily an embodied experience? While the idea of "contact," primarily regulated via spatial encroachment and distance, may scratch the surface but not be "embodied," the idea of incorporating and expelling the desired object in the realm of fantasy involves no actual contact. French and French-inspired critical theories have made possible an extensive reading of touch, in which space, interruption, and gap themselves create contact, by encroaching and distancing—in my view, treating contact mainly from a spatial perspective. Here I am imagining Roland Barthes's concept of the "Neutral" as "spacing (production of space)" of time and of space, with reference to the concept in Japanese *ma* (often translated as in-between-ness),[8] Jacques Derrida's concept of "con-tact" as interrupted contact, a "hiatus at the core of contact" as the possibility of

---

6. Mark Paterson, *The Sense of Touch: Haptics, Affects and Technologies* (Oxford; New York: Berg, 2007), 145.

7. Those who withdraw from human relationship and stay at their home in contemporary Japan are called *hikikomori*, literally meaning "withdrawal." Saitō Tamaki, *Hikikomori Bunkaron* [*Cultural Analysis of Hikikomori*] (Tokyo: Kinokuniya Shoten, 2003), 149.

8. Roland Barthes, *The Neutral: Lecture Course at the Collège de France (1977–1978)*, trans. Rosalind E. Krauss and Denis Hollier, text established, annotated and presented by Thomas Clerc, directed by Eric Marty (New York: Columbia University Press, 2005), 146–147. Barthes notes of *ma* as "Every relation, every separation between two instants, two places, two states" (notes, 243).

contact with alterity,[9] and Jean-Luc Nancy's concept of the body as being a space, the "departure of self to self," and of touching that impedes itself.[10]

Psychoanalytic accounts of internalization and externalization/incorporation and excorporation have also expanded understanding of the subject's fantasy related to the object, though without always taking into account how the object may feel about it. These include: Sándor Ferenczi's analysis of introjection (and exteriorization), by which he means "an extension of the ego" to the external world and a taking-in of an image of the loved object[11]; and Melanie Klein's introjection and projection where infants internalize or introject a good object, while splitting the bad object, later theorized as "projective identification," that is to say putting a part of oneself onto an other with whom one identifies.[12] In such approaches, bodily encounter (which would involve contact) largely remains in the realm of fantasy.

My hypothesis is that reading touch in terms of the pre-verbal interpersonal sensations expressed in the texts (not-yet-uttered yet written) advances our understanding of inter-personal/object affect, as well as concepts of touch, the body, and intimacy in a way that might not have been captured through accounts that have thus far been mainly phenomenological or psychoanalytic. This is because the literary touch I investigate translates the (imagined) felt experience, moving between the embodied experience of touch formed via repetitive surface contact or weight touch over time and the verbalized (and thus disembodied) form of touch in written texts. Once touch is written, it is disembodied, its desire is displaced, and thus it is no longer there. And yet,

---

9. Jacques Derrida, *On Touching—Jean-Luc Nancy*, trans. Christine Irizarry (Stanford, CA: Stanford University Press, 2005), 63, 70. Originally published as *Le toucher, Jean-Luc Nancy* in 2000 by Éditions Galilée.

10. Jean-Luc Nancy, *Corpus*, trans. Richard A. Rand (New York: Fordham University Press, 2008), 33; Jean-Luc Nancy, *Noli Me Tangere: On the Raising of the Body*, trans. Sarah Clift, Pascale-Anne Brault, and Michael Naas (New York: Fordham University Press, 2008), 42. The text "Corpus" is based on the French text, published by Éditions Métailié in 2006. *Noli me tangere: Essai sur la levée du corps* was originally published in 2003 by Bayard Éditions.

11. Sándor Ferenczi, "On the Definition of Introjection" (1912), in *Final Contributions to the Problems and Methods of Psycho-analysis*, trans. Eric Mosbacher et al., and ed. Michael Balint (New York: Brunner/Mazel, 1980), 316.

12. Melanie Klein, "The Psychological Principles of Infant Analysis" (1926) and "A Contribution to the Psychogenesis of Manic-Depressive States" (1935) in *The Selected Melanie Klein*, ed. Juliet Mitchell (New York: Free Press, 1987). Hereafter abbreviated as *SMK*.

writing itself can also re-activate or re-embody what has been disembodied. In the same way that touch mediates bodily encounter, literary touch translates what the body feels and that which it is possible to express through language.

In discussions of pre-verbal feeling, theorists tend to distinguish "affect" from "emotion," giving a lack of clear agency to the former, and associating subjectivity more with the latter.[13] This is a not a distinction I wish to uphold. Feelings in the writing of contemporary female writer Matsuura Rieko, for example, whom I examine in this book, are often portrayed almost like physiological responses to stimuli, sensations in characters' relationality as experienced through the skin and pre-verbal: in her writing, sensations are feelings, affect is emotion. Also, the word "touching" can apply to emotions and feelings, implying that one's emotions are "touched," with many equivalent expressions in Japanese (ふれる, 触れる, 触る, etc.), which have a physical and emotional side. All the works I examine in this book effectively awaken awareness to feelings and sensations that have not been completely illuminated either in discourses on contact and embodiment, or in psychoanalytic categorical frameworks where feelings are replaced by language to produce meaning: they do so, by translating the felt and non-verbalized and crossing sensory modalities such as visual, auditory, and olfactory across time and space. Above all, touch as expressed in the pages of texts constructs the body of characters, writers, and potentially also of the reader, presenting selves encountering others and the forming and transforming of feelings, perceptions, and awareness.

---

13. Gregory J. Seigworth and Melissa Gregg define affect as "visceral forces beneath, alongside, or generally *other than* conscious knowing, vital forces insisting beyond emotion" ("An Inventory of Shimmers," in *The Affect Theory Reader*, Gregory J. Seigworth and Melissa Gregg, eds (Durham, NC: Duke UP, 2010), 1). Affective intensity, when considered as a social experience, is thought by Raymond Williams to be the change in "structures of feelings" that are still in process (*Marxism and Literature* (Oxford: Oxford UP, 1989), 132). Silvan Tomkins, comparing affects to drives, illuminates transformable and fluide aspects of affects (*Shame and its Sisters: A Silvan Tomkins Reader*, Eve Kosofsky Sedgwick and Adam Frank, eds (Durham, NC: Duke UP, 1995), 45–61). Recognizing the origin of the split between affect and emotion in the psychoanalytic practice (feeling as "affect," described from the observer's perspective and as "emotion," belonging to the speaker), Sianne Ngai demonstrates a nuanced utilization of those terms for aesthetic productivity, by observing one's affective response and relating to the perceived events, instead of creating two different categories of feeling (*Ugly Feelings* (Cambridge, MA: Harvard UP, 2005), 25–28).

In this book I intend to offer neither a mere thematic study of touch and intimacy nor a literary study of the particular authors. By approaching particular themes raised by each author's acute attentions to touch in conversation with the psychological and the bodily, this book posits and develops a model with which to examine intersensorial bodies interacting with an object (or objects) and with the environment through touch. Yoshiyuki's writing questions any tendency to view the body as a material substance that moves independently in space, and suggests rather that the body is in contact with the external, without any assumption that one person can understand the other. In contradistinction to Merleau-Ponty, where touch is conceived through attention to the surface, vision, and language, with scant attention to weight friction,[14] the imaginary membrane in Yoshiyuki, constructed partly through the protagonist's fantasy and partly involving characters' past sensations, functions as a kind of "other" that is indivisible from living bodies and has the properties of a biological organ such as the skin. An examination of touch through the Japanese texts written by other authors further illuminates the gap or in-between space (*aida/ma*) created among hesitations, attempts, and fantasies of reaching others across such a gap. Drawing on Merleau-Ponty's idea of the "untouchable" that resides right in the midst of touch in self-touching, and allowing for a reverse relationship between the untouchable and touch, as well as the invisible and vision,[15] I argue that authors try to touch the other and, in

---

14. Hashizume Keiko, in her study of the body or embodiedness [called *shintairon* in Japanese] of Gaston Bachelard (1884–1962) with reference to Merleau-Ponty and Henri Bergson, points out Bachelard's criticism on Merleau-Ponty's understanding of the bodily perceptions that are supported by totality of the body. In contrast with Merleau-Ponty's understanding of the body as a unity without compartmentalizing the senses, Bachelard's understanding of touch emphasizes partial recognition of things, always expecting weight resistance from the objects. "Shokkaku wo Chūshin toshita Bachelard Shintai ron heno Ichi shiza: Busshitsu teki Sōzōryoku wo chūshin ni" ["A Perspective on Bachelard's Embodiedness focused on Touch: Centered around Material Imagination"], *Bigaku Geijutsugaku Kenkyū* [*Aesthetics and Arts Research*] 31 (2012), 58–59.

15. Merleau-Ponty, "Working Notes," in *The Visible and the Invisible*, 254–255. The word "untouchable" is associated with a certain social class in the caste system and also with diseases, such as leprosy and AIDS (Constance Classen, ed., *The Book of Touch* (Oxford and New York: Berg, 2005), 292–293), in the Japanese context, potentially including the emperor's body as both untouchable and invisible. In this book, I focus on a reading of touch that reflects a dynamic mobility created through desire, sensations, memories, and affects.

so doing, come up against the unknowability of the other as well as of the self. The more they try to write the body, the more they acknowledge something that is unreachable, the recognition of which gives rise to works of literary imagination and the desire for the potentiality for touch. Some psychological accounts have argued that a lack of touch triggers later developmental, psychological, and interpersonal issues.[16] Literary works demonstrate a capacity if not to fill at least to enrich the lack or absence: rather than pathologizing it, they elaborate on and recreate it through the work of imagination.

The word *skinship,* which emerged and was circulated across cultural, linguistic, and national borders, occupies a central place in my discussion of touch in the Japanese context, allowing me to go beyond thus-far distance-based and visually concerned discourses on contact and touch. The term skinship (*sukinshippu, skin* plus the suffix *-ship*) gained circulation in Japan in the early 1970s and was used to refer to intimate interaction via skin-to-skin touch mainly between mothers and small children.[17] It was promoted by Japanese pediatrician and psychiatrist Hirai Nobuyoshi, who was impressed by an American teacher's use of the word skinship in a 1953 World Health Organization (WHO) seminar on child's mental wellbeing, majorly discussing the issues of maternal deprivation and lack of motherly love.[18] The concept of skinship was then taken up by Hirai and others later as a way to redress the lack of intimate familial communication he identified at the core of the collapse of the nuclear family in 1970s Japan. Child-rearing practices in Japan started to change in the 1950s due to the introduction of Western-style practices based on the idea of fostering children's independence, but the same decade, the 1970s, also saw a commonly renewed emphasis on touch in a wider Western context, with Donald Winnicott's publications on child psychology and object relations, which offered a revision of Melanie Klein's observation on infants.[19]

---

16. Hirai Nobuyoshi, *Ushinawareta Boseiai: Kosodate wo Tanoshimutameni* [*Lost Motherly Love: To Enjoy Child-rearing*] (Nagoya: Reimei Shobō, 1981), 1–2, 139–43; Muriel Jolivet, *Japan: The Childless Society? The Crisis of Motherhood* (London: Routledge, 1997), 84–85.

17. Nihon Kokugo Daijiten [*The Unabridged Dictionary of the Japanese National Language*], Nihon Daijiten Kankōkai, ed., vol. 11 (Tokyo: Shōgakukan, 1972), 376.

18. Hirai, *Ushinawareta Boseiai,* 1–2.

19. D. W. Winnicott's *Playing and Reality* examined transitional objects, such as towel, as a way to conceive child's relationship to the object other than the mother. Winnicott, *Playing and Reality* (London and New York: Routledge, 2005).

For French psychoanalyst Didier Anzieu (1923–1999), who criticized Jacques Lacan for his excessive focus on language and incorporated into his own thinking both Kleinian object relations theory and the group theory of the British psychoanalyst Wilfred Ruprecht Bion, the skin is both site and means of communication through its invocation of a host of previous sensations and emotions. For Anzieu, the skin, or "a surface for registering the traces" left by other people, retains the good material that has accumulated through breastfeeding and care.[20] Anzieu claims that previous sensations and emotions stored on the skin affect the formation of identity, which he calls "the skin ego," the concept of which arose in the early 1970s (exactly when Yoshiyuki was meditating on the imaginary "membrane") and uses this as a way to rethink subjectivity as reflected by the other. Scholars have noted how movements and postures become sedimented in the body: how the body is an accumulated collection of body images that involve a non-straightforward narrative of formative and transformative events;[21] how internalized bodily practices become a natural and automatic system.[22] The skin's capacity to accumulate past sensations and feelings and memories, all resulting from (attempts at) relationship with others, to become overlaid with, in the mind of Yoshiyuki's protagonist in the passage I have quoted, a kind of an imaginary membrane, a repository of the ambiguous nature of physical contact and the inevitable uncertainties or failures experienced, suggests that there is much more to "skinship" than a simple tactile-based mutual affirmation between mother and child. My focus on relationship using this understanding of the skin (or "skinship"), as a site of accumulations of sensations and feelings, will enable me to expand what intersensorial communication through the skin might mean in the wider context.

Touch, Embodied, or Fantasized

In the course of my research for this book, I have found myself being repeatedly asked certain questions. "Why touch?" "Why Japanese texts and

---

20. Didier Anzieu, *The Skin-Ego*, trans. Naomi Segal (London: Karnac, 2016), 44. Originally published as *Le Moi-peau* by Dunod in 1995.
21. Harvie Ferguson, *Modernity and Subjectivity: Body, Soul, Spirit* (Charlottesville: University Press of Virginia, 2000), 26–27.
22. Eyal Ben-Ari, *Body Projects in Japanese Childcare: Culture, Organization and Emotions in a Preschool* (Richmond: Curzon Press, 1997), 75.

Western (along with Japanese) theories?" "Why phenomenology and psychoanalysis?" Such questions have kept me on my toes, critically engaging with the topic under analysis. Simply put, I needed both approaches to develop this study. The thinking of Merleau-Ponty has witnessed a resurgence of attention in the humanities and social sciences, especially relating to the notion of embodiment. His theories have been helpful in my consideration of touch as a type of embodied or lived experience. Even so, I considered an exclusively phenomenological approach toward the subject of touch in literary texts held the risk of failing to address psychic–corporeal/inside–outside dynamics, and the role of desire and fantasy (especially the displacement of desire via language), fully. Similarly, if I were to employ only a psychoanalytic approach, this would exclude certain aspects of lived experiences and intentionality created through being embodied; and might not be able to fully grasp the not-yet-namable elements such as affect. In my book, phenomenological and psychoanalytical approaches are cross-culturally interrogated to constantly challenge what may seem like the limit of transferability regarding concepts, words, and practices. The two inform each other to develop our understanding of touch—that is, of the mediated construction of the self. As early as the 1910s Japan, a number of literary critics, authors, and intellectuals had become interested in (Freudian) psychoanalysis[23] and (Husserlian) phenomenological

---

23. This includes Tanizaki, Satō Haruo, Hasegawa Tenkei, Noguchi Yonejirō, and Ohtsuki Kenji. According to Sone Hiroyoshi, the introduction of Freudian psychoanalytic theories by psychologists in Japan started around 1910, with the translation of psychologist Stanley Hall's *Adolescence* from 1904 by Motora Yūjirō as *Seinen ki no Kenkyū* in 1910, and with Ohtsuki Kaison's essay on forgetfulness ("Monowasure no Shinri"), published in the journal *Shinri Kenkyū* [*The Study of Psychology*] in 1912, as the first psychoanalytic source published in Japan, followed by Kimura Kyūichi's article on repression in 1912, Ueno Yōichi's articles on Freudian dream theories in 1914, and Kubo Yoshihide's extensive work on psychoanalysis, introducing Freudian theories with reference to such analysts as Alfred Adler and Wilhelm Stern, in 1917 (Sone Hiroyoshi, "Freud no Shōkai to Eikyō: Shin Shinrishugi Seiritsu no Haikei" ["The Introduction and its Influence of Freud: The Background of Establishment of New Psychologism"], in *Shōwa Bungaku shi no Shomondai* [*Issues of Showa Literary History*] [Tokyo: Kasama Shoin, 1979, 80–81]. Also see *Two Millennia of Psychiatry in West and East*, ed. Toshihiko Hamanaka and German E. Berrios (Tokyo: Gakuju Shoin, 2003). However, the psychotherapeutic practice of the self, such as psychoanalysis, has never become widespread in Japan. Okonogi Keigo writes that, after Freud's ideas were introduced in Japan in the 1910s, their translations were published from 1929 to 1933, and Marui Kiyoyasu's writing and teaching of psychoanalytically-oriented psychiatry at Tohoku University (Japan's first generation of such group collectively known as the Tohoku

study.[24] In the 1960s and 1970s, provoked by the translation of Merleau-Ponty's *The Structure of Behavior* in 1964 and further introduction of Merleau-Pontean phenomenology by scholars such as Takiura Shizuo, Kida Gen, Nitta Yoshihiro, there was a veritable boom in phenomenology. Both theoretical approaches, the psychoanalytical and the phenomenological, have long been part of modern Japanese intellectual and literary life.

The creative use of psychoanalytic theory in Japan has so far received relatively limited discussion. Comparisons of Japan and Western countries regarding psychoanalytic culture tends to focus on the difference in subjectivities, nurtured through national, geographical, and linguistic boundaries.[25] Yet in cross-cultural theoretical analysis to do with the self and

---

School), the 1930s saw a certain albeit limited expansion of psychoanalytic practice, psychoanalysis was viewed with suspicion; Kosawa Heisaku from the Tohoku School came under surveillance at this point Japan's ally Germany regarding psychoanalysis a "dangerous Jewish system of thought" (Okonogi Keigo, "Psychoanalysis in Japan," in *Freud and the Far East: Psychoanalytic Perspectives on the People and Culture of China, Japan, and Korea*, ed. Salman Akhtar (Lanham, MD: Jason Aronson, 2009), 11).

24. "Phenomenological studies" in Japan also emerged in the 1910s especially at Tohoku University. Keiichi Noe writes of Takahashi Satomi's essay on the phenomena of consciousness in 1912, published as a critical response to Nishida Kitarō's *Zen no Kenkyū* (*An Inquiry into the Good*), and the philosophical exchanges between the two as "the first full-fledged philosophical debate" in modern Japan (Keiichi Noe, "Phenomenology in Japan: Its Inception and Blossoming," in *The Bloomsbury Research Handbook of Contemporary Japanese Philosophy*, Michiko Yusa, ed. [London: Bloomsbury Publishing, 2019], 24). Nishida had studied under Husserl at Freiburg and introduced Husserlian phenomenology, with further development in the interwar period such as by Kuki Shūzō. Takahashi studied with Husserl at Freiburg in the mid 1920s and started writing about the phenomenology related to the body upon his return to Japan.

25. Despite the attention to psychotherapy and the uses of psychoanalytic therapy during the 1960s for the psychological problems that seemed to be emerging as a result of rapid Westernization and urbanization, certain conditions, including a resistance to verbal treatments and antipsychiatry movement, prevented psychoanalysis from making much headway in Japan. See Kitayama Osamu, *Prohibition of "Don't Look": Living through Psychoanalysis and Culture in Japan* (Tokyo: Iwasaki Gakujutsu Shuppansha, 2010), 106–09; Okonogi, "Psychoanalysis in Japan," 13–14; Nishizono Masahisa, "Culture, Psychopathology, and Psychotherapy: Changes Observed in Japan," in *Asian Culture and Psychotherapy: Implications for East and West*, eds. Wen-Shing Tseng, Suk Choo Chang, and Masahisa Nishizono. (Honolulu: University of Hawai'i Press, 2005), 48–49. Also, despite the numerous Japanese translations of psychoanalytic works and a certain international interest in the theories of Japanese psychoanalysts such as of Doi Takeo and Okonogi Keigo, the

the body in literature in particular, attention to the body expressed via a facet of language is surely critical. On one hand, the body itself "speaks," sometimes more profoundly than through words. This is in fact a central premise of this book. On the other, language tends to remain one of the principal means to access bodily vocabularies when one tries to communicate them to other individuals, even if some elements remain irreducible to language. Language reflects the desire to bridge the ever incompletely bridgeable gap; or at least, it marks the absence as the displacement of desire. My methodology, which combines texts and theories that transcend geographical boundaries beyond the places where they arose, reflects, quite simply, my wish to create a fruitful dialogue that goes beyond the limitations of assumed cultural boundaries. When this intricacy between the body and language comes together with touch and Japanese writing, one may attend to what remains outside of language—the moment in which the body or the physiology surprises the awareness of the self or presses the limit of linguistic representation. Writing and reading about touch thus renews the sense of the self as well as of the other. Jean-Philippe Mathy writes: "What dominates in Japan is not the love of knowledge 'contents' or the celebration of speech (as in the West) but the cult of the letter, that is, of pure form without content."[26] I do not necessarily read the body as a pure form or sign, but I consider that writing allows access to unnamable psychical or physiological conditions of the subject while allowing and respecting some degree of the subject's anonymity and obscurity, in comparison to the way the psychoanalytic speaking body reveals him or herself at the moment of utterance. Especially in a cultural context where explicit bodily and oral expression of the self tends to be hesitant, an analysis of the writing subject along with the speaking one advances further understanding of the ties between literature and psychoanalysis, the written and the spoken, and the body and language. All the more so when the

---

contemporary psychoanalytic field remained small, a situation exacerbated by a widespread prejudice in the popular against mental and psychological infirmity, as documentary film *Seishin* [Mind] by Sōda Kazuhiro illuminates (2008; Tokyo: Kinokuniya Shoten, 2010, DVD).

26. Jean-Philippe Mathy, "From Sign to Thing: The French Literary Avant-Garde and the Japanese Difference," in *Confluences: Postwar Japan and France*, ed. Douglas Slaymaker (Ann Arbor: Center for Japanese Studies, The University of Michigan, 2002), 44.

writing hand touches the surfaces of different textures with various media, including pen, brush, and keyboard.[27]

My concept of the unreachable—that is, the lack of complete ability of characters to touch what they try to reach for—provides an effective way to allow readers to reflect upon touch in writing and also allows me to make a critical intervention on the issue of intimacy. Heretofore, discourse on the body and intimacy in Japanese literary analysis tend to focus on gender and sexuality—there is also an assumption, perhaps, that touch is sexual. The comments and questions I have received along these lines throughout this research themselves indicate why I needed to choose a different angle from which to focus on touch, in order to liberate readings of certain authors and texts that I consider to have been limited by particular critical lenses. The most effective way of doing so was to create continuous dialogues among phenomenological and psychoanalytical (as well as psychopathological) approaches towards touch that would allow me to recognize the verbal representations of lived experience, and acknowledge and examine the implications of the disembodiment that occurs when lived experience is written. For example, observation-based Kleinian theory—rarely utilized in Japanese literary analysis even though its strongly maternal orientation has a clear synergy with the Japanese cultural context and it has certainly been read by Japanese poets/writers and scholars—is an effective way, as I demonstrate in the chapters related to Kawabata and Matsuura, to raise issues around touch beyond gender configuration. Psychoanalysis generally focuses on verbal representation of bodily symptoms, but Kleinian analysis has a unique way of presenting the body and mind through the observation of child's relation to the objects, even attracting psychologically-informed phenomenologist Merleau-Ponty's

---

27. While some French writers were fascinated by writing on a fiber surface with brush and ink, as observable in Philippe Sollers's "Sur le matérialisme" ["On Materialism"] (1974) and Roland Barthes's *Empire of Signs* (*L'Empire des signes*, 1970), Japanese writer Abe Kōbō was intrigued in the 1980s by the word processor, which helped him sort out overabundant adverbs of Japanese language, due to its ability for cutting and transferring, Abe aiming at an inorganic writing style. Fusako Innami, "The Touchable and the Untouchable: An Investigation of Touch in Modern Japanese Literature" (PhD diss., University of Oxford, 2014), 150–151.

attention for this reason.[28] My monograph thus brings phenomenological and psychoanalytical approaches together to think about touch in literature within the cultural context of Japan.

The psychoanalytic theories I engage with in my book are diverse in nature, with my fundamental question being how to engage with theories cross-culturally, especially those having to do with subjectivity, without falling into the trap of cultural determinism and without simply "applying" Western theories in an imperialistic manner. That is my longstanding journey, my questions starting from, for example, how to engage with postcolonial theories in the post-economic-miracle Japanese context or Freudian psychoanalytic theories in a patriarchical Japanese society that yet possesses strong maternal aspects. In area studies, there might have been resistance against the weight placed on theoretical frameworks arising from the West almost as if those theories are unnecessary in discussion of Japan, or as if theory-heavy works are somehow not "Japanese" enough. The argument is sometimes made that indigenous texts should guide theories, instead of the other way around. In this book, texts raise questions and problematize the manner in which touch has been conceived and discussed in theoretical frameworks and in society in general. At the same time, a certain range of phenomenological and psychoanalytical thought has become so ingrained in artistic and literary thinking and practices especially regarding the body in postwar Japan that it may not be always possible and sensible to try to discern which should or might come first. For me, texts and theories inform one another or live together; one may engage with creative writing critically, or critical writing creatively, and engage with creative critical writing. Having been exposed to phenomenological thinkers and creative workers who are engaged in pondering on the

---

28. In his "The Child's Relations with Others" (1951, as a part of the lecture series at Sorbonne) and in "Man and Adversity" (presentation in 1951 in Geneva), Merleau-Ponty refers to Melanie Klein's idea of ambivalence in which child has two alternative images on the same object as the "good" as well as "bad" mother, as opposed to ambiguity as non-pathological adult phenomenon in which one admits that the *same* object, good and generous, could be bad and annoying. Merleau-Ponty, "The Child's Relations with Others," in *Primacy of Perception: And Other Essays on Phenomenological Psychology, the Philosophy of Art, History and Politics*, ed. James M. Edie (Evanston, IL: Northwestern University Press, 1964), 102–03; "Man and Adversity" in *The Merleau-Ponty Reader*, ed. Ted Toadvine and Leonard Lawlor (Evanston, IL: Northwestern University Press, 2007), 217.

body as a phenomenon in the Japanese context, for me, phenomenological and psychoanalytical approaches are not exclusively "Western," despite their origins. Discussing touch through such a dynamic interaction of texts and theories provides me with a way to critically engage with thinking and writing about it and, above all, to make contact with things, as if forming relationship, that might have dwelled in different spaces and times.

During the 1960s and 1970s, a period which saw, as Mathy puts it, "another wave of *Japonisme*,"[29] Francophone writers and philosophers visited Japan and left observations on what they saw as an erasure of content, emptiness, de-centeredness, and meaning without content, which they saw as uniquely "Japanese." Jacques Lacan's attention to what he saw as a perpetual translation in the Japanese language (through the Japanese reading of the Chinese characters *kun-yomi*, the Chinese reading of the Chinese characters *on-yomi*, and the interaction between all three different types of characters) suggested that Japanese subjects are always already involved in the translation of the unconscious to the conscious or communication between the unconscious and *parole* (spoken language), telling the truth via lies without being liars.[30] Shingū Kazushige, acknowledging this fragmentation of the self arising from the use of language, sees instead the possibility of discovering oneself through the viewpoint of the Other on an alienation from one's own culture, while still living within.[31] If the prevalent phenomenon in Japan is not the speech but the cult of the letter as Mathy puts it, the literary expression of touch in the Japanese context may provide another, much broader reading of psychoanalysis or another way of analyzing the self, especially regarding the verbalization of desire and bodily senses through writing. While some ethnographic work on touch in Japan illuminates an embodied aspect of touch,[32] verbalized literary touch is, in a sense, already disembodied. The verbalized is no longer

---

29. Mathy, "From Sign to Thing," 34.

30. Jacques Lacan, "Nihon no Dokusha ni yosete" ["For the Japanese Readers"] (1972), in *Ecuri* (*Écrits*), trans. Miyamoto Tadao, et al. (Tokyo: Kōbundō, 1972), iv. Originally published as *Écrits* in 1966 by Éditions du Seuil.

31. Shingū Kazushige, "Freud, Lacan, and Japan," in *Perversion and Modern Japan: Psychoanalysis, Literature, Culture*, ed. Nina Cornyetz and J. Keith Vincent (Abingdon: Routledge, 2010), 266–268.

32. Diana Adis Tahhan's works on touch with phenomenological approach were helpful for my research, especially Tahhan's "Blurring the Boundaries between Bodies: Skinship and Bodily Intimacy in Japan," *Japanese Studies* 30: 2 (2010): 215–230; and *The Japanese*

there, except for what may be stored in the unconscious.[33] To write is to make a contact, even if it is either early or belated; language itself is a displacement of desire such that literature conveys desire as absence.

Phenomenology and psychoanalysis have been generally considered incompatible: while the former acknowledges intentionality for human actions, the latter gives priority to the workings of the unconscious as the vehicles of human actions.[34] Japanese thinkers, on the other hand, such as philosopher Ichikawa Hiroshi and psychiatrist/psychopathologist Kimura Bin, have frequently employed both phenomenology and psychoanalysis on the same horizon to expand their respective studies on the phenomenal body and schizophrenic self in the 1970s and onwards.[35] Their work has

---

Family: Touch, Intimacy and Feeling (Abingdon: Routledge, 2014). For other anthropological works on touch and *skinship* relevant in Japan, that are referring to relationality between the mother and infant, see Edward T. Hall, *The Silent Language* (New York: Doubleday & Company, 1959), Eyal Ben-Ari, *Body Projects in Japanese Childcare*, and Tiffany Field, *Touch* (Cambridge, MA: MIT Press, 2001).

33. Freud associates the motif of the "mystic writing pad," where, while certain stimulations are erased through the work of protective shield, others are inscribed on the wax slab as if they are unreachable in the unconscious. On this pad associated with the system of perception-consciousness that receives perceptions without retaining permanent traces, and the unconscious traced on wax slab as permanent traces, the pointed stimuli scratch the surface and leave traces on the wax slab through the medium of two layers of sheets, which will be erased once the layers are lifted from the slab from the unfixed end. Sigmund Freud, "A Note upon the 'Mystic Writing-Pad,'" *The Standard Edition of the Complete Psychological Works of Sigmund Freud*, vol. 19, trans. James Strachey et al. (London: Hogarth Press, 1964), 228–231. Hereafter abbreviated as *SE*.

34. As the subject has intentionality and agency in phenomenology, compared to psychoanalytic lack of self-control due to the unconscious, Jean-Paul Sartre explored the possibility of existential psychoanalysis, which recognizes human freedom before anything else, rejects the presupposition of the unconscious, and which looks for "choice," rather than the state, based on conscious intention. Jean-Paul Sartre, *Being and Nothingness: An Essay on Phenomenological Ontology*, trans. Hazel E. Barnes (Abingdon: Routledge, 2003), 590–595. Originally published as *L'Être et le néant* in 1943 by Éditions Gallimard.

35. The concept of *aida* in Kimura as the space between one and the other, as well as the internalized space between the self and self, is reflecting the self as internalized difference through temporal and spatial aspects in his clinical study. Kimura Bin, *Bunretsubyō to Tasha* [*Schizophrenia and the Other*], (Tokyo: Chikuma Shobō. 2007), 14. Ichikawa Hiroshi's concept *mi* emphasizes mutuality between the body and the world, much like Merleau-Ponty's idea of "flesh," while starting his analyses of *mi* with one's prenatal stage inside the womb and passive separation from the mother with reference to Otto Rank's idea of birth trauma. Ichikawa Hiroshi, *Mi no Kōzō* (Tokyo: Kōdansha, 2007), 10–12.

overlapped with a time when various psychic disorders started to appear in Japanese society after the postwar economic expansion, along with the disintegration of nuclear families—problems prevalent in contemporary society. Especially in such a context, my work offers an urgent scholarly intervention, rethinking ways to construct and regenerate self-other relationships as well as advancing the understanding of the interconnectedness between the body and language. My question is, rather, why this has not been done thus far. My method of working with literary and theoretical texts not only bridges cultural gaps beyond geographic and linguistic constraints, but also aims to decentralize a Eurocentric hegemony in its production and use of theories and brings Japanese cultural and literary analyses into further productive and stimulating intellectual dialogues. Writers' attempts at approximation of touch in their depictions of it provide a crucial way of problematizing the extent to which we can verbalize what we feel or how we desire the other. It is not only theorizations that contribute to our understanding of literary texts: the texts also advance our understanding of theories related to touch and relationality, in a way that goes beyond cultural and linguistic boundaries. Indeed, it may be that the particular contribution of Japanese texts, set side by side with phenomenology and psychoanalysis, is their recognition and treatment of the unreachable.

My textual analysis regarding the interstice in the work of Yoshiyuki, for example, tries to expand the theoretical discussion of touch through the play of weight—pushing, being pushed against, dissolving, and mutual pressing in touching the other. In Merleau-Pontean understanding of touch, including self-touch of the left hand on the right hand, emphasizes the reciprocal nature of touch, or rather, the "circle" of the touched and the touching, the visible and the seeing, and my body and another.[36] In this account, what is tangible and what is touching are considered inseparable. Luce Irigaray criticized Merleau-Ponty for his solipsism and his lack of consideration of otherness, where the subject–object relationship

---

36. Merleau-Ponty, *The Visible and the Invisible*, 143. In Merleau-Ponty, the subject–object relationship oscillates: "a touching of the sleek and of the rough, a touching of the things— a passive sentiment of the body and of its space—and finally a veritable touching of the touch, when my right hand touches my left hand while it is palpating the things, where the 'touching subject' passes over to the rank of the touched, descends into the things, such that the touch is formed in the midst of the world and as it were in the things." Merleau-Ponty, *The Visible and the Invisible*, 133–134.

understood as "two leaves" of body and of the world seem to make it impossible for the other to be seen for itself.[37] While Merleau-Ponty takes account of the depth and thickness of the body in thinking on the mutuality of flesh between self and world, I argue that his idea of reversibility omits friction and weight, as Jean-Luc Nancy reminds us that the body is also a weighty mass.[38] And yet, Yoshiyuki's literary depictions can also suggest that the bodies in fiction are almost already touching even when they do not have actual contact—characters come in to contact with others through mediation over time.

While Merleau-Pontean understanding of touch proposes a mutuality of the body and the world, Derrida disagrees with, in his reading of Husserian phenomenology, Merleau-Ponty's ambiguous treatment of the relationship between touching one's own body and seeing another person and the relationship between touch and vision.[39] Derrida explores the possibility of "interrupted contact"; as he writes, "*I* self-touches spacing itself out, losing contact with itself, precisely in touching itself,"[40] by discussing Nancy's contact that necessarily coincides with departure.[41] In this

---

37. Luce Irigaray, *An Ethics of Sexual Difference*, trans. Carolyn Burke and Gillian C. Gill (London: Continuum, 2004), 131. Originally published in French as *Éthique de la différence sexuelle* in 1984 by Les Éditions de Minuit.

38. Nancy, *Corpus*, 7.

39. Derrida, *On Touching*, 190–191. For Derrida, such ambiguity seems to negate the alterity of the other, as Christopher Watkin puts it, "reducing the other person to the same quality of otherness of one's hand: that is to say, to an alterity very much less 'other' than Derrida would like." Christopher Watkin, *Phenomenology or Deconstruction? The Question of Ontology in Maurice Merleau-Ponty, Paul Ricœur and Jean-Luc Nancy* (Edinburgh: Edinburgh University Press, 2009), 15. Watkin further investigates a mutuality (rather than reciprocity) of body and world, from the fact that meaning for Merleau-Ponty is *of* the world rather than *in* the world in the same way that the body is *of* the world, where encountering others *alters* participants' lives. Thus, rather than mutuality eliding the alterity of the other, Derrida "risks not respecting the other at all" in "respecting the *otherness* of the other" (64–65).

40. Derrida, *On Touching*, 34.

41. Nancy's interpretation of *Noli me tangere* (a Latin phrase meaning "Do not touch me," the words the resurrected Jesus said to Mary Magdalene when she recognizes him) is also based on distancing: "a touching that, of itself, distances and impedes itself," in which touch is identical to its withdrawal. Nancy, *Noli Me Tangere*, 42. See also Martin Crowley's reading, through Nancy, for a thought of the artwork as the offer and the promise of contact "whose excessively proximate touch is nowhere other than in the departing movement" of the promise. Martin Crowley, "Contact!," *L'Esprit Créateur* 47: 3 (2007): 3.

account, touch is an act of moving away from the other while attempting to reach the other in the very invisible tension between these antagonistic directions. The relationship between phenomenology and deconstruction has provoked a continuous ongoing discussion, by critiquing and informing one another, comparable to how I engage with phenomenology and psychoanalysis together in this monograph on touch.

The relational aspect of experience, which is visible from Merleau-Ponty's 1942 *The Structure of Behavior* (translated into English in 1963 and into Japanese in 1964), opens a way in which our relation and perception, rather than objective knowledge, create the value and meaning of the other. As Merleau-Ponty puts it, the objects are "lived as realities," instead of "known as true objects."[42] Merleau-Ponty's works provoked an enormous response in Japan. This included Kamei Hideo's phenomenological literary analysis involving the senses and sensibility. Kamei, through his works on expression and the body, examined modes of expression and the self-consciousness achieved through language. In his introduction to the English translation of Kamei's 1983 *Kankaku no Henkaku* (*Transformation of Sensibility*), Michael Bourdaghs writes: "For both Kamei and Merleau-Ponty, because we come to self-consciousness only through the language that we share with others, the subject produced through language is inherently intersubjective, a subject with others. Moreover, since the subject is produced through expressions, a change in mode of expression necessarily means a change in our self-consciousness—and in our way of relating to others."[43] As discussed here, the appearance of word, in character's utterance, affects one's self-consciousness. It is my premise that this intersubjective relationship, in the context of my analysis of literary touch, depends not only on language but also on time; the invisible traces appear and disappear on the body surface over time, like a palimpsest, questioning

---

42. Maurice Merleau-Ponty, *The Structure of Behavior*, trans. Alden L. Fisher (Pittsburgh, PA: Duquesne University Press, 2015), 168. Originally published as *La Structure du comportement* in 1942 by Presses Universitaires de France.

43. Michael Bourdaghs, "Editor's Introduction: Buried Modernities—The Phenomenological Criticism of Kamei Hideo," in *Transformations of Sensibility: The Phenomenology of Meiji Literature*, trans. and ed. Michael Bourdaghs (Ann Arbor: Center for Japanese Studies, the University of Michigan, 2002), xvii.

the extent of what the body can voice. Most of the literary texts Kamei examined were from the Meiji period (1868–1912): he left it to others to examine the transition of self-expression of the "I" in later literary texts. However, the fact that various Japanese critics, intellectuals, and writers and artists were keen to engage with phenomenological thought (or at the very least the body and self reflected by the world), in the 1970s and the 1980s, leading to the emergence of the discourse of the body or embodiedness called *shintai ron* signals a particular set of interests and questions posed at the time—precisely when the idea of skinship was also promoted by medical practitioners.

The ideas surrounding the distance-based notion of contact—touching due to leaving in Nancy, the Neutral in Barthes as spacing, and *aida* in Kimura—suggest that we have (or are) a space or distance between one and the other and within oneself at the time of making contact. We make contact due to and within the place of this gap, and we also leave this place due to contact. To touch the other, or even being in contact with the other to begin with, is fundamentally to pose a question about the possibility of reaching the other; the trial of reaching the other reminds the touching subject of the gap between one and the other—or, as Yoshiyuki constantly suggests, the gap within oneself. As examined throughout this book, touch in Japanese literature exhibits indefinable tension between the touchable and the untouchable, mediation and immediacy, desire and hesitation, and repression and fantasy of touch. Thus, although the idea of "contact" in French theories and of the tension between mediation and immediacy, or what I conceive of the unreachable in Japanese writing, arise from different cultural, geographical, and linguistic contexts, a common aesthetic involves the pursuit of the unattainable in the midst of conflicting impulses, such as reach and withdrawal, rise and fall, the urge to reveal and what is kept unrevealed, and the desire to possess and the unwillingness to be taken hold of. It is therefore important to situate the above theorizations on touch and contact beside literary texts and thoughts to analyze the phenomenon of touch. Touch in Japanese writing raises questions, engages, and makes contact with temporally and geographically dislocated thought systems, just like touch itself bridges and unbridges entities. Furthermore, writing about it adds another layer to the attempt—not just to represent but to relive sensations.

Translating Sense Experiences into Language in Context

Sense experiences, despite the vocabularies used to express them, are never fully verbalized. Anthropologist C. Nadia Seremetakis, through her work on the gradual disappearance of a type of peach known as "the breast of Aphrodite" from the markets and a growing oblivion of its taste and texture, writes: "[A]lthough the senses are a social and collective institution like language, they *are not* reducible to language … What is being said may be relativized, contradicted or confirmed by embodied acts, gestures, and sensory affects … Truth therefore is extra-linguistic and revealed through expression, performance, material culture and conditions of embodiment."[44] It is right that the senses are a valid social register— contemporary female Japanese writer Ogawa Yōko's 1994 novel *Hisoyaka na Kesshō* (translated as *The Memory Police* in 2019) comes to my mind as a case of collective sensory oblivion where people living on the islands throw away objects and corresponding memories one by one, as directed by the secret police—even though the memories are not completely reducible to language. Bodily performances (conceived broadly here, to include everyday gestures, facial expressions and other un/intended actions and stillness) translate between verbal and bodily expression.

It is possible to question the veracity of what is expressed: in terms of the sincerity of the narrative or the reality of the bodily trace that appears to underly the spoken narrative or the interpretation of what is communicated, whether it is inside the fiction or in the therapeutic setting. (Un)controlled acts and gestures combine words and wordless vocalizations— such as breathing, groans, and moans—in a way that can seem artificial to one party and authentic to another. Yoshiyuki's protagonists tend to be troubled by this, as they are often at once physically entangled with, and wishing to be emotionally distanced from, others whose voices they cannot ignore. In the therapeutic setting, one of the main criticisms against psychoanalysis has been its tendency toward categorical judgement, as well as listening from a position of authority; analysts translate patients' verbalized symptoms into their readings and then put them into categories, even

---

44. C. Nadia Seremetakis, "The Memory of the Senses, Part I: Marks of the Transitory," in *The Senses Still: Perception and Memory as Material Culture in Modernity*, ed. Seremetakis (Chicago, IL and London: University of Chicago Press, 1994), 6.

though in some cases patients might, potentially, construct false narratives. All of which points to the gap between linguistic and extra-linguistic expressions or, more broadly, verbal and bodily expressions: the possibility that narratives that rely on language may not be true to what the body feels. And yet, I would like to suggest the viability of the idea that sensory experiences might be conveyed and translated into language in a person-specific manner. I would challenge the idea that sensory experiences are completely irreducible and untranslatable to language, and suggest instead that one uses a dual scheme of private and public and individual and collective, in order to write about the senses.

Touch in late nineteenth-century and early twentieth-century Japan is often thought of as being not something that one sees: expressions of contact, at least in public, are subtle, indirect, modulated, and mediated. Everyday life had not been without forms of tactile communication: as Western painters and journalists such as Georges Ferdinand Bigot and Charles Wirgman observed the piggy-back ride (*onbu*; a way of carrying others, used not only by children on each other, but also the way a mother might carry her young baby, or an adult might carry another perhaps elderly person), breastfeeding, co-sleeping between the mother and child, and massage.[45] However, the adoption of Western social mores in the Meiji period saw the introduction of several unaccustomed touch-based gestures such as hand-shaking and ballroom dancing (albeit only among certain classes of society). A form of everyday skinship, also, may not have been thought of as intimate communication in quite the way that the poet Yosano Akiko (1878–1942), for example, described. In the 1914 account of her travels in Europe with her husband, *Pari yori* [*From Paris*], she records the day they left the house they had stayed at in London, and how the eyes of their hostess filled with tears as she put her hand in through the car window to shake theirs. This gesture, or experience, Yosano wrote, was the first thing that came to mind when she thought of England.[46] She remembers a comment from a certain Japanese painter whom she and her husband met on their journey in France, who contrasted the kiss he

---

45. See *Bigō Gashū* [*Collected Illustration by Bigot*], commented by Sakai Tadayasu (Tokyo: Iwasaki Bijyutsusha, 1982 [1973]), images 3, 8, 57, 61.
46. Yosano Akiko, "Pari yori," in *Teihon Yosano Akiko Zenshū* [*The Complete Works of Yosano Akiko*], vol. 20 (Tokyo: Kōdansha, 1981), 560.

saw between Western parents and their children and the educational slap Japanese fathers administered to theirs.[47] Japanese people who travelled abroad in Europe in the early twentieth century were quick to notice the prevalance of physically affectionate modes of communication (even if there were variations) when compared to Japan.

At the Rokumeikan, a controversial building that was seen as a symbol of Westernization in the Meiji period, ballroom dance in which men and women linked arms or held each other in intimate embraces allowed limited touch between the sexes in a public space. Some considered this inappropriate and injurious to public morals, while others (a limited few) approved, finding in such activities a beneficial manner of communication. While the Rokumeikan had only a very brief heyday, ballroom dance continued to be practiced among some in the upper classes, was introduced into women's physical education,[48] and stimulated authors' literary imagination. Akutagawa Ryūnosuke (1892–1927) used ballroom dance in his 1920 story "Butōkai" ["The Ball"], and Tanizaki depicts ballroom dancing in his 1924 *Chijin no Ai* (*Naomi*). In one scene in *Naomi*, the male protagonist Jōji dances with Kirako, a dancer from the Imperial Theatre who seems to embody the West even more eloquently than the Western-looking Naomi:

> I noticed that Kirako's lips were just below my temple. This seemed to be a habit with her: just as with Hamada a few minutes before, her sidelock touched my cheek. The caress of her soft hair ... the faint whispers that escaped from her lips from time to time ... For me, having been trampled so long by that unruly colt Naomi, this was a height of feminine refinement that I'd never before imagined. I felt as though a sympathetic hand were tending the wounds where thorns had stabbed me...[49]

---

47. Yosano Akiko, "Pari yori," 567. Also about the same time, Marcel Proust was depicting the habitual goodnight kiss Marcel receives from his mother (which irritates his father, who calls it an "absurd" ritual). Marcel Proust, *In Search of Lost Time, Vol. 1. The Way by Swann's*, trans. Lydia Davis (London: Penguin Books, 2002), 17. Originally published as *Du Côté de chez Swann* in 1913.

48. Nagai Yoshikazu, *Shakō Dansu to Nihonjin* [*Social Dance and the Japanese*] (Tokyo: Shōbunsha, 1991), 26–28.

49. Tanizaki Jun'ichirō, *Naomi*, trans. Anthony H. Chambers (New York: Vintage International, 2001 [1985]), 100. Originally serialized as *Chijin no Ai* of the journals *Osaka Asahi* and *Josei* in 1924.

Despite the Japanese tendency to conflate what was Western with whatever was modern or new,[50] touch-based dancing was in fact a modern development even for Europeans, as Marcel Mauss associates dancing in a partner's arms as a historical "product of modern European civilisation." [51] Literary representations of touch are more often than not muted and understated. And yet, an awareness of the possibility that mediated modes of physical interactions may actually heighten the desire for touch offers a nuanced understanding of distance, hesitation, and fantasy.

In early twentieth-century Japan, a literary group that came to be known as the *Shinkankaku-ha* (the New Sensationists; so named by the critic Chiba Kameo), formed around the journal *Bungei Jidai* in 1924, attempted to conceive of the senses in a new way fitting the group's literary creations. The New Sensationists attempted to capture stimuli with maximum immediacy, using a temporally and spatially dislocated immediacy with an object (as in a film). Kawabata Yasunari, in particular, seems to have aimed for the sensory organs to be simultaneous with the phenomena, composing texts out of sensory perceptions. In his 1924 essay "Shinshin Sakka no Shinkeikō Kaisetsu" ["Analysis of the New Writers' New Trends"], which was on the theoretical basis of new sensationist expression, Kawabata contrasts the literary styles of authors who describe the connection or lack thereof between an eye and a rose. Whereas conventional authors divide the eyes from the rose blossom and say, "My eyes saw the red rose," the new authors, Kawabata said, unite the eyes and the rose and say, "My eyes are the red rose."[52] Through a mixture of what Kawabata calls an Eastern subjectivistic objectivism (*shukaku ichinyo shugi*), where the author's scattered subjectivity is identified with objects; psychoanalytic free

---

50. Miriam Silverberg attends various ways of representing modern experience, including: *modernization* as an economic process; *modernity* as a philosophical inquiry referring to a post-traditional temporality; *modernism* as a set of cultural practices, mirroring the Japanese term *seikatsu* concerning the everyday; the Japanese terms of *kindai*, implying a presentist temporality in *modernity*; *modan*, indicating the dynamic post-traditional capitalistic world; and *modanizumu*, characterized by the western "liberation of mores." Miriam Silverberg, *Erotic, Grotesque, Nonsense: The Mass Culture of Japanese Modern Times* (Berkeley: University of California Press, 2006), 13–14.

51. Marcel Mauss, "Techniques of the Body," *Economy and Society* 2: 1 (1973): 82–83.

52. Kawabata Yasunari, "Shinshin Sakka no Shinkeikō Kaisetsu," in *Kawabata Yasunari Zenshū* [*The Complete Works of Kawabata Yasunari*] (hereafter abbreviated as *KYZ*), vol. 30 (Tokyo: Shinchōsha, 1982), 175. Translation mine unless otherwise indicated.

association, where ideas appear in a unregulated manner; and Dadaist idea generation through free association in order to be faithful to an intuitive subject, Kawabata considered that the free association offered by psychoanalysis would liberate the human imagination and render it immediate.

Haptic elements appear explicitly in modernist art and film, as discussed by Walter Benjamin, Filippo Tommaso Marinetti, and others. European avant-garde art movements articulated new ways of thinking about the senses. Marinetti (1876–1944), the founder of the Futurist movement, states in his 1924 manifesto, "Tactilism": "[Tactilism's] purpose must be, simply, to achieve tactile harmonies and to contribute indirectly toward the perfection of spiritual communication between human beings, through the epidermis."[53] The work of the Dadaists was also described by Walter Benjamin as "acquiring a tactile quality," especially in his famous 1936 essay "The Work of Art in the Age of Mechanical Reproduction": here he argued that the work of the Dadaists (that functions like a bullet) promoted the demand for the film, which is also tactile, "being based on changes of place and focus which periodically assail the spectator."[54] Sudden changes of place or focus—or what Benjamin calls "shock effect"—became a part of composing a filmic surface. This reminds us of similar "tactile" elements in Kawabata's script for the 1926 silent film *Kurutta Ippēji* [*A Page of Madness*]—in which an iron barrier appeared in between a dancing girl and the spectator transforming the scene into a mental hospital—to reflect Kawabata's search for a partcular immediacy of perception. While manifesting some confusion of Dadaism with its surrealist predecessors as promoted by Takahashi Shinkichi's Dadaist manifesto in 1921 and Kawabata's understanding of it in relation to surrealism, such a heightened attention to the haptic in modernist art was concurrently occurring in Japan, prompted by new technologies.

Writing, by and large, served as a way for Kawabata to reflect on his life and approach the unreachable, including emotions he had repressed from his childhood. He made use of the technique of free association in his literary creations.[55] This method is observable in Kawabata's "Hari to Garasu

---

53. F. T. Marinetti, "Tactilism," *Marinetti: Selected Writings*, ed. R. W. Flint., and trans. R. W. Flint and Arthur A. Coppotelli (London: Secker & Warburg, 1971), 111.

54. Walter Benjamin, *Illuminations*, trans. Harry Zohn, ed. Hannah Arendt (London: Jonathan Cape, 1970), 240.

55. Kawabata's reference to psychoanalysis appears especially through Dadaistic idea generation. See Sone Hiroyoshi, "Furoito no Shōkai to Eikyō," 95–96.

to Kiri" ["Needle, Glass, and Fog"] from 1930, in which he writes about various phobias including touch phobia (*sesshoku kyōfushō*) and "Suishō Gensō" ["Crystal Illusions"] published in 1931 which is an experimental writing on embryology. Both of these works use stream of consciousness, in creating a series of fragmented narratives that discuss topics such as phobias, embryology, and artificial insemination, by writing "the world via the unconscious."[56] Various attempts to touch the unreachable thus conversely elevated the literary imagination and even formed a new literary device. The New Sensationists' attempt was ultimately, I claim, to decompose language, to narrate the senses in way that could be as true as possible to what the body perceives: to make the relationship between self and other as bare and naked as possible.

Kawabata's writings reveal a continual search for the unreachable. For example, in his quasi-autobiographic work "Shōnen" ["The Boy"], published in 1948–1949,[57] he includes letters, narratives, and recollections to delay the protagonist's enactment of and sharing of written feelings. Kawabata allows his male protagonist to retrospectively become aware of his feeling toward the intended loved object, his dorm mate, in an adolescent friendship. Kawabata lets his characters talk and act out their (or his) repressed experiences to potential readers through writing; the words are in and of themselves a revelation of the unconscious. Kawabata here utilizes psychoanalysis as a creative device, beyond its theoretical function to interpret literature, in an attempt perhaps to work through childhood experiences. It is as if to write gives him the chance to reflect and act on the loved object.

Many of Kawabata's protagonists approach the issue of contact with an other with marked hesitation. This is true even in works by Kawabata published after the war. In the novel *Senbazuru* [*Thousand Cranes*], published in 1949–1951, the protagonist Kikuji tries and fails to touch the trace of his dead loved one's lips. The tea bowl Mrs. Ota uses has been left with a brown stain where it has been touched by her red lips, which arouses in Kikuji "a nauseating sense of uncleanness and an overpowering

---

56. Sharif Ramsey Mebed, "Kawabata Bungaku ni okeru Furoito Shisō no Eikyō wo meguru Ichi Kōsatsu - Jiyū Rensō kara 'Bukimi na Mono' made" ["An Analysis Tracing the Freudian Influence on the Writing of Kawabata: from Free Association to 'the Uncany'"], PhD diss., Nagoya University (2015), 93.

57. Kawabata Yasunari, "Shōnen," in *KYZ*, vol. 10 (Tokyo: Shinchōsha, 1980). Originally published in six installments in the journal *Ningen*.

fascination."[58] The story portrays Kikuji's subtle attempts to touch his loved one through this mark as the presence of her absence. While Kikuji hesitates to touch the stain, which seems to symbolize an intimacy, an actual union with Mrs. Ota is unattainable. In his analysis of aesthetic modernism in postwar Japan in relation to that of France, Matt Matsuda writes, with reference to French Japanologist Jean-Jacques Origas, "Kawabata's [narrative view] is so much the opposite of a European monumentalized past, weighted in heritage, ill-suited to change and an acceleration of history."[59] Kikuji remains undecided, in a liminal space between his desire and his hesitancy to touch the mark, its reachability and unreachability, and his communication with the absent body represented in the mark in relationship to the living body. Eventually, Mrs. Ota's daughter Fumiko throws the tea bowl onto the stones in the garden and the trace of the lips is lost among the fragments of the broken bowl. The trace of the lips is possibly not only lost, but fragmented—not just as a mark on a surface but as a material thing in and of itself. The trace subsequently attains in Kikuji's fantasy the status of a symbol of the loved one that invokes her imagined presence.

Not realizing the wish to fully touch the intended heightens the desire to do so, which leads to an expansion of the space of the readers' imagination, as if the author has invited the readers to feel the sensations that are (un)written in the texts. In Tanizaki Jun'ichirō, there is a much more insouciant search to satisfy a seemingly instinctual carnal desire, and this is shared by postwar literature of the flesh (called *nikutai bungaku*) generally. However, while the later writers pursue carnal desire as a necessity (comparable to sustenance like food and drink), and with a political agenda that is opposed to an idea of the national body politic, Tanizaki pursues fantasy so as to continually produce a literary space, both for tangible objects and for the imagination, both for the author and for his readers. Douglas Slaymaker writes: "[I]f we are to speak of *nikutai bungaku* [the literature of the flesh] before the war, one thinks of Tanizaki's work and a sexuality that follows an instinctual carnal desire, the sense in which individuals are

58. Kawabata Yasunari, "Thousand Cranes," in *Snow Country and Thousand Cranes*, trans. Edward G. Seidensticker (London: Penguin Books, 1986), 179. Originally published across multiple journals and completed in 1952.
59. Matt Matsuda, "EAST OF NO WEST: The *Posthistoire* of Postwar France and Japan," in *Confluences*, 25.

unable to resist natural instincts, no matter the cost in terms of morality and social ostracism."[60] If Ibuki in Tamura Taijirō's "Nikutai no mon" ["The Gate of the Flesh"] (1947) meets his physical needs through eating, drinking, and sex, Seikichi in Tanizaki's "Shisei" ["The Tattooer"] (1910) realizes his desire merely through visualizing his image on the other's skin, penetrating the desired object with only a needle, merging his own sweat with the blood of an idealized customer. Filled with unrealized possibility the story leaves ample space for the reader's imagination to come into play.

Tanizaki elevates pleasure through the duality of touch and vision, or even inter-sensorial (here I mean encompassing and translating multiple senses) stimulations by lengthening out both the time in which desire is felt, and the time in which it reaches its intended object. Literary critic Isoda Kōichi, associating Tanizaki with Mishima Yukio (1925–1970) in the immediate postwar period, writes that Tanizaki was the only author who chose art or artificiality (*jinkō*) over nature (*shizen*), claiming that this is the result of some sense of having acknowledged the loss that had taken place in the period following the Russo-Japanese war (1904–1905).[61] In a well-known dispute on "novels without plot" in 1927 between Tanizaki and Akutagawa, Akutagawa advocated the non-narratival style of a plotless novel and the importance of a poetic spirit (*shiteki seishin*) or its depth, while Tanizaki proposed the construction of beauty in the literary style within the solid structure and progression of a story.[62] Tanizaki creates an architectonic beauty with the development of plot, his characters often interacting with others within a limitation based on a contract between them. And yet, in depicting physical details of the incompletely reachable or visible objects, Tanizaki stimulates reader's desire particularly when he succeeds in letting touch and vision merge. Although an extensive study on touch in Tanizaki has yet to be conducted, touch as a dynamic potentiality for reaching the other (even when actual touch is not realized) is arguably visible from his first work, "Tattooer."

---

60. Douglas Slaymaker, "Sartre's Fiction in Postwar Japan," in *Confluences*, 101.

61. Isoda Kōichi, *Sajō no Kyōen* [*Feast on the Sand*] (Tokyo: Shinchōsha, 1972), 10.

62. Tanizaki Jun'ichirō, "Jōzetsuroku" ["Garrulous Jottings"], in *TJZ* vol. 12 (Tokyo: Chūoh Kōronsha, 2017), 291–294, 318–322; Akutagawa Ryūnosuke, "Bungeitekina, amarini bungeitekina" ["Literary, all too literary"] in 1927, *Akutagawa Ryūnosuke Zenshū* vol. 9 (Tokyo: Iwanami Shoten, 1978), 3–9, 50–53, 67–68. See also Karatani Kōjin, *Nihon Seishinbunseki* [*Japan Psychoanalysis*] (Tokyo: Bungei Shunjyū, 2002), 88–92.

The thirst for carnality in postwar Japan allowed authors to use the body more freely and explicitly than previously, raising challenging questions regarding how to regulate relationships between the individual and national bodies, or beyond the nation. Freed from the unitary state focused on the national body/body politic (*kokutai*), soon after World War II an existential inquiry and a sense of individuality with a focus on the individual flesh (*nikutai*) came to occupy an explicit position in Japan through what was soon dubbed the literature of the flesh. Writers of literature of the flesh included Sakaguchi Ango (1906–1955) and Tamura Taijirō (1911–1983). Tamura, recognizing how thought is slippery, careless, and fuzzy through his experience at the war-front, brings mind and language back to the body—the body as the very basis of the human condition.[63] Sakaguchi argues for the discovery of language of the flesh itself, emphasizing what the body itself speaks instead of mind talking about thought, with reference to Jean-Paul Sartre's short novel *Intimacy*.[64] Sakaguchi's famous account on "daraku"—fall, fallness, often translated as decadence, from which he argues humans are born, like a mother's womb (*botai*)—further emphasizes falling as a living condition through which the individual, only by thoroughly falling, discovers and rescues oneself.[65] Post-surrender concerns of Japanese writers and critics convoluted existential and phenomenological concerns, as Slaymaker points out,[66] regarding individual subjectivity, body awareness, intentionality, and responsible actions.[67] Writing posed a

---

63. Tamura Taijirō, "Nikutai ga Ningen dearu" ["The Flesh is the Human"] (1947), in *Tamura Taijirō Senshū* [*Selected Works of Tamura Taijirō*], vol. 5 (Tokyo: Nihon Tosho Sentā, 2005), 187–191.

64. Sakaguchi Ango, "Nikutai Jitai ga Shikō suru" ["The Body itself Meditates"] (1946) *Sakaguchi Ango Zenshū*, vol. 4 (Tokyo: Chikuma Shobō, 1998), 268–269. *Intimité* was published in 1938 in France, translated as "Mizuirazu" in Japanese in 1946.

65. Sakaguchi Ango, "Discourse on Decadence" ("Daraku ron"), trans. Seiji Lippit, *Review of Japanese Culture and Society* 1: 1 (1986), 5.

66. Slaymaker, "Sartre's Fiction in Postwar Japan," 100–101.

67. The first publication of Sartre to be translated into Japanese, goes back to 1940, and is of "Le Mur" ("The Wall"), trans. Horiguchi Daigaku. "La Nausée" ("Nausea") was translated in 1941 by Shirai Kōji, followed by "Intimité" ("Intimacy"), translated by Yoshimura Michio in 1946. *Sarutoru Zenshū* [*The Complete Works of Sartre*], is from 1950, and had sold more than one million copies by the time of Sartre's visit to Japan together with Simone de Beauvoir in 1966. Takeuchi Yoshirō translated Merleau-Ponty's *Phénoménologie de la perception* (*Phenomenology of Perception*) and *Signes* (*Signs*) in 1967 and 1969 for the first volumes, respectively.

fundamental question about the distance between the body and language, mind and extra-linguistic experiences, or, potentially, what Miryam Sas has called language and "what language cannot attain,"[68] in the postwar context.

What is written often calls into question both the division between sensory modalities and the validity of constructed time periods such as the pre- and post-war. Male writers of the literature of the flesh recognized the radical possibilities in, as Yoshikuni Igarashi puts it, "the language of the body," treating the (women's) bodies as "ambivalent symbols" of liberation and subjugation.[69] Women's bodies under the U. S. occupation (from 1945 to 1952) became "a battleground," as Mire Koikari observes: regulation of gendered bodies became "a source of tension and controversy."[70] The radical liberation of the flesh in postwar Japan, in short, occurred at the expense of the commodification of female bodies. Advocates of the flesh believed, Harry Harootunian argues, that "Japanese had been denied 'sensory stimuli' down to the end of the war."[71] Yet, the shift from the pre- to the postwar period complicates the distinctions—in some cases marking historical ruptures and discontinuities—between the collective and the individual, and repression and liberation.[72] Indeed, many literary characters of the authors I discuss such as Kawabata and Tanizaki who lived through two world wars continued to approach intimate contact with a sense of hesitation and restraint even after World War II. In Kawabata,

68. Miryam Sas, *Experimental Arts in Postwar Japan: Moments of Encounter, Engagement, and Imagined Return* (Cambridge, MA: Harvard University Asia Center, 2011), 7.
69. Yoshikuni Igarashi, *Bodies of Memory: Narratives of War in Postwar Japanese Culture, 1945–1970* (Princeton, NJ: Princeton University Press, 2000), 57–58.
70. Mire Koikari, "Gender, Power, and U.S. Imperialism: The Occupation of Japan, 1945–1952," in *Bodies in Contact: Rethinking Colonial Encounters in World History*, ed. Tony Ballantyne and Antoinette Burton (Durham, NC: Duke University Press, 2005), 356.
71. Harry Harootunian, "Japan's Postwar and After, 1945–1989: An Overview," in *From Postwar to Postmodern: Art in Japan 1945–1989*, ed. Doryun Chong, et al. (New York: The Museum of Modern Art, 2012), 19.
72. Slaymaker, through his research on the literature of the flesh, contests the historicizing of such distinctions through the very notion of the "postwar" period, including when the war started and ended; for him and many others the term "postwar" indicates a prolonged time period, beyond just "after WW2." Douglas N. Slaymaker, *The Body in Postwar Japanese Fiction* (London: Routledge/Curzon, 2004), 5–6. Sas likewise suggests, looking at postwar experimental arts, that it may be more worth looking at the continuity, rather than the "rupture" between prewar and postwar. Sas, *Experimental Arts in Postwar Japan*, 221.

whose work I examine in chapter 1, the loved object, which is rendered unreachable, is shaped by a strong yearning to touch through the gaze and language. Here the objectified body, often female, affects the viewer. Tanizaki, whose work I examine in chapter 2, allows partial realizations of touch with the enticing lure of fetishization, as if the partially reachable or the invisible becomes tangible through the work of the imagination to touch, lick, and form the imaginary body. As I will show in this book, (the repressed or diverted desire for touch leads to detailed observations of the loved object, as if the narrators' language and the characters' gaze do indeed almost succeed in touching the other.)

A focus on the autobiographical elements in his writing is not enough to explain how Yoshiyuki constructed his characters' relationality through embodied experiences (even if they are his own and mapped onto the characters), how his language capturing bodily perceptions symbolically "touches" characters, and the ways in which his characters try to reach their intended object. As if at odds with one of the fundamental ideas in psychoanalysis, that bodily stimuli can be replaced with words for a cure of symptoms, Yoshiyuki's descriptions of perceptions and feelings blur the clear distinction between body and mind. In Yoshiyuki, as I show in chapter 3, sensations are described in a semi-autobiographical yet distant manner, as the verbalization of the senses serves also to visualize the characters' contact traces and entanglements with other beings. Works by Yoshiyuki and other writers of a group dubbed by critics *daisan no shinjin* (the third generation of new writers)—including Kojima Nobuo (1915–2006), Yasuoka Shōtarō (1920–2013), and Endō Shūsaku (1923–1996), all of whom appeared in literary circles after the Korean War, which was instrumental in bringing economic prosperity to Japan—have long been criticized as demonstrating a flight from political engagement, being devoid of ideology, or "regression" to the effeminate prewar "I-novel" (*shi-shōsetsu*), as well as "reclusion" in the personal everyday life.[73] They seem concerned only with the everyday and were often seen as employing the I-novel approach.[74] Despite

73. Tomiko Yoda, "The Rise and Fall of Maternal Society: Gender, Labor, and Capital in Contemporary Japan," *The South Atlantic Quarterly* 99: 4 (Fall 2000), 868–869.

74. Yoshiyuki himself was aware of these "characteristics" subject to criticism, first proposed by Hattori Tatsu. Yoshiyuki Junnosuke, "Watashi no Bungaku Hōrō" ["My Wandering Journey through Literature"], in *YJZ* vol. 8 (Tokyo: Shinchōsha, 1998), 95–96. Yoshiyuki's partner Ōtsuka Eiko, apparently the model for Natsue in *The Dark Room*, claimed

such critiques, including ones that make an assumption about the identity of the author with his protagonists, Oka Fukuko sees in Yoshiyuki's use of distance a way of transposing the said into the seen, and the seen into the felt.[75] Others have seen in the third-generation authors' explorations evidence of the major preoccupation with relationality in the 1970s, which is to say the confirmation of the relationship between self, ego, and the external world through the verbalization of physiological imagination.[76] Yoshiyuki's works have been the subject of psychological readings, partly because Yoshiyuki used the autobiographical novel to sketch out his own mental states.

Postwar economic expansion, rapid industrialization, and the mass consumer society that developed in mid-1950s and 1960s Japan, brought disruptions and contradictions to established norms in societal, familial, and personal relationships. The dissolution of the national body and the rise of the nuclear family from the traditional *ie* system (based on a principle of male primogeniture),[77] which had pertained before and during the war, was accompanied by the growth of all-powerful corporations that now took fathers away from the physical space of the family, rendering the father absent and the mother a sometimes overbearing psychological presence.[78] Despite the legal advancement for gender equality, such as the Equal Employment Opportunity Law (*Danjo Koyō Kikai Kintō Hō*) of 1985, many barriers to women remained, in conditions in the internal

---

in her books that the characterization of Nakata reflects Yoshiyuki's own experiences. See Ōtsuka Eiko, "*Anshitsu*" *no Nakade* [*Inside the Dark Room*], 1997.

75. Oka Fukuko, "Katoki no Dorama" ["Drama of Transition"], in *Yoshiyuki Junnosuke no Kenkyū* [*Studies of Yoshiyuki Junnosuke*], ed. Yamamoto Yōrō (Tokyo: Jitsugyō no Nihonsha, 1978), 186.

76. Miyoshi Yukio, *Nihon Bungaku Zenshi - Gendai* [*Complete History of Japanese Literature: Modern*], vol. 6 (Tokyo: Gakutōsha, 1978), 444–45. Also Murakami Haruki mentions his interest in the third-generation authors related to the relationship between the self and the ego. Murakami Haruki, *Wakai Dokusha no tame no Tanpen Shōsetsu Annai* [*Guide to Short Stories for Young-generation Readers*] (Tokyo: Bungei Shunjū, 2004), 35–38.

77. Ochiai Emiko, *The Japanese Family System in Transition: A Sociological Analysis of Family Change in Postwar Japan* (Tokyo: LTCB International Library Foundation, 1997), 58–62.

78. Yoda, "The Rise and Fall of Maternal Society," 872–875. Also, the disruption of the kinship system in 1960–1990s Japan ascribed the absence of the father. Margaret Hillenbrand, *Literature, Modernity, and the Practice of Resistance: Japanese and Taiwanese Fiction, 1960–1990* (Leiden and Boston, MA: Brill, 2007), 183.

labour market, job training, and promotion systems.[79] Interpersonally, many gender-related expectations about women in the workplace and the home pertained. Discrepancies between legal developments, social shifts and their actual implementation remained, along with vestiges of familial patriarchy and corresponding gender roles and modern family based on "good wife, wise mother" ideology.[80] It was this kind of contradiction in the postwar era, where the family became a void, that gave rise to the depiction of a disfunctional family in Kojima Nobuo's 1965 novel *Hōyō Kazoku* [*Embracing Family*], featuring a housewife's affair with an American GI. A further question of how children were to be raised became a fundamental problem in the 1980s Japan.[81] Meanwhile, the permeation of the family by the principles of capitalism prompted, via women's liberation and the feminism movement of the 1970s and 1980s, the emergence of female writers who wrote against the lives of housewives.

Female characters in Kōno Taeko (1926–2015) and Takahashi Takako (1932–2013) decide and act from themselves, with clear agency, much more radically than those in Yoshiyuki, who at first sight seem subjugated to male characters. The female protagonist in 1961 "Yōji gari" ["Toddler-Hunting"] by Kōno, contemporary to Yoshiyuki, lacks motherly love (*bosei ai*) and has lost her fertility, imagining children being beaten and punished.[82] Fantasies of violence against children and hatred toward blood relations also appear in Takahashi's works, opposing an assumed motherly love and instead depicting female subjects as autonomous individuals. The female protagonist in *Sora no Hate made* [*To the Far Reaches of the Sky*] from 1973 considers motherly love (*bosei ai*) as a "deformation of egoism"

79. Mary C. Brinton, *Women and the Economic Miracle: Gender and Work in Postwar Japan* (Berkeley: University of California Press, 1993), 146–47.

80. Hasegawa Kei, "Sekushuaritī Hyōgen no Kaika—Feminizumu no jidai to Mori Yoko, Tsushima Yūko, Yamada Eimi" ["Flourish of Expressions about Sexuality: The Era of Feminism and Mori Yoko, Tsushima Yuko, and Yamada Eimi"], in *Ribu toiu Kakumei: Kindai no Yami wo Hiraku* [*The Revolution Called Women's Liberation: Opening the Darkness of the Modern*], *Bungaku shi wo Yomikaeru* [*Reflecting the Literary History*] Vol. 7, ed. Kanō Mikiyo (Tokyo: Impact Shuppankai, 2003), 104.

81. Tanaka Kazuo, "Kazoku Shōsetsu no Genzai" ["The Current State of Family Novels"], *Gunzō* 61: 5 (2006): 203–204.

82. Kōno Taeko, *Toddler-Hunting: And Other Stories*, trans. Lucy North (New York: New Directions, 2018), 45–68; "Yōji gari," in *Kōno Taeko Zenshū*, vol. 1 (Tokyo: Shinchōsha, 1994), 7–23.

(*egoismu no henkei*)[83] and wishes for a dry and cold human relationship, stealing her friend's baby whom she decides to raise with mental deformity in the postwar confusion. Takahashi's "Ningyō Ai" ["Doll Love"] in 1976 further brings the touching female subject to the fore. The female protagonist meets, during the day, an eighteen-year-old Tamao in a tearoom staying at the same hotel, whom she identifies with a wax doll and, at night, she caresses the wax doll Tamao in her room, strokes his skin, forehead, ear, and nipple, making her feel almost as if all her body has become a tactile sensory organ and giving him the warmth of life, thoroughly as a subject (*tetteishite shutai*) by touching him.[84] In the works of following generations to reconsider familial relationship marked by these female writers, Hasegawa Kei sees evidence of a longing for a "post family"—a family beyond bloodline—in writing by Tomioka Taeko, Tsushima Yūko, and Yoshimoto Banana.[85] This was the context in which authors like Matsuura Rieko emerged.

The writing of Matsuura, which I examine in chapter 4, occupies rather a unique place in contemporary Japanese writing. It is marked by an obsessive attention to bodily intimacies[86] that are unrestricted to categories of gender, sexuality, and species. In particular, by constructing characters' relationality by employing pleasure based on a skin sensuality, intimacy invests the surface of the skin as irresistible touch. Furthermore, skinship in Matsuura emerges in an alternative, imaginary "familial" bond. In her 2017 novel *Saiai no Kodomo* [*The Most Beloved Child*], three high-school

---

83. Takahashi Takako, *Sora no Hate made* (Tokyo: Shinchōsha, 1973), 63.

84. Takahashi Takako, "Ningyō Ai," in *Takahashi Takako Jisen Shōsetsu shū* [*Takahashi Takako Self-Selected Works*], vol. 4 (Tokyo: Kōdansha, 1994), 414.

85. Hasegawa Kei, "Feminizumu/Jendā Hihyō de Yomu <Kazoku> Hyōshō—Nihon no Kingendai Bungaku, Media ni Miru Kindai Kazoku no Hensen to Gendai Kazoku" ["The Representation of Family through Feminism and Gender Criticism: The Transition of Modern Family and Contemporary Family in Modern and Contemporary Japanese Literature and Media"], *Jōsai Tanki Daigaku Kiyō* 29: 1 (2012): 3–4.

86. Allison Alexy writes of intimate relationships in contemporary Japan as emotional, physical, or informational closeness, within realms of private, often through love, desire and contact, focusing on the active part of intimacy such as "actions, practices, and patterns that are always shaped by imagination, fantasies, and various mediations." Allison Alexy, "Introduction: The Stakes of Intimacy in Contemporary Japan," in *Intimate Japan: Ethnographies of Closeness and Conflict*, Allison Alexy and Emma E. Cook, eds. (Honolulu: University of Hawai'i Press, 2019), 6.

girls act out a kind of pseudo-family in which exchanges of touch and intimacy between them have much more meaning than any blood-based family bonds.[87] The active return to skinship in pediatrics occurred together with the dissolution of nuclear families depicted in literary texts around the 1970s. It seems then that the skin-to-skin relationship was not necessarily readily available when Matsuura debuted with her 1978 "Sōgi no Hi" ["The Day of the Funeral"]. Or rather, it may have seemed present but was actually absent and thus longed for—with the gap between its assumed presence and its actual absence producing a desire to "shape" a relationship through the skin. Matsuura depicts a transferable, non-motherly, yet individually-specific skinship. The use of touch in Matsuura's works suggests a new relationality mediated by the skin beyond the family construct. In the 1987 "Nachuraru Ūman" ["Natural Woman"], too, the main female character Yoko has remarkable memories of touch with her beloved Hanayo that serve as a sort of primary memory to refer back to even without a familial presence. In Matsuura's writing, there is often neither a lived mother nor a family for her literary characters to return to, so a sense of relationality has to be re-generated. This type of renewable relationship, which is constructed in relation to the new object/person, while reforming the self, within psychological and physiological turmoil—which may be depicted by the author without the literary characters being conscious of it—would suggest the possibility of a critical reading of object-relations psychology, focused on otherness, the reconstructive possibility of language, and a reconceptualization of relationality.

The "other" in Matsuura refers not only to other persons with whom characters in the narrative attempt to construct a relationship through the skin—for example, in an intimate relationship. I want to suggest that the process of othering also has a literary analogue, in which characters are constructed through a decentering of both social norms and readers' likely expectations. For the male protagonist in Yoshiyuki, touch in his relationships with other (female) characters enhances his awareness of the otherness of both the other and the self, as narrated in a third-person perspective that mirrors what we know to be the author's experience. In

---

87. Matsuura Rieko, *Saiai no Kodomo* (Tokyo: Bungei Shunjū, 2017). As the narrator of this story is a collective of high-school girls, one may translate the title as "The Most Beloved Children." But illuminating the singular child of the pseudo-family inside the story, I here use the translation of singular form "child."

[margin handwritten notes: "what kinds of relationality are suggested" and "individual/family/nation"]

Matsuura, touch becomes the point of pluralistic intimate encounters, often involving bisexual female protagonists, who seem, at least from their outward appearance, naive and docile.[88] The narrative engagements offered in Matsuura's writing dissolve the singular "I" as of Yoshiyuki's middle-age male protagonists; the sexually indeterminate self here does not come back to the singular "I."

Yoshiyuki's works have not attracted much academic attention in the English-speaking world and, in Japan, have tended to be criticized for conveying a heterosexist viewpoint: through the use of females (such as prostitutes) as a means of eliminating male anger and emotional turmoil; and also for exhibiting a sexual double standard—that is generous to the male, but strict to females,[89] requiring of females both chastity and a non-reproductive sexuality. Their effacement of female subjectivity and otherness have also come in for criticism: the protagonists both yearn for communication with women, and fear them.[90] And yet, the recognition of the self even in Yoshiyuki always occurs through being in contact with others. I would counter the claims of male solipsism with the counterobjection that Yoshiyuki's reflexive awareness of the self perceived through the senses, especially touch, demands the other.

Toward the Unreachable

My chapter on skinship via Matsuura is where I most explicitly problematize the issue of gender difference and power imbalance—between the genders as well as between mother and child—in any intimate communication through touch, utilizing Matsuura's own at times explicit critique of

---

88. Matsuura aims to write about an in-between (*hanpa*) sexuality that is neither completely hetero- nor homosexual, neither male nor female, neither adult nor infantile. Matsuura's 2012 novel *Kika* [*Rarity*]—in which the main male character eavesdrops his lesbian roommate's romantic conversations—refers to *hanpa hetero*, an odd or incomplete heterosexuality, fundamentally heterosexual, but also interested in the same sex to some extent; this *hanpa* sexuality is not as sexualized as bisexuality, and not particularly active either, swaying toward the same sex to occasionally have sexual intercourse, but relating to the same sex only incompletely (*chūto hanpa*). Matsuura Rieko, *Kika* (Tokyo: Shinchōsha, 2012), 16–17.

89. Ueno Chizuko, Ogura Chikako, and Tomioka Taeko, *Danryū Bungakuron* [*The Discourse of Men's Literature*] (Tokyo: Chikuma Shobō, 1992), 29–30, 35.

90. Sekine Eiji, *"Tasha" no Shōkyo: Yoshiyuki Junnosuke to Kindai Bungaku* [*The Erasure of the Other: Yoshiyuki Junnosuke and Modern Literature*] (Tokyo: Keisō Shobō, 1993), 7.

masculine forms of misogyny, homosociality, distorted interest in homosexuality, and phallocentrism.[91] However, I must emphasize that each time
the abovementioned male authors (Tanizaki, Kawabata, and Yoshiyuki)
"objectify" women or female bodies, they also nevertheless portray characters' feelings such as uncertainty, anxiety, and fear about gendered other(s)
and make their characters react. One of the main contributions that my
book makes through its close reading of texts is to illuminate long-dismissed
or misunderstood aspects of particular texts and authors. There seems to
be a perception in Japanese literary scholarship that working exclusively
on female writers rather than critically and thoroughly engaging with male
writers' works enables provocative feminist readings and important interventions related to gender. And yet, the most critical moment for gender
politics arises, I believe, when assumed (gender) difference is played out
in texts and when characters across genders and sexes interact, even when
authors do not explicitly write against or act upon gender issues. This
is potentially more critical than a discussion of gender politics based on
gender similarity, or solidarity based on being a "woman."

While I have sympathy with collective voices, for me the issue is first
and foremost one of the individual voice, even as one shaped by cultural
and social contexts. When characters are situated in a confined space, such
as in Yoshiyuki's *The Dark Room*, and Kawabata's *Nemureru Bijo* [*House
of the Sleeping Beauties*] from 1961, and others examined in the monograph, they are primarily single individuals who decide, utter, and act.
My monograph offers a critical reading of texts by both male and female
writers in the hope of contributing also to the study of gender politics via
the reflexive recognition and transformation of the self. A critical reading
of gender politics is possible and still provocative when it comes via a thor-
ough reading of male writers' works, even when authors such as Kawabata
and Yoshiyuki problematically depict objectified female characters. This is
precisely because these authors write about them with extensive attention,
which conversely allows gendered others to speak or act out. Neglecting
such authors' depictions would mean missing ample opportunities to

---

91. Matsuura Rieko, "Kore ga Nihon no Homosōsharu" ["This is a Japanese Homosociality"], *Gunzō*, 61: 5 (2006): 234–237. See also discussion between Matsuura Rieko and
Kawakami Mieko, "Taidan Matsuura Rieko and Kawakami Mieko: Sei no Jubaku wo
koete" ["Conversation between Matsuura Rieko and Kawakami Mieko: Beyond the Sexual
Spell"], *Bungakukai*, 62: 5 (2008): 172.

rethink not only gender politics but also the whole issue of self-other construction in modern Japan.

My point discussing touch throughout this book is that one may not know what another end of touch might be feeling; one does not know and does not fully understand the other so that one tries to reach another's existence. Each of the writers I engage with in this book— Kawabata, Tanizaki, Yoshiyuki, and Matsuura—writes in way that presents a particular obsession with objects or relationality to the other constructed via the desire for touch. To give a very broad summation of these individual obsessions: In Kawabata, it is a withdrawal from touch followed by an eternal yearning for the loved object. In Tanizaki, it is the partial reachability of the other, which then elevates characters' desire to close the remaining distance via touch. In Yoshiyuki, it is the contemplation of an imaginary interstice formed through a repetitive contact with the other which then raises awareness of the self. And in Matsuura, it is a preoccupation with fluid skinship beyond the construct of an existing family that allows for a reorientation and regeneration of a sense of intimacy and relation to the other. These writers all depict intimate interactions that occur—whether due to desire or necessity—outside the traditional marital or family relationship. Sometimes the interactions turn into a yearning for skinship with the mother. At other times they turn into a negation of the mother. Taken together my readings of these writers suggest that one cannot assume that one can "touch" the other in reaching the other. Touch is an ongoing attempt at constructing a relationship with the other and a continuous process in which one become aware of oneself in the face of another.

The Japanese writers I examine are, most likely, skeptical about any assumption that one can easily construct an intimate relationship with an other, and therefore also similarly skeptical about the feeling called love— heterosexual love, familial love, or any love in other normative form. The characters in the writings of Kawabata and Yoshiyuki, for example, are often too fearful to try to construct a human relationship even if they desire it. Those in Tanizaki may not be afraid but may set particular barriers to reach the intended objects by themselves to elevate their desire for erotic communication with others, offering a landmark of tactile imagination. Those in Matsuura actively pursue intimate relationships, but without a sense of the so-called primary loved object, such as the mother. How can one love the other as well as the self? How does one deal with a situation in which the primary loved object is not available? How can one reconstruct relationality with an other? These are the questions that I believe these texts ask, and that I will be asking of them.

When characters are hesitant about direct contact (and indeed writers are hesitant about writing direct contact), the act of reaching toward the other often becomes intersensorial: the sense experience will involve the connection of one sense modality to another. The writers I deal with in this monograph commonly offer an intersensorial account of touch; by touching the other, one listens to it, or makes contact with it through gaze, shadows, or smell. This also includes when that "other" is a non-human presence, an entity such as air, dampness, or wind. One sense modality compensates another, but also allows access to another, exactly like touch itself, which lies in "between," connecting yet separating. My analysis of touch will treat the mediating nature of touch in a three-fold way: touch itself, sense modalities (touch's relation to other senses such as vision and sound), and their relation to language (embodied/disembodied). In my book, authors bring these questions and advance them further in such a way that they cannot be examined otherwise, in conversation with phe-nomenological and psychoanalytical thoughts—despite that touch has been neglected compared to other senses such as vision and sound (or "prohibited" in the case of psychoanalytic practices). All of my chapters respectively present a feature of touch, explored by each of the authors, the whole contributing to thinking about how to (try to) touch unreachable others. Touch is always an attempt to make contact with, reach, and to embrace the other beyond distance.

One of the agendas for this book is to discuss Japanese texts that have not been given enough attention in (English-speaking) academic circles but that pose critical inquiries about relationality. The lack of critical works on Matsuura, for example, might be explained by contemporaneity and limited translated works especially into English. Her 1993 novel *Oyayubi P no Shugyōjidai* (translated as *The Apprenticeship of Big Toe P* in 2009) is the only fictional work as yet to be translated into English. Yet, a careful reading of Matsuura's works show she is demanding a reconsideration of relationality through the skin especially in an extra-familial context, specif-ically how the body affects and is affected by the other in a non-verbal way. Similarly, despite his considerable stature in Japan, Yoshiyuki remains rela-tively little researched in Western academia, and afforded limited attention and interpretation in Japanese scholarship. The distinctive way in which he verbalizes physiological sensitivities and emotion, and illuminates the body breathing in an environment, requires a reading based on an understanding of the body as more than a solid mass. My study draws attention to this mode of bodily existence and attempts to attend to ambient effects[92] beyond objects. I suspect the lack of an effective framework is one of the reasons why writers like Yoshiyuki are under-researched in the English-speaking context, adding to the reason related to the I-novel style in which seemingly nothing dramatic happens,[93] as well as gender-related problematics discussed above. This book attempts to formulate an effective way to bring Japanese works to the global context, connecting the idea of the self, skinship, and writing. Thus, it offers both a thematic study of touch in literature and a theoretical tool to aid the nuanced reading of texts in their psychological and physiological surrounding, rather than focusing on the historical reading of the texts.

Touch in a written form includes not only depicted physical touch but also symbolic touch through language or the imaginary; touch is not only represented in the texts but is lived, missed, enacted, and re-experienced. When readers project themselves onto a particular literary character through the reader–character relationship, which Jean Laplanche and Jean-Bertrand Pontalis describe more aptly as identification,[94] touch is not merely written; with its compressed (and repressed) sensations, it invites readers to be in contact with the written. What one senses is not always fully reflected through words, and those who employ language are

---

92. Paul Roquet, in his work on ambience in contemporary Japan, takes its mediatory role of one's perception to another, ambient literature providing "a means for the usual specificities of self to relax into the more indeterminate contours of imagined space." Paul Roquet, *Ambient Media: Japanese Atmospheres of Self* (Minneapolis: University of Minnesota Press, 2016), 166.

93. Michael Bourdaghs discusses possible causes for the lack of visibility of Shimazaki Tōson—whose works often written in autobiographical I-novel style—in Western academic circles: the lack of exotic elements in comparison to authors like Mishima, Kawabata, and Tanizaki; and the discouragement for Western scholars working within the framework of New Criticism, which emphasized the autonomy of literary texts. Michael K. Bourdaghs, *The Dawn that Never Comes: Shimazaki Tōson and Japanese Nationalism* (New York: Columbia University Press, 2003), 20–21.

94. Jean Laplanche, and Jean-Bertrand Pontalis, *The Language of Psychoanalysis*, trans. Donald Nicholson-Smith (London: Karnac Books, 2006), 350–351.

still trying to capture sensations through words, touch, and to open what is invisible—in an invitation to a particular intimate relationship. As film scholar Laura Marks—who advances the idea of haptic that neutralizes the division between sense modalities and the distance created thereby, such as a vision that engages with the haptic function explored earlier by Deleuze and Guattari[95]—puts it, writing "translates" embodie experiences (into words),[96] the tactile aspects of language evoking the sensations to be felt and re-experienced by an audience or a reader. This tactile language evoking sensations, in my view, translates into literary depictions of touch in a form of literary touch. The literary scholar Naitō Chizuko writes of the novelistic wish to verbalize what cannot be verbalized as "romantic tactility" (ren'ai kanshoku) of the novel—a mixed feeling involving a wish to touch the other and a despair of the impossibility of doing so.[97] It is not only that authors write about their characters' trials of touching the other: their palpable depictions also enact touch, as if their necessarily disembodied accounts of embodied experience of touch can be activated by the tactile aspect of author's language.

In sum, paying attention to the experience of touch offers a new way to conceive the narrative "I" or the concept of the self, reflected by the other in reaching and shaping another's body. Writing about touch also lets the the body on the page emerge, in the very trial of touching it; the literary works invite a circuit of people, objects, and the surrounding environment in a contact that is beyond one-to-one, beyond the immediate moment through the work of imagination. An elevated desire to touch others presented by literary characters may also shape the relation beyond the surface of the skin and the page. On top of the fact that relationality through the skin is renewable throughout one's life, imagined touch allows contact

---

95. Gilles Deleuze and Felix Guattari, *A Thousand Plateaus: Capitalism and Schizophrenia*, trans. Brian Massumi (Minneapolis: University of Minnesota Press, 1987), 492–494. The relation between the haptic and the visual became a central focus of art-historical discourse in the early twentieth century, with such as that of Heinrich Wölfflin, Alois Riegl, and Wilhelm Worringer, as noted in Deleuze and Guattari's discussion of the haptic. Originally published as *Mille plateaux* in 1980 by Les Editions de Minuit.

96. Laura Marks, *Touch: Sensuous Theory and Multisensory Media* (Minneapolis and London: University of Minnesota Press, 2002), ix.

97. Naitō Chizuko, *Shōsetsu no Ren'ai Kanshoku* [*The Romantic Tactility of the Novel*] (Tokyo: Misuzu Shobō, 2010), 22–23.

with the loved one beyond space and time. In this book, I shall argue that touch shapes one's relationality to others—even allowing authors to shape a relationship with the reader by writing on an imaginary "skin"—in an attempt to reach the other and shape the body. When authors depict details of characters' experience, they are also reaching their characters as well as readers through the respective features of language they choose to use. Authors' literary touch on to their characters, shared by their readers, transforms and enriches the awareness of those who are involved, through the dynamic interaction with the world. It is with such an oscillatory relation created via touch between characters and authors, and authors and readers, that literary touch exerts a force and makes us "feel."

CHAPTER I

Loved Object

The Unreachable

Loved Object

"'I can let you have one of my arms for the night'," says the girl. She removes her right arm at the shoulder and uses her left hand to lay it on the protagonist's knee. The girl's right arm is still warm.[1] So begins the short story "Kataude" ["One Arm"], written by Kawabata Yasunari in 1963–1964, originally published in five installments in the journal *Shinchō*. In "One Arm," a girl lends the male protagonist her arm for one night, permitting him to replace his arm with hers. He takes her arm home, carrying it under his coat for fear of its being noticed. Once safe in his flat, he observes the arm under the play of the light, gently touches its nails and fingertips, and "talks" with it and embraces it. He replaces his own arm with hers, which then causes him to become conscious of an uncrossable chasm between her arm and his body. Eventually reaching a kind of peace, he sleeps—only to awaken when, accidentally, he touches his own separated arm, which is lying on the floor, at which point he wrenches the girl's arm from his body and replaces it with his own. This story explores the issue of alterity—how can one relate to an other, particularly when that other has become a part of oneself. At this sudden recognition of an alterity within his own body, he encounters "her" (and indeed himself too) with both repulsion and affection. "One Arm," in my reading, depicts the protagonist's oscillating relation with the arm and its unreachable main

---

1. Kawabata Yasunari, "One Arm," in *House of the Sleeping Beauties and Other Stories*, trans. Edward Seidensticker (Tokyo: Kōdansha International, 2004), 103 (hereafter abbreviated as *HSB*).

body, and his negotiation with its otherness, or lack thereof. In this chapter I shall be looking at touch with the loved object, which in Kawabata is yearned for but depicted as infinitely unreachable.

This chapter offers a rereading of intimacy and narcissism in Kawabata, not in relation to male fantasy and the absence of female agency, which have generally been the focus of existing discussions on Kawabata; but rather with regard to reciprocal relationship (or the desire for it). Studies of Kawabata have pointed to the objectification of female body, emphasized feminine passivity, as in "One Arm" and "House of the Sleeping Beauties." The argument is that female characters in Kawabata are "objects," often devoid of identity, anything individual, and seem to have to be rendered unable to speak or to act.[2] While acknowledging the validity of these arguments, and the existence of seemingly objectified bodies, I would like to make the argument nevertheless for a degree of reciprocity in Kawabata's writing, and a degree of a desire for mutual relationship on the part of his male protagonists.

In Kawabata's writings, the characters' strong yearning to reach the other often appears in a form of a gaze, and is verbalized by the author's language. The desired object in Kawabata emerges, in my view, by being longed for. Such a trial of reaching the desired, I argue, necessarily requires the object; love, including narcissism, requires the presence of the object even if sometimes without the clearest difference between the self and the other. In Leo Bersani's account of "impersonal narcissism," as discussed at length later in this chapter, narcissistic love is identical to a "knowledge of otherness,"[3] and the emergence of love of the self necessitates the existence of an object. Reading touch in Kawabata, which illuminates narcissistic nature, rather highlights the active involvement of the object. Even if the protagonists fail to communicate effectively, Kawabata depicts the signals uttered by the objectified bodies, to which we might do well to listen. In analyzing the neglected dimensions of touch and incorporation of the loved object in Kawabata, I will examine in this chapter touch in

2.   Roy Starrs, *Soundings in Time: The Fictive Art of Kawabata Yasunari* (Richmond: Japan Library, 1998), 189; Mebed, "Kawabata Bungaku ni okeru Furoito Shisō no Eikyō wo meguru Ichi Kōsatsu," 163–165; Susan J. Napier, *The Fantastic in Modern Japanese Literature: The Subversion of Modernity* (London: Routledge, 1996), 63.
3.   Leo Bersani, "The Power of Evil and the Power of Love," in *Intimacies* by Leo Bersani and Adam Phillips (Chicago, IL: The University of Chicago Press, 2008), 85.

relationship to the object: the way one relates to, intensifies one's desire for, accepts or rejects the otherness of, and constitutes a loved object. This is the unreachable in Kawabata's writing.

The loved object I examine includes the transitional one in an adolescent friendship, through the quasi-autobiographic novel *Shōnen* [*The Boy*], published in six installments in the journal *Ningen* in 1948–1949, and *Shin'yū* [*Best Friends*], published in fifteen installments in *Jogakusei no Tomo* in 1954–1955. This last was only recently reconstructed and published in 2015. While *Shōnen* illuminates an intimate relationship that the narrator Miyamoto had in his adolescence with another boy, his boarding mate Kiyono, *Shin'yū* depicts same-sex yearning between girls (referred to at the time as "S," for "sisterhood"). Both stories express Kawabata's yearning for the sincerity and beauty of adolescents. This yearning also appears in "One Arm" in the form of the protagonist's preference for a "not-yet-touched" girl over other "touched" women, which is further extended to the dormant body in *Nemureru Bijo* [*House of the Sleeping Beauties*], originally published in seventeen installments in *Shinchō* in 1960–1961, a text that also relies on the fundamental unreachability in touching.

These stories, taken together, tell us much about Kawabata and his depictions of one's relationship to the loved object. Touch in Kawabata in these stories always figures in a partial, mediated, and highly nuanced manner. It speaks of the complexity of this man, especially when the trajectory of his life and the cultural context are read together. Having lost his parents when he was little and his grandparents in his teens, Kawabata had few memories of intimate relationships with his immediate family members, partly reflected in his early writings.[4] He reached maturity at a time when literary representations of sensual expressions such as hugging, kissing, and the touch of the lover's hot skin became subject to severe censorship. The Peace Preservation Law (*Chian Iji Hō*) enacted in 1925 covered

---

4.   See Kawabata Yasunari, "Sobo" ["Grandmother"], in *Kawabata Yasunari Zenshū*, vol. 2 (Tokyo: Shinchōsha, 1980), 439–441. After the death of first-person narrator (I / *watashi*)'s parents, his grandmother loved him unreservedly, two memories of whom remained; when his blind grandfather angrily kept hitting his grandmother who tried to protect him, and when he had her wear a *tabi* and cover herself with a quilt before her death. *Tabi* are the Japanese white socks that go with a kimono; it is common for the dead to be clothed in them at a funeral. See also Kawabata Yasunari, "Koji no Kanjō" ["Orphan's Feeling"], in *KYZ* 2, 155.

the first version, now called "pre-original" version, of his *Yukiguni* [*Snow Country*] in 1935 with deletions, omissions, and corrections. In the first part ("Yūgeshiki no Kagami" ["The Mirror of the Evening Landscape"]) of this pre-original version, the protagonist Shimamura "remembers" his loved one through his left forefinger (although the actual term "forefinger" [*hitosashi yubi*] was omitted in the published text), the forefinger mediating the uncertain memory of woman and its distant physicality.[5] During the rise of a return in all things Japanese in the 1930s, commonly dubbed the "return to the Orient" (*tōyō kaiki*), an attitude that many leading Japanese writers at least professed to share, Kawabata avoided active political engagement, unlike his new sensationist friend Yokomitsu Riichi (1898–1947). He continued to write about female bodies, beauty, and sadness even in the postwar period.

While Nina Cornyetz argues that Kawabata, in turning to Japanese traditional culture, refused to politicize art, yet also refused to depoliticize what was already political,[6] Kawabata Kaori, referring to Kawabata's postwar return to Japanese tradition, suggests that reading this simply as a "return to tradition" is a misrecognition given that vanguard elements and traditional, classical, or indigenous elements coexist and crisscross.[7] In my view, Kawabata was experimental throughout his career in writing about the precarious nature of relationship; his works questioned the extent to which ways of pursuing intimacy could be accepted, some works even foreshadowing and predicting later related social phenomena such as stalking in "Mizuumi" ["The Lake"] in 1954, and the payable co-sleeping services in *The House of the Sleeping Beauties*. Both stalking and commodified intimacy are noticeable phenomena in contemporary Japan.

---

5. Kawabata Yasunari, "Yūgeshiki no Kagami," in "Yukiguni (pure-orijinaru)" ["Snow Country (pre-original)"], in *KYZ*, vol. 24 (Tokyo: Shinchōsha, 1982), 73–74. The completed version has both parts (*KYZ*, vol. 10 [Tokyo: Shinchōsha, 1980], 11–12), with further intimate descriptions. Kawabata Yasunari, *Snow Country*, trans. Edward G. Seidensticker (London: Penguin Books, 2011), 5.

6. Nina Cornyetz, *The Ethics of Aesthetics in Japanese Cinema and Literature: Polygraphic Desire* (Abingdon and New York: Routledge, 2007), 25–26.

7. Kawabata Kaori, "Sekaiteki Kanten kara Kawabata Yasunari wo Miru" ["Seeing Kawabata Yasunari from the World View"], *Kokubungaku* 46: 4 (March 2001): 22. Kawabata Kaori, a scholar of Russian literature, is Kawabata's son-in-law (the husband of Kawabata's adopted daughter Masako).

The characters in Kawabata's works tend to be so hesitant to touch others that they can only reach the objects of their desire through the act of looking or identification with an object that represents the loved object. Some authors and literary critics have noted that Kawabata had a peculiar way of looking at other persons; he would hold them in a fixed stare or gaze; and his eyes gave him a demeanor that was almost ghostly. Kawabata's stare evoked a number of reactions—including cold sweats, tears, and a strong desire to flee[8]—and commentators surmise that his marked preoccupation with life and death stems from his experience of deaths of most of his immediate family when he was little, leading to his eyes to recognize the fugitive beauty (*hakanai utsukushisa*) or ruined beauty (*horobi no utsukushisa*).[9] Yoshiyuki Junnosuke wrote that Kawabata considered female beauty in terms of an idea of "passing beauty" (*toorisugiru bi*).[10] Any direct physical interaction tends to be one-way or to comprise communication with a mere part of the loved one, an arm or an unconscious body like those of the girls in *House of the Sleeping Beauties*, who can only be touched after they have been given sleeping pills and have fallen asleep, as if with a necessary precondition of a certain distance.[11]

In *House of the Sleeping Beauties*, customers sleep overnight with the girls at a particular inn, who are put to sleep with sleeping pills. Old Eguchi touches the girl who is sleeping with him, observes her response, and sometimes tries to wake her, although customers are never allowed to retain the same girl on multiple visits. However, in my view, it is not that Kawabata's

8. See Mishima Yukio, "Eien no Tabibito: Kawabata Yasunari shi no Hito to Sakuhin" ["Eternal Traveller: Kawabata Yasunari and His Works," written in 1956 and edited in 1958], in *Kindai Bungaku Kanshō Kōza*, ed. Yamamoto Kenkichi, vol. 13 (Tokyo: Kadokawa Shoten, 1958), 264. See also Yoshiyuki Junnosuke, "Kawabata Yasunari den Danpen" ["Fragments on Kawabata Yasunari"] (1966) in *Yoshiyuki Junnosuke Zenshū*, vol. 12 (Tokyo: Shinchōsha, 1998), 376–377.
9. Yamamoto Kenkichi, "Kinjū" ["Of Birds and Beasts"] in *Kindai Bungaku Kanshō Kōza*, vol. 13, 138.
10. Yoshiyuki Junnosuke, "Funabashi Seiichi Shōron" ["Short Essay on Funabashi Seiichi"] (1963) in *YJZ*, vol. 12, 238.
11. Van C. Gessel, *Three Modern Novelists: Sōseki, Tanizaki, Kawabata* (Tokyo: Kōdansha International, 1993), 162; Tsujimoto Chizu, "Yama no Oto ron: Sono Ai no Yōsō" ["On *The Sound of the Mountain*: The Appearance of Love"], *Ronkyū Nihon Bungaku* 50 (1987): 64.

literary characters are distant from the possibility of being in touch; in fact, they are still hoping to reach the loved object from afar—even through a piece of broken tea bowl—making sure to have some space in-between to keep themselves as well as the loved objects safe. Even with distance as a necessary precondition, the visual possesses a haptic nature: there is a reaching for the observed other. It is not that the seer/looker is an active subject who looks at the object and the seen/looked-at a passive object is waiting to be seen; rather, there is reciprocity in action. The gaze in Kawabata plays a haptic role, as though the character's gaze replaces actual touch. The protagonist withdraws: he refrains from reaching the object; he touches it through his gaze. The distance is thus required.

At the same time, in verbalizing such an alternative form of touch, Kawabata's language itself begins to serve a haptic function. Speaking of Kawabata's detailed and precise descriptions of the sleeping girl in his *House of the Sleeping Beauties*, Mishima Yukio suggested, "[it is] as if she were being caressed by words alone."[12] Kawabata was an acute observer, even making a profession of his powers as a reviewer of dance and ballet performances.[13] His preparations for writing *House of the Sleeping Beauties* also involved hiring female models, and taking photographs of them.[14] His vision of the objectified sleeping girl invites Eguchi to observe her silent body in detail by participating in an irresistible relationship in which the haptic is led by the visual, but also by the written. In reading this story through two axes of the literal—as the mechanism of the desire to dissect the symbol, trying to open the girls' eyes and coming closer to the surface—as opposed to the "symbolic" eye in the sleeping girls, Hosea Hirata finds that the author's language mirrors his representation of his protagonist's gaze: "Kawabata's words caress the entire body, slowly, in

---

12. Mishima, "Introduction," *HSB*, 9.

13. For Kawabata's contributions as a dance reviewer/critic to a range of dance culture in twentieth-century Japan, see Fusako Innami, "Gendered High and Low Culture in Japan: The Transgressing Flesh in Kawabata's Dance Writing," *The Routledge Companion to Gender and Japanese Culture*, eds. Jennifer Coates, Lucy Fraser, and Mark Pendleton, 373–81 (Abingdon; New York: 2020).

14. Fukuda Junko, "Kawabata Yasunari to Shōsetsu 'Nemureru Bijo'" ["Kawabata Yasunari and the novel 'House of the Sleeping Beauties'"], in performance program, *Opera Nemureru Bijo* [*Opera House of the Sleeping Beauties*] (Tokyo: Tokyo Bunka Kaikan, 2016).

detail, as if casting a tight-fitting net of language over the body."[15] This account of the relation between words (or writing) and touch—or writing as touch and as touched—is thus key to the reading of Kawabata's texts, precisely because he mostly avoids depicting touch between his characters; and yet the male protagonist (or Kawabata himself, as writer) still tries to reach the other through the gaze and through words. Adding to the capacity of a haptic visuality, Kawabata's language reaches from afar and caresses the body by attentively depicting it.

And yet, somewhat in contrast to the careful attention given in most of Kawabata's works to describing physical contact, with a subtle tension between touching and not touching, in "One Arm," a single arm is completely and suddenly joined to another person's body. Mishima points out that it is made possible for the protagonist in "One Arm" to have a dialogue, or interactive communication, with the girl's arm precisely because it is merely an arm, and not the entire body;[16] interactive communication thus depends on the fragmentation of a female body. The unreachability of the other person is figured through that of her body as a whole (the *botai* 母体; literally "mother body"). The story raises questions regarding contact and rupture. A subtle surface contact using the nails and fingertips, and the play of light and smell, suddenly gives way to violent acts such as wrenching off and forced grafting—radical shifts of forms of touch, as well as the haptic in Kawabata, which are still to be addressed.

The communication via touch detailed in this story makes us rethink the relationship to the loved object due not only to the rupture, but also to the shifting distance between the protagonist and the arm, and between him and the girl's main body, by depicting the protagonist as constantly concerned with and yearning for the unreachable. In the reciprocal relationship between the embracing and the embraced in this story (midway through the story her arm embraces his neck; at the end, he embraces the dead arm), the protagonist creates the other, potentially including his own otherness, through the incorporation of the girl's arm, even if he cannot fully accept what he finds. "One Arm" tends to be discussed in terms of

15. Hosea Hirata, *Discourses of Seduction: History, Evil, Desire, and Modern Japanese Literature* (Cambridge, MA: Harvard University Press, 2005), 31.
16. Mishima Yukio, "Kaisetsu" ["Interpretation"] (1967) in Kawabata Yasunari, *Nemureru Bijo* (Tokyo: Shinchōsha, 2011), 246.

disjunction and passivity, as well as fetishism and virginity, all of which make it difficult to understand how the protagonist could relate to the beloved arm.[17] But this is a story in which the loved object is transitive. It is not only acted upon, it affects the other. It is this mutual shaping of relationship in Kawabata that I shall be giving my attention to throughout this chapter.

Jean Laplanche and Jean-Bertrand Pontalis draw a distinction between incorporation, the term of which they note first appeared in Sigmund Freud's *Three Essays on the Theory of Sexuality* (1905), and introjection: "In psychoanalysis the bounds of the body provide the model of all separations between an inside and an outside. Incorporation involves this bodily frontier literally. Introjection has a broader meaning in that it is no longer a matter only of the interior of the body but also that of the psychical apparatus, of a psychical agency, etc."[18] The concept of introjection was first introduced and developed by Hungarian psychoanalyst Sándor Ferenczi, Melanie Klein's mentor, who used it to mean internalizing objects and their qualities from outside through fantasy, without specific reference to the real bodily boundary.[19] Ferenczi's analysis of introjection and exteriorization (by which he meant an extension of the ego and its autoerotic interests to the external world, and a taking-in of an image of the loved object) drew attention to the inside–outside, pleasure–unpleasure, and love–hate polarities, leading to Freud's development of the active–passive and sadistic–masochistic polarities in his 1915 essay "Instincts and their Vicissitudes," in which he first used Ferenczi's 1909 term "introject."[20] Having served as an army physician during World War I (and having developed his psychoanalytic theories through his experience with traumatized soldiers), Ferenczi theorized how one negotiates with the physical

---

17. Fujii Takashi argues that the vanishing of the border between a machine (a girl's arm) and the subject is the mark of an erotic unity of the two. " 'Dokushin-sha no Kikai' to 'Ikei no Shintai' Hyōshō: 'Tanin no Kao,' 'Kataude,' 'Ningyō zuka' no Dōjidai sei." [" 'Bachelor Machines' and the Representations of 'Malformed Bodies': On the Contemporaneity of 'Tanin no Kao,' 'Kataude,' and 'Ningyō zuka' "], *Nihon Kindai Bungaku* 91 (2014): 102.

18. Laplanche and Pontalis, *The Language of Psychoanalysis*, 230.

19. Sándor Ferenczi, "On the Definition of Introjection," 316–18.

20. Sigmund Freud, "Instincts and their Vicissitudes" (1915), *SE*, trans. James Strachey et al., vol. 14 (London: Hogarth Press, 1962 [1957]), 136. Also see Sándor Ferenczi, "Introjection and Transference" from 1909, reprinted in *First Contributions to Psychoanalysis*, trans. Ernest Jones (London and New York: Karnac, 1994).

reality inside one's psyche, while also delivering his psychoanalytic theories to a new readership with an interdisciplinary mindset.

If we define "tactile" to mean "involving touch" and "haptic" to mean "involving touch as possibility," introjection suggests a potentiality that lies between the internal and external worlds in the realm of fantasy, without involving actual touch. As demonstrated in my reading of Kawabata below, Klein's analysis of the incorporation of the loved object further describes the infant's relation to the mother's breast as the prototype of a "good" object, including incorporation through the sense experiences apart from touch, without being confined to the oral stage. Relational dynamics between inside and outside—such as introjection taking in the source of pleasure and projection keeping out the source of unpleasure[21]— raises further questions regarding the relationship between the protagonist and the unreachable in "One Arm," while the latter literary case raising the issue regarding the acknowledgement of otherness in Klein's writing. As the Kleinian sense of "position" is of a state to which one may return later in life, Kleinian incorporation sheds a suggestive light on relation-ships between adults as well as that of infant and mother. With a particular attention to relationship to the loved object in this manner, I will make the case for the yearning for reciprocity in Kawabata's writing, viewed through ruptured communication.

Ruptured Incorporation

The common understanding of physical touch is mostly based rather on a visual understanding by shortening the distance between the touching and the touched. However, defining what constitutes touch is complex. "One Arm" reflects the protagonist's tenderness toward, as well as relation with, the not-fully-reachable girl's arm and, above all, her distant main body (*botai*), rather than toward a touchable "it." And yet, I here go against existing readings regarding the passivity of female characters in Kawabata's works; the girl here, by giving a consent for her arm to be transferred to the

---

21. Especially when the ego projects its feelings into objects which it identifies with, it is called projective identification. See Juliet Mitchell's introduction to Melanie Klein, as well as Klein's "The Psychological Principles of Infant Analysis" and "Notes on Some Schizoid Mehcanisms" (1946) in *SMK*.

protagonist's body, directs the relationship that develops between them: " 'I don't suppose you'll try to change it for your own arm,' she said. 'But it will be all right. Go ahead, do'."[22] With this consent, the girl gives the protagonist a part of her body. Her consent means that her arm is not merely dislocated, touched, and incorporated, but also actively transferred: it leaves her body for that of the protagonist. Despite the starkly depicted motif of bodily incorporation, this story illuminates an uncertainty about touch, depicted through the fragmentation of the body. It seems as if, in touching, the protagonist definitively escapes the presence of her body.

In my introduction to this book, I proposed that touch consists of conflicting forces of reaching and departing, touching and not touching. Touch in shape of pursuit of the other convoluted with hesitancy and withdrawal from touch, prevalent in Kawabata, is theorized in Emmanuel Levinas's account of caress. Levinas writes of caress as a search into the invisible, involving a difficulty in or the impossibility of holding the loved. "It [the caress] *searches*, it forages. It is not an intentionality of disclosure but of search: a movement unto the invisible."[23] Levinas sees the caress as involving a quest for, rather than a taking hold of and a possessing of, the loved object.[24] This view suggests that, moving toward the invisible, the very attempt to reach the other may be what constitutes touching, rather than the actual shortening of the distance. Jean-Paul Sartre further suggests that it is not only that the distance shrinks between the toucher and the touched, but also that the act of reaching indicates the other: "[t]he caress is not a simple stroking: it is a *shaping*. In caressing the Other, I cause her flesh to be born beneath my caress, under my fingers."[25] Touch indicates

---

22. Kawabata, "One Arm," 104.

23. Emmanuel Levinas, *Totality and Infinity: An Essay on Exteriority*, trans. Alphonso Lingis (Pittsburgh, PA: Duquesne University Press, 1969), 258. Originally published as *Totalité et infini: essai sur l'extériorité* in French in 1961 by Martinus Nijhoff.

24. Steven Connor adds here on Levinas: "It is as though a hand were to reach out in a dark place and touch, where it had expected an object, another hand, or the twitching fur of an animal. One recoils from such a touch" due to "the danger of betraying the flesh into the carapace of an outline." Steven Connor, *The Book of Skin* (London: Reaktion Books, 2004), 278.

25. Sartre, *Being and Nothingness*, 411–412. The pronouns in French are masculine (as *autrui*). The use of capital "O" in "Other" appears in writings of Levinas, Sartre, Lacan, and other thinkers, to differentiate the radical "Other" as an element to define or constitute the self from a more general "other."

and brings to mind the presence of the other in the very act of touching. Despite Kawabata's depiction of the pleasure (*itoshisa*) found in the girl's arm, which is focused on purity, evident in such an expressions as "her breasts, not yet touched by a man,"[26] "One Arm" also complicates the boundary of "touch," abruptly progressing from surface contact to incorporation of the arm.

"One Arm" captures the resonance of the beloved's body through its partiality and wholeness. The protagonist narrates, "It seemed to me that the arm and the girl herself were an infinity apart." Writing of the girl's whole body as *botai* (main, or mother, body), he wonders, "Would the arm be able to return to the girl, so far away?"[27] The "distance" interrogated here is not just the distance between him and her, but between her displaced arm and her main body. In touching, he is constantly aware of this distance from the *botai*, which remains unreachable. Her appearance as one arm rather than a whole body also seems to give him easier access to her, since he can keep escaping from the visibility of the body: both his own, as she does not possess the eyes to directly look at him, and thus make him the object of her vision, and hers, since she does not appear as a whole body. However, her arm, though only a part of her body, essentially functions as if it is her subjectivity, her person: it listens to and "talks" to him, moves, watches him, and makes him feel shy. He communicates with her arm, which stands for her wholeness, but without any feeling of pressure, since it is visually merely an arm rather than a whole female body. The sense of unreachability in the distance her partial body indicates with respect to her body and person as a whole confers upon their contact its special character.

Another characteristic of this story stems from the multisensorial effect that the subtle surface contact has on the protagonist before the incorporation of the arm. When he comes back to his room with the girl's arm, a pleasant and calm interaction between the protagonist and the arm ensues. When he touches the girl's fingertip, which he notes is protected by a carefully polished, faintly pink nail, her finger flexes and her elbow bends. Having discovered from experience with another woman that women's fingers are especially sensitive when they have long nails, and regretting the fact that he asked if her fingers were tickled by his touch, he says, "on the

---

26. Kawabata, "One Arm," 106; "Kataude," in *KYZ*, vol. 8 (Tokyo: Shinchōsha, 1981), 550.
27. Kawabata, "One Arm," 111; "Kataude," 557.

body of the girl who had lent me the arm they [her tender spots] would be beyond counting"; that is, they were all over her body.[28] When he takes the girl's arm and flexes the elbow again and again, the arm says, "Behave yourself," as if smiling; a smile that, however, "did come over the arm, crossing it like light. It was exactly the fresh smile on the girl's cheek."[29] Kawabata's narratives access the world, Cornyetz puts it, through "vibrantly tactile, auditory, and visual" senses,[30] or a synesthetic where, as Takayama Hiroshi puts it, "touch and smell smiling at vision."[31] Kawabata translates his protagonist's tactile discovery of the partial body into observation. The subtlest touch that barely connects with the other affects him personally: "The long, narrow, delicate nail scratched gently at the palm of my hand, and the slight touch made my sleep deeper. I disappeared."[32]

Conversely, the drama of this story lies in the fact that such delicate touching may lead to rupture. In a single moment, he throws her arm away from his body, "insisting," as Susan Napier puts it, "on the essential isolation between individuals, the fundamental inability to connect."[33] In "One Arm," when the girl gives the protagonist permission to replace his own right arm with hers, he does so. Soon after that, he feels a spasm, then a break, and a disjunction between the arm and his shoulder. "I could feel the girl's fingers in my mouth, but the fingers of her right hand, now those of my own right hand, could not feel my lips or teeth. In panic I shook my right arm and could not feel the shaking. There was a break, a stop, between arm and shoulder."[34] In the next moment, he is concerned about the detached arm's bleeding, wondering whether the blood is coming from her arm or his shoulder. When her arm covers his ear, he continues noting the motion that comes not of his volition but of the girl's arm, from its heart. Then the protagonist and the arm listen to the sound of the pulse,

---

28. Kawabata, "One Arm."
29. Kawabata, "One Arm," 113.
30. Cornyetz, *The Ethics of Aesthetics*, 18.
31. Takayama Hiroshi, "'Bukimi na Monoga...' Kawabata Gensō Bungaku no Atarashi-sa: 'Kataude' 'Nemureru Bijo' ni Furete" ["The Uncanny ... The Novelty of Kawabata Fantastic Literature: through 'One Arm' and 'House of the Sleeping Beauties'"], *Kokubungaku* 46: 4 (March 2001): 82.
32. Kawabata, "One Arm," 123.
33. Napier, *The Fantastic in Modern Japanese Literature*, 65.
34. Kawabata, "One Arm," 119.

the blood flowing through the arms. He no longer feels any shuddering or spasm, and falls asleep. When he wakes suddenly with a scream, to the repulsive touch of his right arm, he tears off the arm that is attached to his shoulder and replaces his own, trembling. When he regains his composure, the girl's arm is lying on the bed, quite still and growing pale. He embraces it like a dying baby. If the condition of what Levinas would call "a fecund being" is to be capable of a fate other than its own,[35] what is the meaning of the spasm and gap between the arms of the man and the girl, incurred by incorporation?

The struggle between possession or dispossession occurs with a feeling of love that progresses from the part to the whole, which is explained in relation to the ambivalent feeling by Klein. Klein writes:

> Full identification with the object based on the libidinal attachment, first to the breast, then to the whole person, goes hand in hand with anxiety for it (of its disintegration), with guilt and remorse, with a sense of responsibility for preserving it intact against persecutors and the id, and with sadness relating to expectation of the impending loss of it. These emotions, whether conscious or unconscious, are in my view among the essential and fundamental elements of the feelings we call love.[36]

The good object, now incorporated, becomes a source of anxiety as one continues to care about the incorporated loved object. In "One Arm," in the actual process of knowing her arm—through his talking with it, observing the light reflected on it, communicating with it by smell, and spending time with it—he becomes attracted to it. Her body part effectively becomes like a whole body, especially through his identifying the pulse of the arm with his own heartbeat. As her arm and his body lie beside each other, the protagonist's heart becomes overlaid with the delicate pulse that belongs to the girl's arm: the two pulses sound against each other, and it is indiscernible which is which. The presence of her arm beside him is for him like that of her whole body. He is soothed by the presence of her

---

35. Levinas, *Totality and Infinity*, 282.
36. Klein, "A Contribution to the Pychogenesis of Manic-Depressive States" (1935), *SMK*, 125.

arm and decides to take it on. "In a trance, I removed my right arm and substituted the girl's. There was a slight gasp—whether from the arm or from me I could not tell—and a spasm at my shoulder. So I knew of the change."[37]

The physical incorporation of the arm brings about an inescapable chasm involving repulsion at the touch of his own arm, and the ultimate wrenching off of the arm of the other. Being "overtly 'postmodern' in style and setting," as per Napier, "anything can happen."[38] Incorporation, in particular, signifying a greater sense of bodily frontiers than introjection, causes a significant sense of loss both in psychic phantasy and corporeal reality. The arm embracing the protagonist's neck in the middle of the story and the protagonist conversely embracing the girl's dying arm in the final scene, this story reveals the protagonist's ambivalent feelings beyond categories like the erotic or maternal. In particular, the alterity sensed through incorporation and the absence of negotiation at the end impart a subtle sadness about bodily communication, both in the sense of the loss of a loved object, and the inability to accept another's life within oneself. The bodily incorporation and the sensations caused by the alterity of the other's body problematize the standpoint of the incorporated object and the further possibility of an ethical co-existence with the other.

Kawabata tends to depict male protagonists who hesitate and defer an actual encounter with the loved body. This deferral of touch makes the beloved "the untouchable," placing her, as in Levinas in a "future in the present,"[39] and the act of caressing "the anticipation of this pure future."[40] Yet, this un-realization of touch may not always be the product of a male fantasy; Cathryn Vasseleu problematizes Luce Irigaray's caress as "the gesture of touch," instead of touch itself, as well as Levinas's idea of fecundity as "an escape from the universal,"[41] by placing the beloved not in the tangible present but the unknowable future. Insisting that the mark

---

37. Kawabata, "One Arm," 118–119.
38. Napier, *The Fantastic in Modern Japanese Literature*, 64.
39. Levinas, *Totality and Infinity*, 258.
40. Emmanuel Levinas, *Time and the Other*, trans. Richard A. Cohen (Pittsburgh, PA: Duquesne University Press, 1987), 89.
41. Cathryn Vasseleu, *Textures of Light: Vision and Touch in Irigaray, Levinas and Merleau-Ponty* (London: Routledge, 1998), 107, 114.

inscribed during the course of a touch, which "my body" remembers, cannot be made into discourse,[42] Irigaray is attentive to surfaces such as membrane and mucosa. While exploring the possibility of an "invisible" touch, as opposed to the kind discussed by Merleau-Ponty, Sartre, and Levinas, where touching subjects relate to sight, Irigaray implies a kind of mystery to it: "This invisible cannot be seized or be understood."[43] Such theoretical problematics question whether a body ever really encounters another body.

It is here that Kawabata's work would contribute to the conceptualization of touch, with the idea of consent, or "permission" ("*yurushi*" in original Japanese) to replace the arm. In his story, the object saying, "Please" ("*iiwa*" in original Japanese), gives it a degree of agency. There are two permissions in "One Arm." One is given to the protagonist by the girl who lends her arm; the other is given to him by a different woman who decides to give herself to him. The protagonist retrospectively narrates this woman's permission; her voice was trembling, he remembers, and she associated herself with the dead Lazarus.[44] Although the substitution of gender here creates another "beloved" female, this permission is given to actualize the unification of their bodies, not in an unknown time but an impending future. Both the physical exchange with the other woman above and the replacement with the girl's arm occur through a mutual consent between the male protagonist and the female figures. Incorporations here are driven not exclusively by the male fantasy but through consent between those who touch.

Incorporation in Kawabata, as in Klein, is not limited to the sexual kind, and the sadness at being unable to accept otherness indicates an ambivalence of feeling: of love and rejection, desire and hesitation, affection and repulsion. The communication between the protagonist and the arm proceeds not necessarily through visible demonstration, gesture, or abstract erotic energy, but through the experience of finding and feeling the other next to or inside of oneself, or oneself inside the other: through the warmth, the texture of the skin, the smell, the light, the pulse, heartbeat,

---

42. Irigaray, *An Ethics of Sexual Difference*, 178–179.
43. Luce Irigaray, "Perhaps Cultivating Touch Can Still Save Us," *SubStance* 40, no. 3 (2011): 138.
44. Kawabata, "One Arm," 113–115; "Kataude," 559–562, with reference to the Bible: John 11: 35–37.

and blood coming and going between them. This is a visceral way of know-ing the other.[45] This acute awareness of pulse, heartbeat, and blood flow may indicate that the delicate touch discussed earlier—with the body con-toured through surface contact and subtle caresses—still remains in the visible realm. Kawabata's "One Arm" shows a bodily contact that is sensed through light, warmth, and the texture of the surface, or audible through heartbeat and blood flow. The protagonist comes to negotiate with the girl's alterity through a consonance in pulse and heartbeat via incorpo-ration, even if this cannot last for any substantial length of time.

Disjunctions and ruptures felt between bodies might comprise a condition for continuance, in the same way as Levinas suggests that the discontinuity of time renews and resuscitates the time to come.[46] Touch in Kawabata is a matter of subtlety, lightness, and delicacy. At the same time, however, in "One Arm," the protagonist himself resists the continued incorporation of another's body, which might be the cause of subsequent physical rupture. As this suggests, bodies make contact not just through surface touch, but also when they join or separate. A rupture of contact can affect the possibility of touching, incorporating, or sharing another's body, and is what makes both incorporation and surface touch possible. The encounter with the other touches us in the very oscillation between the possibility of accepting otherness and the sadness of its impossibility.

As already suggested, the male protagonist in Kawabata's fiction often distances himself from the possibility of (dis)possession; in the protagonist's search for unconditional love there is not so much a unification with the other as a yearning for the beloved image. The temporary union with the loved arm is conducted during a moment of trance, which subsequently causes the death of the arm. Laura Marks emphasizes the significance of "giving-over"—"concomitant loss of self in the presence of the other"—in the erotic of haptic visuality.[47] Although the concepts of not possessing or

---

45. Kuriyama Shigehisa writes about the complexity in knowing the body through the act of touching; in his account on pulse-taking, while Greek sphygmologist Galen's understand-ing of pulse as comprised of four parts–the diastole, the rest, the systole, and the rest–in Chinese pulse-talking, *mo*, not only the heart but all of the viscera have to be felt, as opposed to the pulse, which is more about rhythm. Shigehisa Kuriyama, *The Expressiveness of the Body and the Divergence of Greek and Chinese Medicine* (New York: Zone Books, 1999).
46. Levinas, *Totality and Infinity*, 283–284.
47. Marks, *Touch*, 20.

reaching for another in their alterity resonate in Kawabata's "One Arm," this is mainly due to the protagonist's feelings of the possibility of rejection and repulsion. The girl, in contrast, keeps her composure throughout the story; perhaps not always as a "self-sacrificing" woman whose arm is metonymic as Hijiya-Kirschnereit puts it,[48] but rather as a being with a body part that itself has volition. While the search for an object outside oneself in a form of eroticism may respond to one's inner experience,[49] Kawabata's protagonist incorporates the loved object so as to secure self-love as well as his desire. Now internalized as an integral part of his body, it reorientates his attention. With the realization of the otherness of his own externalized and discarded arm, he again exchanges arms. His shifts relating to the object are all aspects of his relationship to the world, manifested via ruptured contact.

In a recent issue of the literary journal *Gunzō*, several writers in a roundtable discussion commented on "One Arm" in a discussion about fiction dealing with "weird" or "partial" love (*hen'ai*, 変愛 and 偏愛), stories about love that is particularly grotesque or weird.[50] For Murata Sayaka, the weirdness derives from the obsession with purity in the descriptions in the narrative; for Motoya Yukiko, it is the protagonist's obsession with the woman's arm, which she sees as arising from his reluctance to see a real female body.[51] Motoya claims sex becomes irrelevant during the process of pursuit of love: a world where one does not have to be mindful of others and where mistakes and wrong moves are accepted.[52] Several decades before, Yoshiyuki Junnosuke surmised that Kawabata's preoccupation with

---

48. Irmela Hijiya-Kirschnereit, "Body and Experiment—Reflecting Kawabata Yasunari's Counter-aesthetics," *Japan Forum* 30: 1 (2018): 54.

49. See Georges Bataille, *Eroticism: Death and Sensuality*, trans. Mary Dalwood (San Francisco, CA: City Lights Books, 1986), 31.

50. Kishimoto Sachiko (1960–) translated and edited anthology of Anglophone literature as *Hen'ai Shōsetsu shū* (Tokyo: Kōdansha, 2008). Having realized how many weird love stories there are in Japan as well, Kishimoto asked some Japanese female writers to write such stories, published as "*Hen'ai Shōsetsu shū*," ed. Kishimoto Sachiko, *Gunzō*, February Issue (2014). The recent issue on *hen'ai* in the October 2014 *Gunzō*, which includes "One Arm," invites Kawakami Hiromi (1958–), Motoya Yukiko (1979–), and Murata Sayaka (1979–); "Hen'ai Shōsetsu: Hen'ai Zadan" "[Collection of Weird Stories: Discussion of Partial Love"], *Gunzō* 69: 10 (2014): 53–68.

51. "Hen'ai Shōsetsu," 62–63.

52. "Hen'ai Shōsetsu," 68.

pure, virginal figures arose from his orphan psychology and narcissism: the protagonist in Kawabata, Yoshiyuki argued, is projecting his own misery and needs as orphaned child onto the pathetic but virginal pure figures.[53] Kawabata describes the girl's arm as having a beauty beyond humanity, and the protagonist treats it with exceeding delicacy (except when he wrenches it off), attracted to her purity and imagined virginity, in contrast to the already touched female body that he recollects as an object of dislike. Kawabata represents the protagonist as being abnormal, yet still wanting to be accepted by the other. Although his orphan background may indeed have determined this depiction of pursuit of love for its lack, in my view, the pursuit of a tolerant space of "no matter what" is also the flipside of self-love. Below, I focus on the object relationship in Kawabata with an attention to orientation and narcissism.

Love of the Object and of the Self

Kawabata's preferences and dislikes have often been discussed in relation to his orphan background. A part of his fixation being dissolved by writing the autographical story, Yamamoto Kenkichi argues that it was Kawabata's homosexual desire toward Kiyono, his boarding mate in junior high school, that made his fiction preoccupied with "the erotic rather than the romantic" (*ren'ai teki dearu yorimo seiai teki*).[54] Kawabata's fiction makes autoerotic extension of the ego corporeal, by incorporating the body part and extending the self (through language, smell, and the gaze, even when physical contact is not involved) out into the world, in a way close to Sarah Ahmed's discussion of object relations and sexuality. Ahmed writes, "the differences between how we are orientated sexually are not only a matter of 'which' objects we are orientated toward, but also how we extend through our bodies into the world."[55] By her account, the individual's

---

53. Yoshiyuki, "Kawabata Yasunari den Danpen," 363–364.

54. Yamamoto, "Kawabata Yasunari: 'Hito to Sakuhin' Josetsu" [Kawabata Yasunari: Introduction, 'His Personality and Works'"], *Kindai Bungaku Kanshō Kōza*, vol. 13: 13. Yamamoto sees the example of Kawabata's autobiographical writing in relation to his orphan background as in the smell of oil as a reminiscent of his parents' death, written in *"Abura"* ("Oil," 1921). Yamamoto, "Kawabata Yasunari: 'Hito to Sakuhin' Josetsu," 5–10.

55. Sara Ahmed, *Queer Phenomenology: Orientations, Objects, Others* (Durham, NC and London: Duke University Press, 2006), 68.

actions on the object shape the object, which in turn affects the individual. The author's depictions of obsession to a particular object shows weirdness or queerness not only in object choice—whether it is the virgin girl, the partial arm, or the same-sex friend, discussed below—but also in the object relations. Mishima Yukio claims that in Kawabata, "life was the senses" (*seimei ikōru kannō*),[56] but it is nevertheless conceivable that, as Yamamoto also suggests, having witnessed a number of deaths in his early life, Kawabata came to understand life and death as being essentially interchangeable, and not necessarily existing in sequence but in continuation.[57] Kawabata's acute attention to the loved object seems inseparable from his fundamental awareness of its unreachability.

In addition to stories for adults, Kawabata also wrote for adolescents. He wrote *shōjo shōsetsu* (girls' novels), which involve girl–girl intimacy, such as "Otome no minato" ["The Girls' Port"], originally published in ten intallements the journal *Shōjo no Tomo* in 1937–1938, and "Shin'yū" ["Best Friends"] in 1954–1955. Throughout his career Kawabata engaged in discovering new writers, and Kawabata Kaori suggests that he seemed to read women's writings more than men's, and children's writings more than adults'.[58] In the late 1930s Kawabata was an advocate of *tsudurikata*, writing in which children depict their everyday lives in plain language: in 1939 he selected children's works for a collection of exemplary *tsudurikata* writings. Perhaps, as Chen Wei puts it, Kawabata saw *tsudurikata* as a way for adults to recover an understanding of human nature through contact with children's minds.[59] At the same time, here too we may recognize an attempt to reach toward the not-quite-reachable. It is not surprising that the eroticism in his fictional accounts of the unreachable is directed towards the immature body rather than the fully mature.

Detailing the sensibility of not-yet-mature girls, "Shin'yū" depicts quotidian events in plain language through the perspectives of two junior-high

---

56. Mishima, "Eien no Tabibito," 268.

57. Yamamoto, "Kawabata Yasunari," 7.

58. Kawabata Kaori, "Kaisetsu: Kawabata Yasunari to Shōjo Shōsetsu" ["Interpretation: Kawabata Yasunari and Girls' Novels"], in Kawabata Yasunari, *Shin'yū* (Tokyo: Shōgakukan, 2015), 243.

59. Chen Wei, "Kawabata Yasunari to *Tsudurikata*: Senjichū no Teikokushugi to Tsunagaru Kairo" ["Yasunari Kawabata and *Tsudurikata*: The Way that is Connected to Japanese Imperialism"], *JunCture: Chōikiteki Nihon Bunka Kenkyū* 5 (2014): 111–112.

school students Megumi and Kasumi, who look so similar they are often mistaken for twins, and who are best friends. Megumi, raised in a warm family environment, radiates cheerful and positive feelings, while Kasumi, an only child raised by a single mother, expresses lonely feelings, and is unable to be honest with others. Kasumi feels through her "girl's sensibility" that her beloved mother will be taken away from her (by her uncle and cousin).[60] Megumi, finding that her beloved friend is surrounded by untrustable people, feels protective of her. When the two end up living some distance apart due to Megumi having to move house, Kasumi sends her a red bag that is identical to her own, as if to suggest that she wishes Megumi to like the bag, almost like a replacement for her own body. Girls' stories developed especially in the interwar period, often emphasizing sisterhood (at the time referenced as "S" or "*esu*"), and attracted the readership of young girls. Those stories in fact served to "discover" the period of adolescence, which previously had been perceived, as Hiromi Tsuchiya Dollase has argued, only in terms of a "lack."[61]

The girls often yearn for (as a matter of *akogare*) upper-grade girls like ideal elder sisters, who are soon to become adults, acting as if they are unaware of what awaits them.[62] In Kawabata's "Otome no Minato" ["The Girls' Port"], which is about sisterhood at a Christian girls' school in Yokohama, the girls, not wanting to graduate and satisfied with remaining in the bubble of their lives at the school, feel at a loss when they encounter the residents of a poor neighborhood in the world outside the school.

---

60. Kawabata, *Shin'yū*, 64.

61. Hiromi Tsuchiya Dollase, "Mad Girls in the Attic: Louisa May Alcott, Yoshiya Nobuko, and the Development of *Shōjo* Culture," PhD diss., Purdue University (2003), 96. See also critic Katarani Kōjin's analysis on the division between the child and the adult; the appearance of "youth" created this division, and conversely, the division guaranteed the appearance of youth. Karatani Kōjin, *Origins of Modern Japanese Literature*, ed. Brett de Bary (Durham, NC and London: Duke University Press, 1998), 119.

62. Highlighting Kawabata's praise of Dazai Osamu's (1909–1948) story "Joseito" ["The Girl Student"] from 1939, in which the girl thinks of womanhood as in part a hatred of female sexuality, Tsuboi Hideto observes that girls' narratives evidently interested Kawabata. The seemingly solid border between adult men and the girl actually dissolves in her narrative in Dazai; the more explicit the hatred toward maturity, the more noticeable the maturing body and voice becomes in her narrative, as a matter of "coquetry" (*bitai*). Tsuboi Hideto, "Odoru Shōjo, Kaku Shōjo: Dōyō Buyō, Tsudurikata, Sonota," ["Dancing Girls, Writing Girls: Children Dance, *Tsudurikata*, and Others"], *Nihon Kindai Bungaku* 72 (2005): 96.

Michiko, the main character, collapses, and consequently feels as if she has suddenly realized what it means to be alive.[63] Written with the help of Kawabata's assistant Nakasato Tsuneko, this story illuminated girls' sensibilities and brought same-sex intimacy into the literary mainstream. The girls described in the "S" stories—which features in girls' magazines often accompanied with images of idealized girls' bodies with large round eyes and thin torsos, and whose illustrators included Nakahara Jun'ichi (1913–1983)—communicate with gestures of physical affection, hugging, linking arms and holding hands, expressing a desire to assimilate the loved one. Such (lesbian) intimacy—often evoking the mother–daughter relationships—is read as "the foundation of feminine sexuality,"[64] while creating an ambiguity between the desire to remain eternally a young girl and to become a fully mature woman, between remaining as is and an irresistible becoming. The attraction of Kawabata's male protagonists to immature girls is characterized by the maintenance of a distance from them, by their being somewhat hesitant about acting on the desire to touch. The instability of the loved object and one's distance from it heighten the yearning to reach it, as if such an unbridgeable gap and incomplete maturity are necessary.

While unrealizable yearning (*akogare*) was mostly directed towards young girls in Kawabata's writing, he also represents intimacy between boys, as in his story "Shōnen" ["The Boy"]. In this story the uncategorizable character of intimacy seems to problematize the division between the erotic and the romantic as proposed by Yamamoto. In "Shōnen," the main narrator Miyamoto combines diaries, recollections, and letters exchanged with Kiyono and tells a retrospective account of Miyamoto's teenage memories at the dormitory in the mid Taishō period (1912–1926), including his intimate desires, his homoerotic experience with Kiyono, and his yearning for the beauty of the flesh. The story tells the type of yearning, described by Barbara Hartley, as an expression of "ambivalent desire," the sexually aware eye of Miyamoto roving across the desired pure objects with a focus on Kiyono.[65] The narrator Miyamoto records a moment of touching with

---

63. Kawabata Yasunari, "Otome no Minato," in *KYZ*, vol. 20 (Tokyo: Shinchōsha, 1981), 63–64.
64. Dollase, "Mad Girls in the Attic," 112.
65. Barbara Hartley, "The Ambivalent Object of Desire: Contesting Gender Hegemonies in Kawabata Yasunari's Shônen," *Asian Studies Review* 30: 2 (2006): 125.

his roommate Kiyono, in which Miyamoto held Kiyono's warm arm at dawn, in his diary: "I felt the warmth from Kiyono's skin flowing into my left arm. Kiyono, as if not knowing anything, held my arm in his sleep."[66] When Kiyono is absent, Miyamoto plays with the hands of another dormmate, Koizumi, sleeping next to each other. He sometimes sleeps holding Kiyono's arm on his right and Koizumi's on his left. Kiyono's fortunate background with a warm and loving family makes the orphaned boy feel miserable: his own background is lonely. The contrast repeats that of the Megumi-Kasumi contrast in "Shin'yū." Kiyono's innocent, strange purity soothes him, making him feel welcomed and accepted, with a calmness he has never experienced before. This comforting feeling goes hand in hand with his feeling that Kiyono loves him the most and will forgive him anything.

With an understanding that intimacy in "Shōnen" presupposes the clear differentiation between the self and the other and in a reciprocal respect with the other who is attractive and also a friend, Takahara Eiri differentiates this story from a narcissistic boys' love story (or the direct expression of narcissism).[67] And yet, read together with Kawabata's girls' stories and especially his involvement with children's *tsudurikata*, I wonder whether this reciprocity is not more a self-mirroring—or whether the self-other differentiation is as clear as if it might be if another person were truly involved. If, as Bersani writes, "Love is an exemplary concept in all philosophical speculation about the possibility of connectedness between the subject and the world,"[68] being attracted to someone as if it is self love might further illuminate the presence of the object.

Different feelings toward the same loved object—what Klein calls ambivalent feeling—bring an imbrication of sensations and memories regarding the loved object. Especially in writing of this type—combining diaries, letters, and protagonist's reflections that may also partly reflect author Kawabata's background—sensations and memories are recollected from the past and relived through the writing. J. Keith Vincent argues for human desire that is not only communicated between two different historical eras of writing, readership, and enactment by different readers

---

66. Kawabata, "Shōnen," 200.
67. Takahara Eiri, "Kawabata Yasunari no Shōnen Ryōiki" ["Kawabata Yasunari's Boy's Territory"], *Kokubungaku* 46: 4 (2001): 111–112.
68. Bersani, "The Power of Evil and the Power of Love," 75.

and narratees, but that foregrounds it with "deferral and between-ness," mediating categorical divisions created between the homosocial and the homoerotic.[69] In my view, this mediation of writing about queerness in "Shōnen" suggests the wilful presence of the author, arising from how Kawabata relates himself to writing. Kawabata lets Miyamoto write about him being freed from his fixation to an orphan mentality and sentimental feeling of depending (*amaeru*) on his abnormal circumstance. After such a reflection, Miyamoto writes that he managed to make an escape from "the dark place" to the town square where he could walk more freely.[70] For an author to relate part of his real-life experience to his literary characters— whether inside a fictional novel as the protagonist or in the form of auto-biographical essay—involves a literary projection, and a manner of acting out repressed feelings through verbalization. Kawabata's language enables Miyamoto to go outside the small space, getting out of the dark place; the adolescent body and author Kawabata encounter each other beyond temporal and spatial distance through the reflection of the repressed, made into language. This language interconnects these figures, as well as the past and present, calling for a moment of negotiation between nearness, distance, and intimacy.

A recent theatrical production based on this story[71] represented Miyamoto's relationship with Kiyono through a particular attention to narcissistic self-touch. In this production, an adult male performer Kawaguchi Takao, to play the role of Miyamoto, narrates Kiyono's story, randomly picking up papers, mostly letters, that litter the stage, and reading them out aloud. At the end of the performance, one of Kawaguchi's

---

69. J. Keith Vincent, *Two-Timing Modernity: Homosocial Narrative in Modern Japanese Fiction* (Cambridge, MA: Harvard University Asia Center, 2012), 15. See also 8–11. Vincent's argument pays attention to the fact that Kawabata's 1926 novel *The Dancing Girl of Izu* [*Izu no Odoriko*] and "Shōnen" were originally part of the same text, but that while the latter remained unpublished until 1948–1949, a piece of its essay was read by his teacher, in a way that its queerness is recognized in retrospect with mediation.

70. Kawabata, "Shōnen," 227–228.

71. The performance *Shōnen*, directed by Liang Yen Liu and performed by Kawaguchi Takao (a former member of the Japanese performance/media art group Dumb Type, active since the mid-1980s), premiered in Tokyo in 2012 as part of the Yasunari Kawabata Trilogy, produced by Yamagata Mirei. In 2012–2014, the Kawabata Trilogy toured in Tokyo, Taipei, and Shanghai, representing Kawabata's stories "One Arm," "The Boy" ["Shōnen"], and "Crystal Illusions" ["Suishō Gensō"] in theatrical performances.

hands starts touching his arm, while the other holds an elbow, and he begins to laugh as if he is tickling himself and being tickled. He then puts his fingers in his mouth, his hands caress his body from head to toe, moving from one body part to another. Moving from a standing posture to sitting down on the stage, he confesses, "I was in love with you" (*watashi ha omae wo koi shiteita*) (Figure 1).

Figure 1 *Shonen* – The Yasunari Kawabata Trilogy (Producer: Mirei Yamagata, Director: Liang Yen Liu, Performer: Takao Kawaguchi) copyright of Hideto Maezawa.

The touching between two adolescent bodies of Miyamoto and Kiyono, performed by one adult body of Kawaguchi, all the intimate feeling directed toward the other is now invested toward one flesh. When Merleau-Ponty discusses self touch, he argues that it is a way to reflexively confirm the self by being externally touched by oneself. The way in which Kawaguchi performs adolescent two-body touch with one adult body seems a particularly perceptive way of reading Kawabata. This is because: firstly, the enactment of repressed feeling is to be performed in a delayed manner (potentially by an older body than the actual body that lived the actual moment of given feeling); secondly, one might come back to the adolescent moment of intimate relationship with a combination of friendship and eroticism. Lastly, when one belatedly liberates the repressed, one may no longer have "another" body to share that intimate feeling with. Now the intimate feeling originally addressed to another is, without reaching the intended, left adrift or reorientated to the self. The enactment or the return of the repressed is always belated, occurring after the actual moment in which the sensation is "felt." By the time it is verbalized, the message has lost its original addressee and can only reach someone else, in this case, including the reader or audience. The delayed enactment becomes further prominent when the text is performed by the actual living flesh, involving temporality and maturity of those who are involved, even though the theatrical adaptation is beyond the control of the author's original intention.

The phrase, "I was in love with you," occurs in Kawabata's writing and is repeated in the play. This phrase, which appears in the original text as of the unsent letter of Miyamoto to Kiyono, written in his teenage days and later recollected, needs further attention: "I liked your fingers, hands, arms, chest, cheeks, eyelids, tongue, teeth, and legs. I was in love with you. And I could say you were in love with me, too."[72] Kawabata's use of the term *koi* to indicate Miyamoto's feelings for Kiyono, and the different term *ai* when emotional struggles are involved (when he found in Kiyono a "savior god" to love him)[73] will recall for readers the debate on love in

---

72. Kawabata, "Shōnen," 161.
73. Kawabata, "Shōnen," 163.

early Meiji Japanese literature, when sensuous erotic feelings were referred to as *koi* (恋) and love in a more spiritual sense was called *ai* (愛).[74] Saeki Junko analyzes the distinction between *ai* and *iro*, the latter indicating sensual and carnal love. With the introduction to Japan of Christianity with its emphasis on an ethics of *love,* the term *ren'ai* (恋愛) was coined to refer specifically to an intimate heterosexual relationship, prioritizing spirit over body.[75] Kawabata's use of *koi* for physical intimacy with Kiyono recall Mishima's contrast between Kawabata, a writer whom he says stands against the intellect, and Yokomitsu, who, for Mishima, "sank into the intellectual delusion."[76] In "Shōnen," reflecting the boy's memories of his youth in the early twentieth century of the Taishō period, the different terminologies employed for matters of same-sex intimacy may illuminate the shifting conceptualizations for it at the time. The author explains such same-sex intimacies among boys not necessarily as homosexuality (*dōsei ai*) but as something like longing or yearning (*shibo*) for the opposite sex, equivalent to the feeling toward loved ones; without seeing those one may feel restless.[77] While the text potentially hints at the then more socially accepted character of a homosocial bond, it also questions the categorical reading of same-sex feelings.[78] If we allow that the story holds within itself

---

74. The now commonly-used word *ren'ai* (恋愛) was adopted in the late 1880s to translate the English "love" and French "amour" that signifies a deeper, spiritual, and mutual affection between a man and a woman, one that reflected Christian values, as compared to the traditional word *koi,* which is associated more with physical intimacy. See Tomi Suzuki, *Narrating the Self: Fictions of Japanese Modernity* (Stanford, CA: Stanford University Press, 1996), 74.

75. Saeki Junko, Iro *to* Ai *no Hikaku Bunka shi* [*Comparative Cultural History of* Iro *and* Ai] (Tokyo: Iwanami Shoten, 2000 [1998]), 8–16. Karatani Kōjin further observes that, while intimate love in Edo literature was exclusively referred to as *koi,* connoting sexual love, *ren'ai,* which might include sexual love, more often had the sense of a platonic, idealized love, translated into English as "romantic love" due to associations with Japanese Christianity and romanticism (Karatani, *Origins of Modern Japanese Literature,* notes in 201–02).

76. Mishima, "Eien no Tabibito," 267.

77. Kawabata, "Shōnen," 155.

78. Both Mori Ōgai's *Vita Sexualis* (1909)—which, with its autobiographical analysis of the protagonist's sexual development, was initially banned as inappropriate for circulation—and Natsume Sōseki's *Kokoro* (1914) illuminate an aspect of same-sex intimacy. Medical

different time frames, Kawabata has Miyamoto make a personal recollection of his intimate desire, and simultaneously distance himself from his own orphan psychology.

Writing, as a specific kind of medium, enables Kawabata to approach the unreachable; it connects past and present, repression and liberation, words and the not-yet-verbalized, or embodied and not-fully-verbalized. Beyond the analysis of same-sex feeling vis-à-vis adolescent developmental process and the use of psychoanalysis for literary creation, Miyamoto's comments quoted above on overcoming adolescent orphan psychology illuminate the process of analyzing oneself, living through the experience, acting it out through writing, and then being freed from it. In the protagonist's yearning and in Kawabata's writing, the very act of trying to reach the loved object "marks" the emergence of the desired objects through the interaction with the loved one.

On the object relation (or object creation, objectualization), André Green states, "The object is created at the very moment that the subject is going to reach it in reality, just before he reaches it; it is created, and this is the subjective object."[79] It is not that the subject and object stand separate from each other and come into contact only through touch, by shortening the distance between the two; rather, they inform and affect

---

practitioners perceived a set of dangers in the same-sex relationship in the early twentieth century, seeing it on one hand as pathological, as a disease to be cured, and on the other hand as a cause of further disorders, such as neurasthenia. The discourse on neurasthenia and mental disorders was intrinsically linked with sexual behaviors, and this linkage bore a specific political significance for Meiji Japan, in which neurasthenia was seen as weak and effeminized, a problem that had to be overcome in order to build a strong nation. Despite wartime censorship, writings related to sexual health and strength were tolerated to promote the nation's procreative potential. See Sabine Frühstück, "Male Anxieties: Nerve Force, Nation, and the Power of Sexual Knowledge," *Journal of the Royal Asiatic Society of Great Britain & Ireland*, 15: 1 (April 2005): 76, 88. As Jeffrey Angles argues, however, a single text could present dissonant images of same-sex desire—illuminating male–male desire as deviant, on the one hand, and as a form of homosocial brotherhood on the other (Jeffrey Angles, *Writing the Love of Boys: Origins of Bishonen Culture in Modernist Japanese Literature* (Minneapolis: University of Minnesota Press, 2011), 12).

79. Gregorio Kohon, "The Greening of Psychoanalysis: André Green in Dialogue with Gregorio Kohon," in *The Dead Mother: The Work of André Green*, ed. Gregorio Kohon (London: Routledge, 1999), 29. Green uses French word "*objectal*" instead of the English word "objective" for this "objectualizing" function, the creation of objects through negation.

each other, processes through which one is constructed and (re)constructs itself. Because of his characters' frequent withdrawal from actual interactions with their desired objects in a process that is nonetheless written, Kawabata convincingly illuminates one's relation to the object. Rather than being one-way communication, it is mutual, and this feeling of mutuality is created by leaving an ambivalent feeling about the relationship between the two and potentially ambiguous separation between author and some of his characters.

Kawabata's use of the medium of writing to approach the unreachable can be understood in terms of what Mishima sees as Kawabata's failure to develop a literary style (*buntai*). Kawabata's works were often completed over a period of years as they were being serialized, making it difficult for readers to tell whether or not the stories were finished. They often lacked dramatic catastrophes or familiar narrative structures. Remarking on Kawabata's fearlessness and lack of a plan, Mishima glossed these as passion (*junan*): "while a powerful intellectual force would reconstruct the world [Mishima wrote], the more powerful this sensibility became, the more he would need to accept the chaos of the world within himself."[80] For Mishima, Kawabata lived his life by eliminating his own fear and anxiety in making himself powerless. Writing provided a way for him to accept the world within himself and to access the unreachable. It may well be that he did not feel the need to establish his own particular literary style because this "style" is precisely what exploratory and experimental writing seek to undermine. Writing—as a medium—is a mode of connection; it is a continuous process between approaching the object while simultaneously distancing oneself. The examples discussed above suggest that what Kawabata was looking for through his writing was the possibility of being connected with and being accepted by others, rather than to create a specific image related to a body. An awareness of the other and of the self goes hand-in-hand with the construction of both self and other, which would be a necessary element for the emergence of love. Attracted to the untouched or unreachable—whether it is an arm, the idealized other, the dormant body, or a missing lip print—his writing about reaching them creates and re-creates the loved object; thus, objects are shaped in the attempt to touch them.

---

80. Mishima, "Eien no Tabibito," 267.

Reciprocity in Sleep

The unreachable in Kawabata is further problematized in the earlier-mentioned *House of the Sleeping Beauties*, where, as Mishima interprets, it is avoided for the loved objects to approach Eguchi, so that his sexual desire will remain a pure sexual drive, preventing an interaction-based love.[81] Beyond the mutual effects and the communicability between him and the girls, the story further complicates the remembrance of touch, raising the question of whether touch that is conducted in the absence of clear consciousness can be remembered. While medical discussions about the brain may highlight the importance on the world represented in the brain for activities including waking and dreaming,[82] for Ivri Kumin, the pre-object relations period (the stage before the infant achieves an ability to objectify the mother as an object) stresses the importance of the sensorimotor or bodily sensations.[83] The protagonist's relationship with the dormant bodies, prompting the fluid circulation of tactile memories and imagination, again question what is (un)reachable. This section reconsiders the desire for reciprocity—whether "mutual" communication is possible when one counterpart cannot consciously register being in touch due to an absence of consciousness (as would occur in sleep).

The girls in this story sleep from the beginning to the end, and are entirely without autonomy. They are unlike people in contemporary payable co-sleeping (*soine*, sleeping with another person) services who decide when they want to be awake or doze off.[84] They know nothing, and are completely unaware of who has slept beside them. The sleeping girls remain unreachable, with no waking consciousness or memory to refer back to. The sleeping girl does not shame the old men, who are no longer "manly"; for them, she is "life to be touched with confidence" (*anshinshite furerareru*

---

81. Mishima, "Kaisetsu," 243.

82. See John Allan Hobson, *Dreaming: An Introduction to the Science of Sleep* (Oxford and New York: Oxford University Press, 2002).

83. Ivri Kumin, *Pre-Object Relatedness: Early Attachment and the Psychoanalytic Situation* (New York and London: The Guilford Press, 1996), 7–8, 82–83.

84. Fusako Innami, "Co-sleeping: Engaging with the Commodified Dozing Body in Kawabata, Yoshimoto, and Yamazaki," *Contemporary Japan* 27: 1 (2015), 37.

inochi).[85] Communication between Eguchi and the girls is doubly distanced from two-way communication: by the girls' lack of consciousness, and by Eguchi's withdrawal from excess interaction, which could harm either the girl or himself. Eguchi knows that he is safe, obtaining a sense of security from the absence of the other's awakened consciousness. For Susan Napier, the girls are "objects in the most fundamental sense": they exist only to be gazed on, neither having sexual activity nor seeing the men who sleep next to them,[86] and this absence of consciousness raises the ethical question of their subjectivity being ignored. Noting that there is no two-way communication that the girls can remember, Eguchi says: "I see. It's not a human relationship."[87] The pursuit of physical intimacy seemingly requires warmth, moisture, and weight, but the "intimacy" here is not sharable, since the consciousness of the other is not actually present. When Eguchi awakens toward the end of the story, he notices that the co-sleeping girl is cold and without a pulse. Her body is simply taken away from the house as if it means nothing.

However, the absence of the other and the lack of interactive communication opens up a wider circuit than the two-person relationship, prompting imagined memories. In "One Arm," the protagonist's contact with the fragmented arm prompts him to imagine the ever-unreachable distance between the arm and her main body, as well as between him and her main body. In *House of the Sleeping Beauties*, in contrast, touch prompts the protagonist's memory of his mother, as well as memories of other girls. While Eguchi gazes at the sleeping girl and feels for a breast, the sensation reminds him of the breast of his mother and, when he withdraws his hand, the sensation travels from his chest to his shoulders.[88] This touch of the girl connects to Eguchi's own childhood memory or imaginary recollection. Even in Kawabata's *Yama no Oto* [*The Sound of the Mountain*], published in multiple journals in 1949–1954,[89] the protagonist Shingo, in sensing his approaching death and feeling the burdens of taking care of

---

85. Kawabata, "House of the Sleeping Beauties" (hereafter HSB) in *House of the Sleeping Beauties and Other Stories*, 20; "Nemureru Bijo," *KYZ*, vol. 18 (Tokyo: Shinchōsha, 1980), 142.

86. Napier, *The Fantastic in Modern Japanese Literature*, 63.

87. Kawabata, "HSB," 38.

88. Kawabata, "HSB," 36.

89. Kawabata, "Yama no Oto," in *KYZ*, vol. 12 (Tokyo: Shinchōsha, 1980), 241–541.

family members, entertains various intimate desires with a number of figures. Prompted by his daughter-in-law Kikuko—who resembles the now-dead older sister of his wife Yasuko, for whom he yearned when he was younger—he marks the revival of his love (*koigokoro*) for Yasuko's elder sister,[90] who is Shingo's real eternal (and unreachable) loved object. The ever unreachable loved one revives, via the chain of imaginary memories of other figures, when he faces his death.

The contact with the girl also invokes bitter memories, as if the loved object appears at the same time as the disliked counterpart. Eguchi remembers being criticized by his former lover, a geisha, for coming to her with the smell of milk on him, a result of embracing his baby daughter shortly before his visit to the brothel. The smell of milk is out of place in a brothel; it highlights only the exclusion of the lover from the conventional family circle and also from traditional family registers. Eguchi has a dream that his daughter's baby is born deformed, and in the dream feels that his search for distorted pleasures is somehow responsible for this "misshapen" birth. Waking, he looks at the sleeping girl, who lies with her back to him, and tries to turn her to him: "Look this way." As if in answer she turns, emitting a small cry that sounds like she is having a nightmare.[91] While the house excludes procreative sexuality, the imaginary arising in between his dream and his co-sleeping with the girl manifests his anxiety and powerlessness about life as well as death. Some have pointed out that the sleeping space in this story, surrounded by the crimson velvet curtains, is a closed internal space, like an imaginary mother's womb: either a place to develop pure ideas, or to yearn to return to, with Eguchi's association of his mother as the first "woman" in his life.[92] The internal space where their bodies sleep, representing both the psychological and physical, leads sleepers to reminiscence about the past. While Eguchi's conflicting attitudes—gratification at the love received by touching the other, and yet anxiety about giving

---

90. See Yamamoto Kenkichi, "Yama no Oto," in *Kindai Bungaku Kanshō Kōza*, vol. 13, 237.

91. Kawabata, "HSB," 33.

92. See Ōkubo Takaki, "Kōki Kawabata Yasunari Sakuhin no Nisō (2) 'Kataude'" ["Two Aspects of the Later Works of Kawabata Yasunari: 'One Arm'"], *Tokyo Jyoshi Daigaku Kiyō Ronshū* 34: 1 (1983): 76; Napier, *The Fantastic in Modern Japanese Literature*, 63; Mebed, "Kawabata Bungaku ni okeru Furoito Shisō no Eikyō wo meguru," 168.

love and supporting a family—questions what it means to welcome touch, insofar as he receives comfort.

"EVERY THEORY OF LOVE IS, necessarily, a theory of object relations," writes Bersani. "Love is transitive; to conceptualize it is to address not only the question of how we choose objects to love, but also, more fundamentally, the very possibility of a subject loving an object."[93] Bersani asks how we can love others for themselves, exploring the reconciliation of narcissism and love that connects one to the world in the name of an "impersonal narcissism." In Kawabata, the protagonist is able to love another insofar as the object appears safe for him. Yoshiyuki, on narcissism in Kawabata's works, refers to Mishima's comments that Kawabata's eroticism is an attempt to reach the voluptuous substance—the life:

> The reason why it is truly erotic lies in the mechanism that the object, or to put it simply, life, cannot be eternally touched. And the reason why he prefers to write about a virgin is perhaps due to his interest in the function particularly of a virgin, that she is forever untouchable [*fukashoku* 不可触/觸] insofar as she remains a virgin but that she is no longer a virgin when she has been violated.[94]

Both Yoshiyuki and Mishima see Kawabata's erotic fixation on virgins as objects be touched, and in the division between the "life" that is to be touched and Kawabata's own life. But Bersani's idea of a narcissistic love that is also a pure object love complicates this reading.

For Bersani, "backlove" or counterlove is a type of self-love in which the loved longs for the lover much like the lover longs for the loved, for the mirror image of the self in the other; the lover's desire is "the reality of the other that he remembers and embraces as his own."[95] This love is caused by the very existence of another. The self whom the loved desires in the other and the self who is the lover itself are almost inseparable. This mode undoes the dichotomy between the active subject and passive object in a different manner from, for example, Deleuze and Guattari's or Marks's dynamic subject–object relation via the haptic. Bersani's approach attests

---

93. Bersani, "The Power of Evil and the Power of Love," 72.

94. Yoshiyuki, "Kawabata Yasunari den Danpen," 362–363. Mishima, "Eien no Tabibito," 269.

95. Bersani, "The Power of Evil and the Power of Love," 84.

to a reciprocal relationship, based on the presence of the other. Bersani's narcissistic love is, at the same time, love for the other.

A rupture of communication in *House of the Sleeping Beauties* due to the absence of girls' awakened consciousness complicates gender dynamics by putting the several sleeping girls in a position to "recognize" the male customers, instead of the men simply objectifying the girls. The girls do not know what is happening during their sleep, including how their bodies might be touched and be treated. Even so, the fact that the male customers have seemingly more agency to approach girls' bodies necessarily make them feel they are committing an ethical violence. The sleeping girls' lack of awakened consciousness does not drive Eguchi into a posture of doing whatever he wants. Rather, he cares for the object of his intimacy, feeling as if handling "a breakable object."[96] Eguchi avoids affecting the girl too much with his contact, conscious that love is too demanding an emotion.

Amazed at the first girl's beauty and youth, Eguchi looks at her body in detail and asks her, "'Are you asleep? Are you going to wake up?',", as if asking the permission for him to touch her hand.[97] Although Eguchi accepts all the conditions posed by the woman at the inn, including that customers cannot stay until the girl wakes up, he nevertheless desires a human relationship in which he can feel her presence and her response. Kawabata carefully describes Eguchi's desire for reciprocity through the fantasy of communicating with an awakened girl. Attracted to the scent of the third girl, he slides his body toward her. She, as if in reply, turns toward him with her arms extended as if to embrace him. "'Are you awake?',", Eguchi asks; and Eguchi shaking her jaw, she turns her face down as if to avoid it, in a deep sleep.[98] After some attempts to breach the house's rule that one should not try to awaken sleeping girls, he decides to stick to the rule, feeling in himself an emptiness at not being able to "communicate" with the girl. Despite the objectification of the girls, it is Eguchi who attempts to be recognized, but goes unnoticed. The fragmentation of the consciousness, I argue, paradoxically makes the "two-way" communication possible between Eguchi and female figures.

The new girl, who is more alive than the previous girl, turns away from him and, with her back toward him, seeks him with her arm, while talking

96. Kawabata, "HSB," 23.
97. Kawabata, "HSB," 18.
98. Kawabata, "HSB," 40.

in her dream. The arm seeks, searches, and tries to reach the other, without reaching the intended in her dream. And yet, he is excited about the idea that he might indeed have something like a conversation with her:

> "Mother." It was like a low groan. "Wait, wait. Do you have to go? I'm sorry, I'm sorry."
> "What are you dreaming of? It's a dream, a dream." Old Eguchi took her more tightly in his arms, thinking to end the dream. The sadness in her voice stabbed at him. Her breasts were pressed flat against him. Her arms moved. Was she trying to embrace him, thinking him her mother?[99]

Trying to approach her mother in her dream, the girl reaches for Eguchi, an unknown man, without recognizing his identity. His thoughts roam, and he even wonders if the touch of old customers has trained her to talk in her sleep, as a form of resistance. Then he starts to touch her, wondering what she should say and where he should touch her to get an answer, just as the protagonist in Yoshiyuki's *The Dark Room* touches his lover in his search on the clean film of her skin.

It is possible that these responses by the girls might be of Eguchi's imaginative creation; however, in the light of Bersani's idea of a reciprocal love that flows from an impersonal narcissism, one might also see the extent of interaction between Eguchi and the sleeping beauties. Eguchi's touching of the sleeping girls, hesitant yet occasionally firm, is to reassure himself of his own existence. He waits to see and feel the girls' responses to check if his touch has been received, and then attempts to find some part of their bodies where they might particularly react, as if to receive a response. Self-recognition and self-awareness stem from confirmation by others. Kawabata's depiction suggests that, even in a state of fragmented consciousness, this wish for a reciprocal relationship to others still survives. Kawabata writes of a subtle form of love that is almost unattainable, violent, and imperceptible, searching for the type of female agency even when the female subject is asleep.

Touch calls up others beyond the two people involved in a relationship; the intimate feeling prompted by contact in Kawabata's fiction is

---

99. Kawabata, "HSB," 46.

repeatedly projected onto different figures, and often recalls Eguchi's imagined memories of his life. Toward the end of this story, he dreams of his mother's death, of the smell of the foods she prepared for him and his new wife, and about the red flower she prepared for their arrival. Between his dreams, he touches the sleeping girl's breast with strength, and is reminded of his own stroking of his mother's bosom; this brings on further memories of the same thing. Touch develops in a throng of Eguchi, the memory of his mother, and the sleeping beauties. The yearning for affection and love is heightened due to the absent presence of the other, while shaping the imagined object, across the divisions between individuals and time. The ultimate goal of this reciprocal relationship is a connectedness between them, fostered in the tumult of temporality by the wish to meet again in the future and a recollection of the past. Touch develops through the presence of the other and circulates between the self and those others with whom one comes into contact, even via memory and association. Love is the pursuit, search, and refinding of the intended object, being "inseparable from memory."[100] As Eguchi gazes at a red drop oozing from the petals of the red flower that his now-dead mother prepared for his wife, he awakens from his dream to find the girl sleeping beside him cold without a pulse. The pursuit of the unattainable circulates, arising from birth and approaching death, partaking in the wandering of consciousness. Beyond the fragmentation of the body and consciousness, these imaginary experiences in co-sleeping open up another dimension of subjectivity.

The girl's breath, scent, and touch evoke a series of fantasy and memories in Eguchi, signaling the vulnerability of shared-ness, making shared intimacy uncertain, and projecting the bodies' impending deaths. Touching the sleeping beauties, Eguchi is unable to receive a response specifically directed to him, as the state of sleeping involves a detachment or absence from the quotidian.[101] During the sleep stages—from the transitional period of drowsiness where a sleeper finds his thoughts flowing, in a light sleep, followed by a deep-sleep stage in which the mind is unfocused

---

100. Bersani, "The Power of Evil and the Power of Love," 72.

101. Jean-Luc Nancy writes of the presence of the sleeper as "the presence of an absence" and is "the return to the immemorial world" (Jean-Luc Nancy, *The Fall of Sleep*, trans. Charlotte Mandell (New York: Fordham University Press, 2009), 15, 22; Simon Williams puts it as involving a certain "absence" from both self and others (Simon J. Williams, *Sleep and Society: Sociological Ventures into the (Un)known* ... (Abingdon: Routledge, 2005), 70).

and drifting, and then the period of rapid-eye movement (REM), when the brain is most active and dreaming occurs—the sleeper experiences different types of perceptions of and reactions toward external stimuli, as the apparent responses of the dozing girls while Eguchi is drifting off to sleep manifest. The line between absence and presence, consciousness and sleep, openness and closure, becomes blurred, the sleeping body losing full access to itself as well as to the other.

The absent or unattainable appears reachable only partially and momentarily through a glimpse when sleeping or dreaming; or when it is written, by bringing the perceived and the unconscious, as well as the self and the object, together through words. Stimuli in pre-object relations are physically communicated through the body, yet are non-repetitive and are thus immemorial, like touch for the sleeping girls. Ivri Kumin calls this double surface—an interface between the surfaces of self and object—a "semipermeable membrane," with an association with Freud's mystic writing-pad, where certain stimulations are erased through the work of an external shield, while some are written on the inner layer, inscribed on the wax slab.[102] There is in this story no assumption that touch on the dormant being has even been perceived or that it can be remembered. The girl's body functions multiply, as if unreachable, though it is physically reachable, and as an absent presence. Or, as Roy Starrs might say, her body "reawakes" his past relationships with other women.[103] While Eguchi's touching of the girls creates for him an imaginary sensual world that he can recollect, it is perhaps a series of passing sensations, which will not even be "remembered" by the girl who might be stimulated by the touch; these two worlds do not meet, unless, possibly, within the male imaginary.

When Eguchi touches the sleeping girl, thinking that she may be the last woman in his life, he goes into a daze, wondering who the first one was; the thought flashes into his mind that it would have been his mother. Eguchi drowsily finds himself thinking of her, remembering his imaginary first "woman," triggered by the touch with the sleeping girls. Meanwhile the girl, stimulated by Eguchi's touch, also dreams of her mother in her sleep. The absentee—the mother figure in this case for both Eguchi and

102. Kumin, *Pre-Object Relatedness*, 120. Freud, "A Note upon the 'Mystic Writing-Pad,'" 227–232.
103. Starrs, *Soundings in Time*, 196.

the girl—reappears in their drowsiness, sleep, and dream and disappears in their death. The girls are sleeping almost as if they were dead, and it occasionally happens at this house that a sleeping girl never awakens, indicating the proximity of deep sleep and death. Eguchi mutters to himself, "As if it were alive,"[104] when looking at the sleeping girl's body part, such as hand and elbow. Death, or the failure to wake up, is depicted not in disjunction from life but as a possible continuation of deep sleep. In a 2006 story by Ogawa Yōko *Mina no Kōshin* [*Mina's March*], a girl, Tomoko, refers to Kawabata's *House of the Sleeping Beauties*, and suggests that Eguchi might be rehearsing his own death; the old man is simply trying to get accustomed to dying, so as not to be scared at his real death.[105] Kawabata suggests the proximity of deep sleep to death with the reference to Lazarus in "One Arm": being asleep signifies being dead, and the dead Lazarus is resurrected because of a "call." Kawabata's works connect this world and other worlds through his attention to the invisible.

Kawabata was the rare author who pursued the motifs of spiritual and erotic love throughout his life. His yearning to touch the unreachable is not only sexual or romantic but also has further connotations of touching the invisible in the interactions between the sleeper, the absent, and the dead. Among authors influenced by the spiritualism movement and psychics from the late nineteenth to the early twentieth centuries, Higashi Masao emphasizes Kawabata's uniqueness: to use elements of clairvoyance, telepathy, ectoplasm, and poltergeists as a central part of his work; his incorporation of psychic elements related to Christian mysticism in the Japanese cultural context; and as a pioneer in uniting psychic motifs and sexual love.[106] Kawabata's protagonists almost never achieve direct touch, because they seek the unattainable, which may be a spirit or an absent

---

104. Kawabata, "HSB," 20.

105. Ogawa Yōko, *Mina no Kōshin* [*Mina's March*] (Tokyo: Chūoh Kōron Shinsha, 2009), 133. In this story, Tomoko, due to her family situation, starts to live with her aunt's family and comes to have a good friendship with Mīna, who is Tomoko's cousin and who likes reading books. Tomoko makes this comment about Kawabata's "HSB" to a librarian, though it is Mīna's comment, as if she reads the story.

106. Higashi Masao, "Kaisetsu: Shinrei to Seiai to" ["Interpretation: the Psychic and the Erotic"], in *Bungō Kaidan Kessaku sen, Kawabata Yasunari shū: Kataude* [*Selected Ghost Stories by Great Writers, Volume on Kawabata Yasunari: One Arm*], edited by Higashi (Tokyo: Chikuma Shobō, 2006), 377.

consciousness. The body becomes necessarily unreachable. The touching of the unreachable is an attempt to reach beyond the confinement of the body with a visible form.

As a young and aspiring writer, Kawabata was particularly concerned with catching immediate sensations, rather than being subject to the two-stage process of first receiving a perception and then writing it down through language. The irony is that despite his early attempts at being progressive and experimental, he was made an icon of "traditional" Japanese writing; and despite his reaching towards a greater immediacy in his writing, his protagonists are hesitant and instead create a space between themselves and the intended objects with which they wish to interact. A strong, almost possessive, yearning for the intended object that he cannot even reach shapes a particular object relationship. Above all, in his desiring it and gazing at it, Kawabata not only depicts but demonstrates how one might relate to, know, and try to love an other. The discussions above illuminate, on the one hand, how the subject may relate to and create the object in the trial of reaching it. On the other hand, Kawabata re-creates an aesthetic, wherein one never over-touches the other and keeps the loved object intact so as to protect it from any harm. The toucher also remains protected, untouched, blurring the boundaries between the (un)touchable and (in)visible. Kawabata develops his model of touch, the fundamental unreachability of the other, through writing that reproduces the unreachability. Kawabata's works offer suggestive accounts of object relations and communication, especially regarding the potentiality of the loved object in his works to evoke the ambivalence of love. As the protagonist experiences various types of psychological and bodily turmoil with the object—whether the object is the arm, girl, or boy—it is not that a passive object waits to be contacted by the toucher. Instead, the unattainable object affects the would-be toucher and shapes relationality between them, as Kawabata desires interactive relationship in maintaining the distance from it. The continual hesitancy and distance toward the loved object in Kawabata conversely heightens the possibility of apprehending the other in the yearning for mutual relationship.

CHAPTER 2

Touch in Plays of Distance, Shadow, Light

The Potentiality of an Unbridgeable Distance

In Tanizaki Jun'ichirō's 1956 novel *Kagi* [*The Key*], a husband and wife each keep their own diaries and secretly (or not so secretly) each reads the diary the other keeps. Meanwhile, the wife, Ikuko, pursues an affair with another man, Kimura, the partner of her daughter Toshiko. Ikuko records the progress of this affair in her diary, aware that her husband will read it—and, in fact, the husband-narrator is anyway cognizant and even supportive of the affair. In one entry, Ikuko gives the following account of a conversation she has had with Kimura:

> —"There's one part of your body I've never touched [Kimura said to me]. He [Your husband] wanted me a paper-thin distance from you, and so I've obeyed his wish. I've come as close as I could without violating that rule."
> —"Oh, I am so glad to hear that!" I exclaimed. "You can't imagine how grateful I am!"[1]

Frustrated by his wife Ikuko's modesty, which makes her feel "ashamed to discuss anything of an intimate nature," the husband-narrator explains that he keeps his diary as a way to address their sexual problems, knowing

---

1. Tanizaki Jun'ichirō, *The Key*, trans. Howard Hibbett (London: Vintage Books, 2004), 82. "A paper-thin distance" is *kamihitoe* in the original Japanese. "Kagi" in *Tanizaki Jun'ichirō Zenshū* (hereafter abbreviated as *TJZ*), vol. 22 (Tokyo: Chūoh Kōronsha, 2017), 146. Originally published in nine installments in *Chūoh Kōron* in 1956.

she will be reading it, and almost as if "talking to her indirectly."[2] Making
full use of the marked visual differences offered by Japanese writing systems
(*hiragana* for her, and *katakana* for him)[3] and forms of address (Figures 2
and 3), Tanizaki foregrounds the role of his characters' imagination, and
through them that of his readers, as if to elicit their hidden desires. Putting
layers of conditions for his characters to reach the yearned-for objects,
Tanizaki subjects his characters' realization of touch to suspension, limitation, and deferral. Continually seduced by the possibility of touch—
almost reaching their desired object, but never quite fully succeeding in

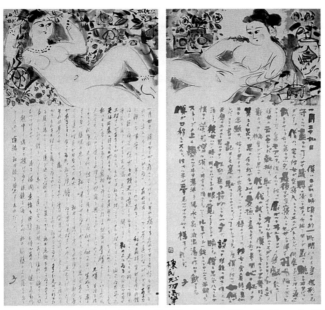

Figure 2 / Figure 3 Munakata Shikō, *Sōhi no Zu* [*The Image of Two Goddesses*], 1958.
Two panel screen, 138.0×69.5 for each panel copyright of Munakata Shikō Memorial
Museum of Art. Folding screen, painting by Munakata Shikō and calligraphy by Kaneko
Ōtei to capture a part of diary entries from Tanizaki's *The Key*, employing different
writing systems (with the use of hiragana for the left screen, and katakana for the right
screen to enact different writing systems employed by wife and husband-narrator,
respectively, as originally written by Tanizaki) and different calligraphic styles accordingly.

2.　Tanizaki Jun'ichirō, *The Key*, 10.

3.　Tanizaki exploits the potentiality of Japanese systems of writing by having the husband
use *katakana*, associated with masculinity, and the wife *hiragana*, associated with femininity.
The different systems also reflect their age difference (mid-fifties and mid-forties respectively).

plays of distance, darkness, and light—they hang in an in-between space, a vital condition for Tanizaki's literary touch.

Tanizaki fuses sensory divisions of touch and vision so that one modality vitalizes another in their mutuality. Further, his descriptions of partially reachable objects, frequently characterized by ambiguity, blurriness, or a shadowy presence, heighten their palpability. It is through this dynamic relationship that the subject and the object reciprocate—as if the seen becomes the seeing, the touched becomes the touching, or the visible becomes the tangible—and the reader grasps a sense of the things depicted. In contrast to Kawabata's works, which seem to work on the premise that the yearned-for objects will always be out of reach, Tanizaki holds out the possibility that the object is always just possibly within reach—except that there are inhibiting factors that get in the way. Haptic visuality carries the idea to blur the division between things seen and touched with haptic functions. As we will see, in his depiction of incompletely visible things, and particularly with his use of light and darkness, Tanizaki complicates touch with vision, and vision with touch. Tanizaki was an author who was consummately skilled in joining sense modalities, together in language.

Tanizaki's characters are commonly impeded to touch the other by, for example, an incompletely bridgeable distance; partially rendered objects as fetish, or "stand-in" object[4]; a partial visibility due to shadows or darkness; a prohibition or condition set by the to-be-touched objects; and a sense experience aided by an alternative sensory faculty, such as touch supplementing impaired vision. This conditioned reachability conversely stimulates the imagination to give specific textures to the yearned-for object. In this chapter, I will analyze specific ways in which Tanizaki deals with

---

4. In his 1867 *Capital*, Marx explains the fetishism of commodities whereby they take on mystical character, once they are produced as commodities, such that social relations between people assume "the fantastic form of a relation between things" (Karl Marx, *Capital: A Critique of Political Economy*, vol. 1, trans. Ben Fowkes (London: Peguin, 1990), 165). For Freud, the fetish is something that comes to play a symbolic substitute for the woman's (the mother's) missing penis, although later object relations theorists highlighted the role of other objects, such as the mother's breast (Melanie Klein), or transitional objects such as a piece of blancket (Donald Winnicott), as having a developmental utility (see Sigmund Freud, "Fetishism" (1927) in *SE*, trans. James Strachey et a. (London: the Hogarth Press, 1961), vol. 21, 152–153. D. W. Winnicott, *Playing and Reality*, 2–12). Any object brings to bear histories that, as Sara Ahmed puts it, are not be available "*on* the surface of the object," apart from traces that may be left behind. "Histories," says Ahmed, "shape 'what' surfaces" (Ahmed, *Queer Phenomenology*, 44).

this "in-betweenness," looking at space, shadow, and light, and how he enlists and/or heightens the imagination of both his characters and (by implication) his readers. *The Key* (1956), "Shun'kin shō" ["A Portrait of Shunkin"] (1933), and *In'ei Raisan* [*In Praise of Shadows*] (1933), and also some earlier works, including his 1910 work "Shisei" ["The Tattooer"] are key works in this discussion. The importance of space was one of the concerns of Japanese philosopher Kuki Shūzō, who wrote contemporaneously with Tanizaki, in the context of (aesthetic) culturalism in the 1930s. Kuki analyzed coquetry (*bitai*), one of the elements in the aesthetic of *iki* (chic)—a value in pre-modern pleasure quarters—as the dynamic potentiality (*dōteki kanōsei*) of a distance (*kyori*) that is forever unbridgeable; a certain distance maintained between two persons of the opposite sex. The closer this distance, the more intense the *bitai* becomes; its essence lies in the dynamic potentiality of the distance being always unbridgeable.[5] Tanizaki's depictions of (desire for) touch written in the texts play with a comparable dynamic. I contend, in Tanizaki's writing, distance (or closeness) enables him to mobilize the relationship between the tangible and the visible, something that I contend lies at the heart of his literary aesthetic, and that also seems to require a similar movement in the reader to see something that is not quite described.

The Key became a public sensation when it was published in 1956, even to the extent that it came under discussion in the National Diet, where Tanizaki, seventy years old at the time and a grand old man of letters, was reprimanded on the grounds of obscenity.[6] Rather than its bold bodily descriptions, what concerned the authorities was surely the way the novel, and particularly its format, seemed to call attention to the role of the

---

5. Kuki Shūzō, *Iki no Kōzō* [*The Structure of Iki*] (Tokyo: Iwanami Shoten, 1971), 21. Kuki studied phenomenology and rethought the traditional aesthetics of *iki*. Japanese poet and critic Kitamura Tōkoku (1868–1894) wrote that in contrast to romantic love (*ren'ai*), the sensibility of *iki* did not require that one lose oneself; he considered self-sacrifice as a requisite for *ren'ai*. Kitamura Tōkoku, "Iki wo Ronjite Kyara-makura ni oyobu," *Gendai Nihon Bungaku Zenshū*, vol. 9 *Higuchi Ichiyō shū Kitamura Tōkoku shū* (Tokyo: Kaizōsha, 1931), 151–154.

6. Akari Chiaki argues that Tanizaki attempts in *The Key* to challenge traditional ideas of public morals, transcending the entire issue of "art or obscenity" that raged for a second time in early postwar Japan. Akari Chiaki, "Kyū Dōtoku wo koete: 'Kagi' no Konnichi sei" ["Beyond the Old Morality: Current Relevance of *The Key*"], in *Tanizaki Jun'ichirō: Kyōkai wo koete* [*Tanizaki Jun'ichirō: Beyond the Boundaries*], ed. Chiba Shunji and Anne-Bayard Sakai (Tokyo: Kasama Shoin, 2009), 56–57.

imagination; the way each of the characters constructs an ideal body based on their own needs and desires and obsessively writes about it for the other to read. The readers are witness to, and also potentially participants in, the obscenity, which is suggested rather than presented—and thus obviously, and self-consciously, eliciting the reader's participation.[7] There is a margin left for reader to fill the gap between what is depicted (suggested by Tanizaki) and what is left invisible (indulged in by the characters but not fully divulged to the reader). By reaching the invisible by way of words, conveyed in a form of characters' diaries in *The Key*, Tanizaki uses these two modalities of reading and writing in the characters' diaries, which are echoed by a secondary plane by the reader. The readers are invited to "read in," to write what is left out of the text, and to engage in an imaginary obscenity of their own. The space left between the depicted and the undepicted is a space for the reader to join Tanizaki in writing the story: imagining the sensory experience with him, in a sense to touch or to be touched by his language. And it is, indeed, a challenge for me to write about touch in Tanizaki, given his sharp yet suggestive and playful use of language; my attempt to write about what happens in this reading experience is in turn another attempt to touch his language along with the reader.

A desire heightened through incompletely available touch is discernible in Tanizaki's 1910 story "The Tattooer," which is notable for the particular attention it pays to the skin. The story starts thus: "It was an age when men honored the noble virtue of frivolity [*oroka*], when life was not such a harsh struggle as it is today … People did all they could to beautify themselves, some even having pigments injected into their precious skins. Gaudy patterns of line and color danced over men's bodies."[8] In a story set in the Edo era, the protagonist Seikichi, a former *ukiyo-e* artist and now a renowned tattoo artist, fantasizes mapping his soul through his tattoos

---

7. As Ohno Ryōji notes, what is central in this work, and in Tanizaki's writing generally, is that the eroticism stems from *reading* the words in the story and their effects, rather than any obscene acts or language in the text. Ohno Ryōji, "Tanizaki Jun'ichirō 'Kagi' ni okeru 'Dokusha' no Yōsō (<Tokushū> Henyō suru Dokusha ron, Dokusho ron)" ["The Readers in/of Junichiro Tanizaki's Kagi" (<Special Issue>Transformations in Reader-Response Theory], *Nihon Bungaku* 52: 1 (2003): 38.

8. Tanizaki, "The Tattooer," in *Seven Japanese Tales*, trans. Howard Hibbett (New York: Vintage International, 2001), 160–161; Tanizaki, "Shisei," in *TJZ* vol. 1 (Tokyo: Chūoh Kōronsha, 2015), 9; originally published in the journal *Shinshichō* in November 1910.

onto a beautiful woman's lustrous skin, and longs for an encounter with someone with sufficiently perfect skin and skeletal structure to appeal to him. Seikichi experiences a sadistic pleasure watching his clients moan in agony, forcing themselves to tolerate the unbearable pain of his needle. The harder they writhe, the more pleasure he derives. One day, Seikichi glimpses a woman's bare foot, its skin white beneath the bamboo blind of a palanquin, and this elevates his imagination to seek a perfect match of his tattoo to her skin, her foot for him being as expressive as a face. Upon finally meeting her, he shows her two picture scrolls, depicting a triumphant woman and her male victims. Seikichi puts the woman to sleep with an anesthetic obtained from a Dutch physician. His spirit dissolves into the charcoal-black ink that now stains her skin, with a drop of cinnabar as a drop of his "lifeblood" (*inochi no shitatari*),[9] and his passions then all merge into one on her skin, forming a spider, which seems to tightly embrace her back. The male bodies are her "victims" (*koyashi*, fertilizer)[10] for her beauty. When the woman recovers from the anesthetic, her eyes are bright, her voice authoritative, and there is a song of triumph in her ears. Seichiki begs her to show him once again the tattoo on her skin where his life is mapped out as her first victim.

The limited interaction between the characters that takes place mainly through the skin, touching the back of the feet, the gaze, and the needle conveying pain, elevates the imagination from the partial to the whole. Making an argument for the eclipse of maternity and the absence of fathers in postwar Japan, Etō Jun reads "The Tattooer" as a story that reflects a fundamental concern of Japanese society in the period following the 1904–1905 Russo-Japanese War; the destruction of motherhood (*bosei*), with his female characters transformed from natural to artificial, is inseparable from the process of modernization, as in "The Tattooer," *Chijin no ai* (*Naomi*), from 1924, and in *The Key*, from 1956.[11] As literary scholar Chiba Shunji puts it, the unnamed woman in "The Tattooer" is the prototype of the transformation that occurs in other female characters, including Naomi in *Naomi*, Shunkin in "A Portrait of Shunkin" in

---

9. Tanizaki, "The Tattooer," 167; "Shisei," 15.

10. Tanizaki, "The Tattooer," 168; Shisei," 16.

11. Etō Jun, *Seijuku to Sōshitsu: Haha no Hōkai* [*Maturity and Loss: The Dissolution of the Mother*] (Tokyo: Kōdansha, 1993), 108–109.

1933, and Satsuko in his last work *Diary of a Mad Old Man* [*Fūten Rōjin Nikki*] in 1961.[12] These women, the object of a male protagonist's desire, become empowered to emit a magical effect on male characters. And yet, as Isoda Kōichi suggests, there is a kind of distancing effect, a kind of coolness, created by Tanizaki's descriptions of tradition and Western civilization, which he imbues with a sense of frivolity and ridiculousness; it is as if Tanizaki suggests that only in being frivolous, ruining oneself, and foreseeing such ruin, can one brighten one's life.[13] This sense of frivolity reminds us of that referred to in the opening passage of "The Tattooer." Tanizaki, fascinated by both Japan and the West, seems himself to be positioned somewhere between them, and they remain forever tantalizingly out of his reach.

Much scholarly attention has been given to fetishization in Tanizaki's writing, but my reading of touch in Tanizaki suggests that the dynamic relationality is mutually shaped in the space in-between. Tanizaki depicts the psychological effects of worshipping the female foot as if it were divine—a foot fetish—in his "Fumiko no Ashi" ["Foot of Fumiko"] in 1919,[14] a part object heightening the desire to reach it fully. In *The Key* the protagonist is obsessed by his wife Ikuko's foot, in self-avowed foot fetishism, which she recognizes and accepts.[15] Even in Tanizaki's last work, *Diary of a Mad Old Man*, where the protagonist is attracted to his daughter-in-law Satsuko, she allows him to lick her calf, her heel, and her big toe. The sight of her partially visible body through the slit of a shower curtain[16] leads him to fantasize about her body further. As Thomas Rimer puts it, "(h)is [Tanizaki's] male characters often find themselves most comfortable when groveling at their [women's or idealized females'] feet."[17] While the fetish

---

12. Chiba Shunji, *Tanizaki Jun'ichirō: Kitsune to Mazohizumu* [*Tanizaki Jun'ichirō: Fox and Masochism*] (Tokyo: Ozawa Shoten, 1994), 21.

13. Isoda, *Sajō no Kyōen*, 12–13.

14. Tanizaki Jun'ichirō, "Fumiko no Ashi," in *TJZ*, vol. 6 (Tokyo: Chūoh Kōronsha, 2015), 257.

15. Foot fetishism in *The Key* is referenced in the Japanese text as "fetishist." See Tanizaki, "Kagi," 94.

16. Tanizaki Jun'ichirō, *Diary of a Mad Old Man*, trans. Howard Hibbett (London: Vintage Books, 2000), 48, 66.

17. J. Thomas Rimer, *Modern Japanese Fiction and its Traditions: An Introduction* (Princeton, NJ: Princeton University Press, 1978), 23.

object marks a seductive distance with the toucher—an incompletely bridgeable distance, the supposedly touched invites the toucher.

In Tanizaki, not only the object but also the distance—the impossibility of actually reaching the object—itself seems subjected to fetish. In *Naomi*, the fetish or incompletely available object emerges through the sense of prohibition. In the scenes of men making fun of the protagonist Jōji for licking the Western-looking, fifteen-year-old Naomi's foot, and with Naomi asking Jōji not to touch her skin while he shaves her, the fetish object conveys a link (based on an agreement) between pleasure and prohibition. Naomi gives Jōji a condition:

"You have to shave me without touching my skin."
"But..."
"No 'buts.' You don't have to touch me. You can apply the soap with
    a brush, and you'll be using a Gillette razor. In a barbershop, the
    assistants don't touch you if they're any good."
"I don't like being lumped together with barbers' assistants."
"None of your cheek! I know how much you want to shave me. But
    if you'd rather not, I won't force you."
"It's not that I don't want to. Let me shave you, please. We've gone
    to all this trouble to get ready." There was nothing else I could
    say as I gazed at Naomi's hairline, exposed where she'd pulled
    back the collar of her robe.
"Do you accept my condition, then?"
"Yes."
"Absolutely no touching."
"I won't touch."[18]

Naomi makes Jōji obey the rule, with agency. As Stephen Dodd suggests in his writing on Tanizaki, Tanizaki's female characters possess an extent of autonomy, a sexual awareness, and "an ability to bite back."[19] The prohibition and partialness of touch heightens Jōji's lust and enjoyment and turns

---

18. Tanizaki, *Naomi*, 227–228.
19. Stephen Dodd, "An Outstanding Storyteller," *Shunkin* performance catalogue (London: The Barbican, 2010), 11.

the gender binary of the active male and the passive female on its head. Suspension and prohibition stimulate the desire for fuller touch.

As the characters incompletely make contact with others, suggestion also plays an important part. In a discussion with writers Ogura Chikako and Tomioka Taeko, Ueno Chizuko notes the implied, never explicit, connotations of sexual acts in Tanizaki's writing, which are highly suggestive to the reader. Ueno refers particularly to the bath scene in *Naomi*. There, the physical interaction between Jōji and Naomi is implied but never stated: "Soon Naomi and I were covered with soap ...."[20] Tanizaki captures characters' bodily interactions with a sense of distance and incomplete reachability in writing. The literary critic Watanabe Naomi argues that indispensable in Tanizaki's masochistic pleasure[21] is an indirectness of shame (*chijyoku no kansetsusei*), which passed through certain artifice (*gitai*) and mediation (*baikai*), instead of a direct approach to the object; at the core of this pleasure is deferral, rather than impetuosity.[22] In elevating desire, Tanizaki fetishizes not only the body part but also the distance, both in physical and verbal senses. Tanizaki indeed offers a literary landmark of the haptic imagination throughout his career—the imagination expanded through the haptic sense beyond distance. Impeded by incomplete visibility, partial reachability to the object, and the mediation of

---

20. Ueno, et al., *Danryū Bungakuron*, 148. Tanizaki, *Naomi*, 231.

21. Laplanche and Pontalis define masochism as a "sexual perversion in which satisfaction is tied to the suffering or humiliation undergone by the subject." Krafft-Ebing's description of masochism, which he named after Leopold Sacher-Masoch, as sexual perversion, included physical pain and moral humiliation. While Freud's description differentiates: "erotogenic masochism," meaning masochistic sexual perversion; "feminine masochism," which does not depend on sex; and "moral masochism," where the subject seeks the position of victim, even without involving sexual pleasure (Laplanche and Pontalis, *The Language of Psychoanalysis*, 244–245). In Freud, erotogenic masochism refers to pleasure found in pain, while moral masochism involves an unconscious sense of guilt. See Freud's "The Economic Problem of Masochism," from 1924, in *SE* 19. Tomi Suzuki notes that Tanizaki read the translation of Krafft-Ebing's *Psychopathia Sexualis* (1886), translated into Japanese as *Hentai Seiyoku Shinri*, in 1913, or possibly read it earlier in English translation. Suzuki, "Jendā Ekkyō no Miwaku to Mazohizumu Bigaku: Tanizaki Shokisakuhin ni okeru Engekiteki, Eigateki Kairaku" ["The Attraction of Transgressing the Gender and Aesthetics of Masochism: Theatrical and Cinematic Pleasure in Tanizaki's Early Works"], in *Tanizaki Jun'ichirō: Kyōkai wo koete*, 46.

22. Watanabe Naomi, *Tanizaki Jun'ichirō: Gitai no Yūwaku* [*Tanizaki Jun'ichirō: Seduction of Mimicry*] (Tokyo: Shinchōsha, 1992), 85.

narratives, the distance to the yearned-for objects becomes dynamic—as critic Isoda Kōichi puts it, the greater the distance, the more powerfully it drives desire.[23] The almost but never quite bridgeable, framed by Tanizaki as a "paper-thin distance," is, I would argue, a necessary element to mobilize the relationship between the tangible and the visible, the written and the read, due to a suspension of realization. This longing—the continuous attempt to close the distance without ever succeeding in doing so, thereby giving the distance a certain oscillatory movement—is the motivation for touch in Tanizaki.

This distance fetish in Tanizaki paradoxically arises from a double range of distance—the "close" surface yearning, such as for the skin, and "distant" cultural yearning. In "Shōnen" ["The Children"] (1911), the protagonist, the first-person narrator, invited for a visit, is involved in a play with his schoolmate Shin'ichi, Shin'ichi's half-sister Mitsuko, and the school bully Senkichi. As part of a game in which Shin'ichi pretends to be a wolf and two boys play travelers to be eaten by the wolf, Shin'ichi crawls on Senkichi, who gets mud all over his body, and nibbles, "smacking his lips greedily," at Senkichi's body parts from his head to his shins (the description features the onomatopoeic word *mushamusha*).[24] When Shin'ichi steps on the narrator, the narrator hears the rustle of the lining of Shin'ichi's silk kimono (*sayasaya*), which also smells of camphor; he feels his cheek being stroked by the cloth, and his chest and stomach also feel the weight of Shin'ichi's warm body. Kimonos are viewed almost as a skin. The narrator's body, "tickled and licked" (*peropero*) by Shin'ichi's damp lips and the tip of his tongue, is gradually bewitched with dream-like intersensorial pleasure.[25] Chiba Shunji argues that this child's play reveals the prototype of Tanizaki's world; reality is denied under the rules of play (*kyōgen*), while children play with illusion.[26] Toward the end of the story, Mitsuko takes Senkichi and the protagonist to the Western house in Shin'ichi's residential compound at night, where both boys are now forced to become Mitsuko's

23. Isoda, *Sajō no Kyōen*, 30.
24. Tanizaki, "Shōnen," in *TJZ* vol. 1, 48; "The Children," trans. Anthony H. Chambers in *The Gourmet Club: a Sextet*, trans. Anthony H. Chambers and Paul McCarthy (Ann Arbor: University of Michigan Press, 2017), 18.
25. Tanizaki, "Shōnen," 48; "The Children," 19.
26. Chiba, *Tanizaki Jun'ichirō*, 48.

slaves, and act as chairs and ash receptacles. Now, when Mitsuko plays a piano, it seems to the narrator like a sound from a different world. And characters' impressions of the real and unreal become conflated. This one-night experience at the Western house suggests what the West may mean to Tanizaki: it is a yearned-for place, that remained tantalizingly out of reach. Distance fetish in Tanizaki works in two ways to engage with the yearned-for: a close range to almost lick the surface, and a far range to yearn for the further unknown.

Light and Darkness

Tanizaki appeared to make an explicit return to traditional Japanese beauty (*Nihon kaiki*) in the 1930s by focusing on shadows, in an apparent reaction to the modernization that was taking place in Japan at the time. In Tanizaki's *In'ei Raisan* [*In Praise of Shadows*] (1933), shadows are clearly a way for him to think about modernization, Westernization, and tech-nological advancement. And yet, shadows were also an aid for Tanizaki to develop his palpable depictions to accompany the invisible—reaching it indirectly. Patrick Maynard writes, "'Shadows for him [Tanizaki] con-noted, as it often does for us all, a *shaded*, protected, indistinct, three-dimensional environment penetrated only by diffused light—which is barred from its deeper recesses—and the soft surfaces that seem to hold it," as opposed to direct rays from two-dimensional hard surfaces or sharp edges.[27] Shadows conceived by Tanizaki touch the surface, encompassing visual and tactile effects. Tanizaki indeed praised the diffusion of light and indirectness of shadows: "The light from the garden steals in but dimly through paper-paneled doors, and it is precisely this indirect light that makes for us the charm of a room. We do our walls in neutral colors so that the sad, fragile, dying rays can sink into absolute repose."[28] It would seem that, as much as the shadows for Tanizaki were a way to mediate

---

27. Patrick Maynard, *The Engine of Visualization: Thinking through Photography* (Ithaca, NY and London: Cornell University Press, 1997), 163.
28. Tanizaki Jun'ichirō, *In Praise of Shadows*, trans. Thomas J. Harper and Edward G. Seidensticker (London: Vintage, 2001), 30. Originally published in the journals *Keizai Ōrai* in December 1933 and January 1934, and *Shinnengō* in January 1934. Translated into English in 1977.

between the East and West, they were a way to mediate touch and vision. Tanizaki attends to shadows as another way of bridging the closing yet distancing space.

Tanizaki often conveys carnality, with the aid of Western-derived visual and lighting technology, such as photography and film, in conjunction with his imagery of the West. In particular, touch in Tanizaki, with the imbrication of light and darkness, makes the image dynamic and oscillatory, instead of being frozen. Tanizaki not only blurs the visual image, but also lets readers form an image in shadow. This happens as readers close their eyes, place themselves in a dim light, imagine listening to the sound of instruments and the voices of birds, feeling the texture and temperature of what their bodies come into contact with, and sensing the world through groping around. Tanizaki suspends the full realization of touch, yet conditioned touch driving dynamic potentiality of movement forward. Through the (masochistic) suspension,[29] Tanizaki mobilizes the image from the frozen to the dynamic when he depicts physical stimulations, blurring the boundaries between light and darkness, touch and vision.

In Tanizaki's 1933 "A Portrait of Shunkin," read together with *In Praise of Shadows*, published in the same year, conveys the lack of clarity of the visible, as in a blurry photograph taken in dim light. The former concerns a story about a blind *shamisen* player Shunkin. The narrator introduces Shunkin's story basing it on a slim volume titled *The Life of Mozuya Shunkin*; at times he functions as annotator, at others as interpreter. Critic Saeki Shōichi describes this narrative strategy as a playful yet experimental literary stunt (*ayauki ni asobu, bungaku teki na hanarewaza pafōmansu*);[30] the narrator himself seems to fade in and out of view as he gives his account of the world of faint light experienced by blind Shunkin. Despite her sadistic, egoistical personality, her servant Sasuke guides her with patience and loyalty, later becoming her student and disciple, and eventually, as a string teacher himself, effectively her partner. After someone attacks Shunkin at

---

29. Deleuze writes about suspense and waiting as essential characteristics of masochistic experience, in referring to the works of Leopold von Sacher-Masoch, especially *Venus in Furs*: "[H]is [Sacher-Masoch's] scenes are frozen, as though photographed, stereotyped or painted." Gilles Deleuze, "Coldness and Cruelty," in *Masochism*, trans. Jean McNeil (New York: Zone Books, 1991), 70.

30. Saeki Shōichi, "Katari no Miwaku" ["The Attraction of Narratives"], in Tanizaki Jun'ichirō, *Mōmoku Monogatari, Shunkinshō* (Tokyo: Iwanami Shoten, 1986), 217.

night and her face is scalded by hot water, she refuses to let anyone see her. Sasuke chooses to prick his eyes with a needle, essentially to blind himself, so as not to see her burns and enters in the world of faint light and darkness. Referring to Deleuze's discussion on fetishistic disavowal as the foundation of imagination, Margherita Long finds it in Sasuke's disavowal; "with the shutting of eyes comes the closing of the distance between subject and object, a distance that must now give way to touching for meaning and desire to exist."[31] Shortening the distance, though, does not necessarily guarantee touch.

The story is set in Osaka and is based on the story of Shunkin, who, the narrator tells us, lived there from 1829 to 1886. The only remaining photo of her, taken at age thirty-six, is blurred. As the narrator says: "the photograph itself is perhaps even vaguer than the impression that my words convey."[32] The reader has no access to Shunkin's photograph, except through the narrator's explanation of it: the text thus conveys the image. Literary scholar Sakaki Atsuko has argued that Shunkin's closed eyes allow the narrator the liberty to interpret her story: "the visual is no more definitive of an image than the textual. The narrator thus disputes photography's claim to absolute truth."[33] The photograph of Shunkin requires the seer's and the reader's reliance upon the imagination. Shunkin's blurred image speaks to both the slow emergence of the developing image as it appears on the photographic surface, and also the inevitable decay of chemical photographs in this still-early stage of photographic technology in Japan.[34]

---

31. Margherita Long, *This Perversion Called Love: Reading Tanizaki, Feminist Theory, and Freud* (Stanford, CA: Stanford University Press, 2009), 131; Deleuze, "Coldness and Cruelty," 127–128.

32. Tanizaki Jun'ichirō, "A Portrait of Shunkin," in *Seven Japanese Tales*, trans. Howard Hibbett (New York: Vintage International, 2001), 9. "Shunkinshō," in *TJZ* vol. 17 (Tokyo: Chūoh Kōronsha, 2015), 53–109; originally published in 1933 by Sōgen sha and translated into English in 1963.

33. Atsuko Sakaki, "Tanizaki Jun'ichirō, or Photography as Violence," *Japan Forum* 22: 3–4 (2010): 386.

34. According to Ozawa Takeshi, a daguerreotype camera set was brought to the port in Nagasaki by a Dutch ship in 1843, though it was brought back without the boat landing, and brought again in 1848. Daguerreotypes—in which one would make a silver panel light-sensitive with iodine fumes, expose it to a camera, and develop it with mercury vapor, a process that took as long as twenty minutes—was followed by the collodion process,

The unstableness and ambiguousness over time of a photographic image, as the lack of certitude, is woven into the very material of the narrative.

As an image consisting only of narration and furthermore interpreted by the narrator, the photo loses its archival function and is dispossessed of authenticity. In *Camera Lucida*, Roland Barthes chooses to see the photograph as a verification, a marker of certainty, as well as of a refusal to change, with reference an orientation toward death.[35] However, Tanizaki, if anything, uses Shunkin's photograph to blur her image, rather than to verify her existence in the past. The image, with its lack of inbuilt perfectibility (photographic technology being in its infancy), appears through its blurriness. Drawing attention to a disembodied aspect of the photographed object, Stephen Dodd states that Shunkin "might be understood as one node in an intertextual web of language," as "an 'abstraction' engendered by the text."[36] The body of blind Shunkin is shaped through the layered accounts by narrator, author, and by the reader who engages with the invisible image in the text. As the reader's relationship to the image remains precarious, the author compellingly invites the reader into the detailed depictions of characters' gestures and the surface materiality of things. Tanizaki develops this literary tangibility, by consciously letting his characters grope in the dark.

Intimate pleasure is in no way dependent on being disabled and, neither, surely, is it necessary to be disabled to know things that abled individuals may not be able to sense. Yet Sasuke's blindness seems to aid his perception to make sense of what he comes into contact with. The narrator says of Sasuke, who starts off as a servant but begins practicing the *shamisen* on his own at night in an attic room after the other servants fall asleep: "Of

---

which was called "*shippan shashin*" (wet-plate photography) and continued to be used until the mid-Meiji period, when one would wet a plate with collodion in silver nitrate, make it photosensitive, and expose and develop it in a period of fifteen seconds. Ozawa Takeshi, *Bakumatsu, Meiji no Shashin* [*Photography in the late Edo and Meiji*] (Tokyo: Chikuma Shobō, 2010 [1997]), 18–21.

35. Roland Barthes, *Camera Lucida: Reflections on Photography*, trans. Richard Howard (New York: Hill and Wang, 1981), 96. Originally published as *La Chambre claire* by Editions du Seuil in 1980.

36. Stephen Dodd, "History in the Making: The Negotiation of History and Fiction in Tanizaki Jun'ichirō's 'Shunkinshō,'" *Japan Review* 24 (2012): 160.

course he had to sing the vocal parts softly and pluck the strings with his fingers, instead of with a plectrum: sitting there in the pitch-dark closet, he played by his sense of touch alone."[37] Never feeling inconvenienced by the darkness, and rather delighting in being able to share it with Shunkin, as a sighted person Sasuke sometimes envies the blind. As Margherita Long writes, "[T]here is … no moment of 'unpleasure' in which the subject perceives it is lacking something."[38] Even the musical voice conveys a surplus of reality-effect. Thus, the narrator tells his readers: "these attitudes in which he persisted since boyhood help to account for his own later blindness. It was something that had to happen."[39] For Sasuke, listening to sonic textures from a standpoint of blindness is a way to get as close as possible to his beloved Shunkin. Tanizaki portrays blindness, often associated with music in traditional culture (the blind masseur Anma in 1931 *Mōmoku Monogatari/The Blind Man's Tale* is also depicted as a *shamisen* player), in the words of Dodd, "as a way of attaining an enhanced state of existence unavailable to those with normal vision"; blindness was "a means [for Sasuke] to gain greater intimacy with his lover."[40] The words Sasuke sings softly at night in the attic comprise another form of approach to the loved one. This is especially the case after Sasuke pierces his eyes: now he can live with his beloved in a world of darkness and mere glimmers of light (despite the variant tonality), sharing the darkness of the condition of blindness and a spatiality within the darkness that ties the characters together.

A dim light that allows only a partial grasp of the vaguely seen object encourages the use of imagination. In looking at a hanging scroll in a dark temple, Tanizaki writes in *In Praise of Shadows* that one must "follow as best as we can the all-but-invisible brush strokes, and tell ourselves how magnificent a painting must be."[41] What is important here is not to take hold of the seen in an attempt to grasp it, but rather to liberate the nearly seen object by seeing it in the mind. Tanizaki later on writes in *The Key* about Polaroid cameras and florescent light as expressions of the search for visibility, but the pictured images still remain ambiguous. When Tanizaki

37. Tanizaki, "A Portrait of Shunkin," 22.
38. Long, *This Perversion Called Love*, 130.
39. Tanizaki, "A Portrait of Shunkin," 22.
40. Dodd, "History in the Making," 161–162.
41. Tanizaki, *In Praise of Shadows*, 31.

moved, after the Great Kantō Earthquake of 1923, to the Kansai area, he was there exposed to temples and shrines, and other works of traditional architecture in Kyoto and Nara. Following the governmental repression of proletarian literature and the pursuit of pure Japanese literature during the early 1930s, Tanizaki began to reflect and to write on the art of the incompletely visible.

In aestheticizing shadows Tanizaki makes surfaces palpable, whether such surfaces are page, lacquerware, sand wall, paper panel, photographic surface, or filmic screen. Chiba Shunji claims that in *In Praise of Shadows* Tanizaki pays particular attention to the haptic sense among other senses.[42] I would go further, and say that Tanizaki, in *In Praise of Shadows* and beyond, brings the duality of senses to the fore by letting the surface bear both visual and haptic functions. In incomplete visibility, importance is placed not so much on comprehension of the viewed object as on imagining how it might be, due to the dimness and shadows that surround it. In haptic visuality, resolving distance, marking the binary relation between the subject and the object, and the seeing and the seen, becomes less important. As Laura Marks puts it: "it is less appropriate to speak of the object of a haptic look than to speak of a dynamic subjectivity between looker and image."[43] An earlier phenomenological investigation of the lived experience by Merleau-Ponty emphasizes the encroachment between the subject and the object, and the self and the world: "the seer and the visible reciprocate one another and we no longer know which sees and which is seen."[44] This reciprocity or reversibility also applies, for Merleau-Ponty, to the visible and the tangible. Such a reversibility—not only of the touched and the touching, the visible and the seeing, but even "an inscription of the touching in the invisible, of the seeing in the tangible"—opens the possibility for an "intercorporeal," if not "incorporeal," being.[45] A doubling of the visible and tangible, in my view, is premised on the incomplete or disabled reach in Tanizaki's writing. Tanizaki lets the invisible objects or

---

42. Chiba Shunji, "Fukusei Gijyutsu no Jidai ni okeru 'In'ei Raisan'" ["In Praise of Shadows in the Age of Mechanical Reproduction"], in Chiba and Sakai, ed., *Tanizaki Jun'ichirō: Kyōkai wo koete*, 13.

43. Marks, *Touch*, 3.

44. Merleau-Ponty, *The Visible and the Invisible*, 139.

45. Merleau-Ponty, *The Visible and the Invisible*, 143.

blind characters complement one sense with another, as if his writing itself "inscribes" the tangible with the invisible.

Tanizaki further complicates the relation between touch and vision when he discusses shadows, especially by bringing haptic qualities in shadows. Patrick Maynard, in his discussion of shadows, brings attention to the distinction between attached shadows and cast shadows; the cast shadow lies on a surface (such as on the ground), projected by rays, which "describes rather than obscures,"[46] while shaded one attaches to the surface. The attached or contiguous shadows accompany the figures or objects, constantly "touching" the surface of those things; the palpability of things arises through shadows. Neither being clearly revealed nor being completely caught by light, the object's shape becomes visible with the touch of shadows in the modulation, or "behaviour" for Michael Baxandall,[47] by light. Light reaches the surface or shadow attaches the body; the body of the object is shaped through a mutual interaction of one sense to another. "Writing" the touch of the invisible thus approaches the surface in multi-dimensional and multimodal manners. Thomas LaMarre writes on the interactions among the senses that Tanizaki treats experiences that are "a-modal" sensory ones instead of mere psychological projection: they involve "an experience in which one sense (seeing) evokes another (hearing)." LaMarre continues: "It is an eerily heightened version of the rather mundane synaesthesia evoked when one speaks of 'loud colors' or 'sharp tones'."[48] Noting the shadow's functions of surfacing the objects while modulating their visibility, and thereby making things appear and disappear, Tanizaki lends his pen to the doubling of the senses—vision and touch.

In *In Praise of Shadows* Tanizaki praises indirect aesthetic perfection through darkness, shadow, and gradations of light. "The lack of clarity, far from disturbing us, seems rather to suit the painting perfectly. For the

---

46. Maynard, *The Engine of Visualization*, 158.

47. Michael Baxandall, *Shadows and Enlightenment* (New Haven, NJ and London: Yale University Press, 1997), 80. Baxandall, focusing on shadows with regard to perception and painting in the eighteenth century, notes that the ways shadows work in our minds have varied according to "people's projects and historical epistemes" (9).

48. Thomas LaMarre, *Shadows on the Screen: Tanizaki Jun'ichirō on Cinema and "Oriental" Aesthetics* (Ann Arbor: Center for Japanese Studies, University of Michigan, 2005), 108.

painting here is nothing more than another delicate surface upon which the faint, frail light can play."[49] Tanizaki laments the ceaseless progression towards illumination, from candle, oil lamp, gaslight, to electric light, and expresses a wish that the Japanese might have achieved modernity in a culturally appropriate manner. How ironic, then, that Japan has become, or was already, one of the "brightest" countries, and indeed, in the 1930s, the Japanese aesthetics of shadows was already to be nostalgically mourned. Miya Elise Mizuta has pointed out the irony of Tanizaki's claims in his praise of shadows: "Electric lighting quickly penetrated the outlying areas of Japan at the turn of the twentieth century, much faster than perhaps any other symbol of modernity. By century's end, Japan led the world in the use of fluorescent lighting (*keikōtō*) as a mainstay and standard of light fixtures in homes."[50] Cities like Tokyo and Osaka were, as Tanizaki himself notes with reference to a novelist who returned from Paris, "far more brightly lit" than any European city."[51] The tendency to pursue light has increased in contemporary Japan, with many city streets and public squares filled with dazzling decorative lights.

In a 2008 theatrical production titled *Shun-kin*[52]—combining Tanizaki's "A Portrait of Shunkin" and *In Praise of Shadows*, with the elements of the *kuroko* in the *bunraku* puppet theater, those who dress themselves all in black to accompany puppets and puppeteers—director Simon McBurney interrogated the gap between Tanizaki's traditional aesthetics and the use of light in contemporary Japan (Figures 4 and 5). In one scene, as the story of Shunkin is recorded by a radio narrator, bright light from vending machines on the street spills against a darkened stage. This is as if to suggest that, on one hand, (the appreciation of) shadows and (the desire

---

49. Tanizaki, *In Praise of Shadows*, 32.

50. Miya Elise Mizuta, "Luminous Environment: Light, Architecture and Decoration in Modern Japan," *Japan Forum* 18: 3 (2006): 339–340.

51. Tanizaki, *In Praise of Shadows*, 54. The co-existence between light and shadow was also noted, according to Daisuke Miyao, by a Hollywood filmmaker who visited Japan in the mid 1930s. Daisuke Miyao, *The Aesthetics of Shadow: Lighting and Japnaese Cinema* (Durham, NC: Duke University Press, 2013), 2.

52. *Shun'kin*, a Complicité co-production with Setagaya Public Theatre and barbican-bite09, directed by Simon McBurney. First performed at Setagaya Public Theatre in Tokyo in 2008.

Figure 4 A Complicité co-production with Setagaya Public Theatre and barbicanbite09 *Shun-kin*, directed by Simon McBurney, inspired by *A Portrait of Shunkin* and *In Praise of Shadows* by Tanizaki Jun'ichirō (First premiered in 2008 at Setagaya Public Theatre) copyright of Robbie Jack.

Figure 5 A Complicité co-production with Setagaya Public Theatre and barbicanbite09 *Shun-kin*, directed by Simon McBurney, inspired by *A Portrait of Shunkin* and *In Praise of Shadows* by Tanizaki Jun'ichirō (First premiered in 2008 at Setagaya Public Theatre) copyright of Sarah Ainslie.

for) light still co-exist in contemporary Japan, while on the other, this was already a reality of "contemporary" life when the original texts were written. With the sense of irony and play in his writing, Tanizaki embraced both wanting the Western-style comforts in real life,[53] and yearning for the return to a Japanese aesthetics—such an aspect is also visible in his 1929 *Tade kū Mushi* [*Some Prefer Nettles*]. In this work, Tanizaki presents another version of East and West comparison inside Japan: the Japanese woman with blackened teeth whose allure still appreciated in western Japan (Kansai) but not in the eastern part of the country (Kantō); the protagonist's fascination with the western wing of his house in contrast to the Japanese one; the protagonist's ambiguous move between the modern Tokyo and the more traditional Kansai, with the *bunraku* puppet theatre as a representative example of Kansai culture.

Tanizaki's use of shadows functions as a trope for rethinking traditional Japanese-ness in the context of rampant modernization and Westernization, as well as the cultural and intellectual movement to *Nihon kaiki* in the 1930s, deliberately created under the expansion of the Japanese empire at the time. Problematizing the notion of tradition with reference to Eric Hobsbawm's idea of tradition as invented, rather than the sum of actual past practices, historian Stephen Vlastos defines tradition as "a modern trope, a prescriptive representation of socially desirable (or sometimes undesirable) institutions and ideas thought to have been handed down from generation to generation."[54] Tanizaki's traditionalist aesthetics of shadow illuminates his ironic project of returning to a tradition that was now lost in the modern era. Although many of Tanizaki's examples are based on a Japanese lifestyle that reflects the experience with shadow and darkness, Japanese lives by that time were being transformed, and for Tanizaki blighted, by the use of Western lighting technologies.

Tanizaki orientalizes the Japanese aesthetics so as to place it as contrast to the West. In so doing, he at times employs a colonizer's perspective when speaking of other Asian countries. LaMarre points out that Tanizaki refers to Japanese aesthetics as both Japanese and "Oriental," suggesting a culture that stems both from China and India: "His turn (or 'return,' if one insists)

---

53. Dodd, "History in the Making," 164.
54. Stephen Vlastos, "Tradition: Past/Present Culture and Modern Japanese History," in *Mirror of Modernity: Invented Traditions of Modern Japan*, ed. Stephen Vlastos (Berkeley and London: University of California Press, 1998), 3.

to traditional aesthetics entails an 'orientalist' or 'orientalizing' gesture that brings Japan into relation to East Asia," with an ambivalence towards the reality of both Western and Japanese imperialism.[55] As Nishihara Daisuke also argues, Tanizaki skillfully switches the object and the subject of his Orientalism—using a double discourse, employing the colonizer's viewpoint, when describing countries such as China, while self-Orientalizing Japanese culture and expressing "the charm and beauty" from a Western perspective.[56] Pursuing the Japanese tradition for Tanizaki functions almost as if it is an extension of his earlier yearning for the West—trying to reach what is not quite reachable or no longer available—as the dually fetishized cultures. Margherita Long recognizes in Tanizaki's aesthetics an investment in interpreting the cultural fetish as "a symptom of the enjoyment it masks and displaces."[57] This is especially so given that the desire for light is not an especially modern construction: we only have to think of Greek and Judeo-Christian thought, the biblical theme of a light and Christian motifs of light tied to enlightenment,[58] Medieval paintings representing God as light or light as wealth, baroque paintings "struck by the light,"[59] and recent adaptations of those where light optically caresses the surface.[60] Inspiration for obscurity is also observable in the Chinese tradition.[61] Tanizaki effectively mobilizes "Japanese" beauty.

---

55. LaMarre, *Shadows on the Screen*, 13.

56. Nishihara Daisuke, "Said, Orientalism, and Japan," *Alif: Journal of Comparative Poetics*, no. 25, special issue on Edward Said and Critical Decolonization (2005): 246.

57. Margherita Long, "Tanizaki and the Enjoyment of Japanese Culturalism," *positions: East Asia Cultures Critique* 10: 2 (2002): 437.

58. M. R. Wright ed., *Empedocles: The Extant Fragments* (New Haven and London: Yale University Press, 1981, 252); John 1: 7–9; 8: 12; Iain M. Mackenzie, *The "Obscurism" of Light: A Theological Study into the Nature of Light* (Norwich: The Canterbury Press, 1996).

59. Umberto Eco, *On Beauty*, trans. Alastair MacEwen (London: Secker & Warburg, 2004), 100.

60. Mieke Bal, *Quoting Caravaggio: Contemporary Art, Preposterous History* (Chicago, IL and London: University of Chicago Press, 1999), 192.

61. A medieval poet Ōe no Chisato took inspirations from Chinese poems by Po Chü-i (772–846), for example, to express the misty moon of spring night. See *The Shin Kokinshū: The Thirteenth-century Anthology Edited by Imperial Edict*, trans. Honda Heihachirō (Tokyo: Hokuseidō Press, 1970). As is well known, Motoori Norinaga (1730–1801) tried to argue for a "Japanese" aesthetics in contradistinction to a Chinese one through native studies Kokugaku, by making the Japanese mind into, as per Ueno Chizuko, "a

At the same time, Tanizaki's shadow occupies a mediatory function. Although ambiguity may generally refer to vagueness or blurriness, as in the sense of grayness as between black and white, or as a shadowy space as between light and darkness, it also manifests a hovering distance in occupying opposite poles simultaneously, as much as shadows are both haptic and visual. Ōe Kenzaburō (1935–) articulates the difference between vagueness (vague as *aimaina*) and ambiguity (in the sense of *ryōgisei*, to possess two meanings), with reference to Kawabata's idea of beauty as extreme vagueness that effectively claims the impossibility of the expression of truth in language; the title of his speech for the Nobel Prize ceremony in 1994 "Aimai na Nihon no Watashi" ["Japan, the Ambiguous, and Myself"] stems from Kawabata's earlier Nobel Prize speech in 1968 "Utsukushii Nihon no Watashi" ["Japan, the Beautiful, and Myself"].[62] Ōe's conscious decision to use the term "ambiguity" over "vagueness" references Japan's state, since its opening to the West to the contemporary after the postwar rapid economic growth, that is "split between two opposite poles of ambiguity": between rapid Westernization and the preservation of its traditional culture, and between being a part of Asia and being an invader in Asia.[63] This notion of ambiguity regarding developmental process and political standpoint also recalls Barthes's idea of "the Neutral," which does not signify the midpoint but rather a form of resistance to choosing either of two opposites: the Neutral as spacing and interruption: suspension of "the will-to-possess."[64] This interruption makes contact possible and creates mediated relations between objects, between self and object, and between the self and itself.

While Tanizaki writes of shadow as being part of traditional Japanese aesthetics, Barthes also calls attention to shadows to achieve the perfection of photographs. Whereas Tanizaki requires a shadow, even on the skin

---

residual category of universalism." Ueno Chizuko, "In the Feminine Guise: A Trap of Reverse Orientalism," in *Contemporary Japanese Thought*, ed. Richard F. Calichman (New York: Columbia University Press, 2005), 225–229.

62. Ōe Kenzaburō, "Japan, the Ambiguous and Myself," in *Japan, the Ambiguous, and Myself: The Nobel Prize Speech and Other Lectures* (New York: Kōdansha International, 1995), 110–111. It was published in Japanese as *Aimaina Nihon no Watashi* by Iwanami Shoten in 1995.

63. Ōe Kenzaburō, "Japan, the Ambiguous and Myself," 117.

64. Barthes, *The Neutral*, 12.

surface, saying, "the Japanese complexion, no matter how white, is tinged by a slight cloudiness,"[65] Barthes professes a desire for the "luminous shadow which accompanies the body."[66] Barthes introduces the concept of *air*, which is something inexpressible, evident, but improbable, intending the expression of truth; this element of air animates the photographed figure. Without this air, the only thing that remains is the body, visible to the eye, and yet incomplete. "It is by this tenuous umbilical cord that the photographer gives life; if he cannot, either by lack of talent or bad luck, supply the transparent soul its bright shadow, the subject dies forever."[67] For both Barthes and Tanizaki, shadows, which are attached to the body, accompany the subject with particular effects on it. Such effects include (in Barthes) the giving of life and value, and even (for Tanizaki) room for imagination and the chance of transformation. Barthes's air, as luminous shadow, illuminates the seen but also puts a shade upon it.

In an essay analyzing a collection of photographs by Shinoyama Kishin, Jacques Derrida writes that photography as skiagraphy is "the writing of light as the writing of shade," reminding him of Tanizaki's use of shadow in which the body immerses and emerges.[68] While Barthes sees the photograph as a unique, absolute singularity, Derrida asks: "How is this (light) clarity *of* the night? Why does it appear not only to come out of and proceed from the night, as if black gave birth to white, but also to belong still to shadow, to remain still *at the heart* of the dark abyss from which it emanates?"[69] Derrida seeks to articulate something that possesses an oppositional tension within itself: a light that illuminates the object but still belongs to the darkness, a shadow created in the midst of light, but that still possesses the darkness—light in the dark, or "Light of the Dark," the title of Shinoyama's collection. Luminous shadow as *air* reaches the photographed object to give to it one final addition: an impression of life. Shadow is thus a dynamic oscillation—between light and darkness, illumination and shade, life and death, and vision and touch—possessing both haptic and visual functions, as one form of touch. Shadow accompanies

---

65. Tanizaki, *In Praise of Shadows*, 49.
66. Barthes, *Camera Lucida*, 110.
67. Barthes, *Camera Lucida*.
68. Jacques Derrida, "Aletheia," trans. Pleshette De Armitt and Kas Saghafi, *The Oxford Literary Review* 32: 2 (2010): 171.
69. Jacques Derrida, "Aletheia."

and gives vitality to the body—as the *kuroko* in the *bunraku* puppet theater support those actors.

The duality of touch and vision in a form of faint light accompanying the body is a vital element for Shunkin to perceive the world. In "A Portrait of Shunkin" the sighted Sasuke guides the blind Shunkin in her daily life but, even after Sasuke becomes blind by his own hand, he anticipates her every possible inconvenience, and solicitously takes care of her. Shunkin comes to require his assistance for almost everything she does, including dressing, bathing, massage, and being escorted to the lavatory, despite the fact that she has a female disciple and attendant Teru (whom she rarely allows to touch her directly). Such communication between Sasuke and Shunkin—one blind person helping another blind person—is described in the following manner, through the narrator's account: "He must have touched her as sensitively as Shunkin had caressed the trunks of the old plum trees ... Sasuke and Shunkin seemed to enjoy the very difficulties, expressing their unspoken love in this way. I suppose we cannot imagine how much pleasure the two sightless lovers took in the world revealed to them by their sense of touch."[70] This blind couple finds a pleasure through the faint light, imagining the world through the sense of touch, hearing, and smelling, beyond the restrictions of vision.

A blind body engages with elements of the other's body surface (texture, moisture, temperature), and with movement, voice, tone, and pitch; the slightest response has the most enormous effect. When Sasuke tells her that he is now blind, Shunkin responds simply with, "Really, Sasuke?", which, we are told, is followed by a long silence. This silence is appreciated by Sasuke as a joyful trembling—leading to his own happiness. As the narrator recounts:

> As they sat facing each other in silence, Sasuke began to feel the quickening of that sixth sense which only the blind possess, and he could tell that there was nothing but the deepest gratitude in Shunkin's heart. Always before, even while they were making love, they had been separated by the gulf between teacher and pupil. But now Sasuke felt that they were truly united, locked in a tight embrace. Youthful memories of the dark world of the closet where

---

70. Tanizaki, "A Portrait of Shunkin," 78.

he used to practice came flooding into his mind, but the darkness
in which he now found himself seemed completely different. Most
blind people can sense the direction from which light is coming;
they live in a faintly luminous world, not one of unrelieved black-
ness. Now Sasuke knew that he had found an inner vision in place of
the vision he had lost. Ah, he thought, this is the world my teacher
lives in—at last I have reached it![71]

The condition that puts Sasuke in a faintly luminous world within darkness enables him to see, touch, and communicate with his yearned-for
object—his beloved Shunkin—in the clearest way possible. Or, as Nosaka
Akiyuki puts it, the abstract beauty of Shunkin for Sasuke becomes nurtured by a vividly skin touch/texture (*namanamashii hada no sawari*)[72] due
to blindness.[73] Sasuke's practice of the *shamisen* in the dark attic, when
witnessed by the readers, is a practice designed to aid Shunkin: he is doing
it as someone who is blind like her. Sasuke's becoming disabled by pricking
his eyes is a way for him to reach his loved one, despite the different body.
Touch blurs the boundaries between the visible and invisible, visible and
tangible, light and darkness, while transforming those involved.

Shadows Animated beyond the Surface

As an avid movie-goer and who had himself been involved in film production particularly in his early days, Tanizaki had become interested in the
play of shadow, the close-up, and dazzling and deadening effect of light.
While Tanizaki was fascinated by new psychological approaches, the haptic
quality of the visual as in European avant-garde art movements was also

---

71. Tanizaki, "A Portrait of Shunkin," 74–75.

72. Nosaka Akiyuki, "Shunkinshō," *Kokubungaku: Kaishaku to Kyōzai no Kenkyū* 23: 10
(August 1978), 91.

73. Arguing for a complex embodiment beyond the specificity of a disability identity, with
reference to Freud's discussion of narcissism, Tobin Siebers draws attention to private emotions and thoughts thinking about disabilities: "We do not love only our own kind or
ourselves. You others are our caregivers—and we can be yours, if you let us. We of the
tender organs are not narcissists." Tobin Siebers, *Disability Theory* (Ann Arbor: University
of Michigan Press, 2008), 52.

emerging in Japan, especially along with cinematic culture—often referred to as *eiga* (cinema) or *katsudō shashin* (animated photographs or moving pictures), developed from the mid Meiji to the early Shōwa (1926–1989) period. The haptic–visual dynamic that fascinated Tanizaki arose in cinema as the oscillations between the still and animated, and between light and darkness, as well as between actuality and illusion. This was especially heightened in the context of urban culture, and *ero guro nansensu* (erotic, grotesque, nonsense) in 1930s Japan—where the "erotic," combined with the elements of mass urban culture, including cinema, functioned as a way to express both sensual pleasure and resistance against business conglomerates; militarization; and social reform amid depression, unemployment, and anxiety. The bodies became illuminated by light, "possessed" by image makers, and animated on the screen's surface. This is, at the same time, the process through which bodies came to bear textures, tangibility, or palpability beyond the distance, via luminous shadows.

Miriam Silverberg explains that while *ero,* or the erotic, was a ubiquitous term in popular media for sexual promiscuity and the configuration of the female body, it also had a much broader meaning of "a variety of sensual gratifications, physical expressiveness, and the affirmation of social intimacy."[74] In eroticized modern industry—including café waitress (*jyokyū,* as Naomi serves in the beginning of *Naomi*)—if *iro* referred to "women's desire for connectedness to men," and *ero* for "male pleasures of physical intimacy with women made available for domination," Silverberg sees a possibility for renegotiating *iro* by women who account for the preoccupation with *ero* in the cafés and in the media at the time.[75] In particular, this seems to be the case when the flipping of the subject and the object, the controlling and the controlled, and the seeing and the seen, is inherently a key element in forming characters' relationality in Tanizaki's works.

The screened female body, which used to be that of a male transvestite kabuki actor, eventually came to be performed by a female actress, with attention to its flesh, for the pursuit of realism and ideas of natural performance that became popular during the rise of pure film movement (*jun eiga undō*) in the late 1910s and early 1920s. As early as in 1911, in "Himitsu" ["The Secret"], Tanizaki knitted the transvestite imaginary

---

74. Miriam Silverberg, *Erotic Grotesque Nonsense*, 29.
75. Miriam Silverberg, *Erotic Grotesque Nonsense*, 107.

together with a spectacle created in the alternations of light and darkness in the modern city. The male protagonist, haunted by the beauty of a silk kimono, feels a need to wear it on the street; the silk textile feels to him like a lover's skin, and wearing it on his own skin suggests to him a physical union with his beloved in its transvestite imaginary. Tomi Suzuki writes that masochistic pleasure in this story is further strengthened through "the reciprocal effects of visual and corporeal, especially haptic, pleasure"[76]; "I," the subject of desire and of gaze, becomes transformed from the looking to the looked through the gaze. Such an imaginary engagement with the loved one through kimono as an extra skin is as if to signal the later Abe Sada incident in 1936, which is known for Sada's strangling Kichizō and cutting off his penis so as to possess him forever. While the Abe Sada incident was sensationalized to be "pathographic" in order to divert attention away from the political tension at the time,[77] it illuminates a mediated unification with the loved one; as screened by Tanaka Noboru and by Ōshima Nagisa,[78] Sada and Kichizō treated the kimonos each had left behind as if they were the loved one's skin, cherishing the smells that had permeated the garments and the interiors of the room, as if they did not want to let go of any element that caused them to feel the existence of the other. Transvestite imaginary, woven together with haptic imaginary, is animated on the surface.

Tanizaki's contemporary Edogawa Rampo (1894–1965) was also pre-occupied by the haptic sense (*shokkaku*). It appears in his 1931 novel *Mōjū*, made into a film adaptation by Masumura Yasuzō as *Blind Beast* in 1969, where a deranged, blind artist constitutes the body parts of a female exemplary model through the haptic sense. Edogawa writes in his 1926 essay "Eiga no Kyōfu" ["The Horrors of Film"] of the terrors of close-up images. Tactile proximity was terrifying, as Thomas LaMarre suggests on this essay: "Madness arises when images come incredibly close to viewers, so close that images are no longer perceived but felt, so close

---

76. Suzuki, "Jendā Ekkyō no Miwaku to Mazohizumu Bigaku," 38.
77. Christine Marran, "From Pathography to Pulp: Popular Expressions of Female Deviancy, 1930–1950," in *A Century of Popular Culture in Japan*, ed. Douglas Slaymaker (Lewiston, NY: The Edwin Mellen Press, 2000), 47, 53.
78. *Jitsuroku Abe Sada* (*A Woman Called Abe Sada*) from 1975 is directed by Tanaka Noboru, and *Ai no Korīda* (*In the Realm of the Senses*) from 1976 is directed by Ōshima Nagisa.

that perception gives way to a shock to the body."[79] But there was another type of terror in film, and this was that of instantaneous extinction of a projected human being; when the projection machine breaks down in the middle of screening and the film reel stops, Edogawa writes in the above-mentioned essay, "A living human being is abruptly transformed into an inanimate puppet. When I see this happen during a movie, it gives me such a shock that I have an uncontrollable urge to jump out of my seat and run away. It is terrifying when a living thing suddenly goes dead."[80] Having written film scripts and various essays on film, Tanizaki himself wrote that seeing a close-up face image caused him more complex, various fantasies than seeing a long drama.[81] Tanizaki's characters, as much as Tanizaki himself, seem to present a particular terror when they are presented with the blurring of the boundaries between actuality and illusion, life and death.

Tanizaki's 1926 short story "Aozuka shi no Hanashi" ["Mr. Bluemound"] further complicates those boundaries between life and death through the engagement with surfaces. The main narrative, which starts after a short introduction, is apparently the testament of Mr. Nakada, a film director and husband, now deceased, addressed to his wife Yurako, who is also an actress. Mr. Nakada confesses to Yurako in his will (*isho*) the real reason for his demise and his encounter with a middle-aged man who was obsessed with Yurako; this man made a practice of examining her body on the screen to constitute her perfect body at one remove and to create perfect Yurako dolls with the surface of thin layer of rubber like the feel of human skin, in various poses would sit on his knee or kiss him.[82] The encounter with this

---

79. LaMarre, *Shadows on the Screen*, 110.

80. Edogawa Rampo, "The Horrors of Film" (1926), in *The Edogawa Rampo Reader*, edited and translated by Seth Jacobowitz (Fukuoka: Kurodahan Press, 2008), 138.

81. Tanizaki, "'Caligari Hakase' wo miru" ["On 'Das Cabinet des Dr. Caligari'"], *TJZ* vol. 8 (Tokyo: Chūoh Kōronsha, 2017), 455–456. Originally published in three instalments in 1921 in the journal *Jiji Shinpō*.

82. In a recent film made by director Kore'eda Hirokazu, *Kūki Ningyō* (*Air Doll*) (2009), where the beloved figure doll functions (physically) as the protagonist's lover, the male protagonist purchases a figure doll, names her, and lives with her as if she were his real lover. She starts to exercise her own agency, moving when she wants to, only to discover that she is replaceable: she discovers that her master has purchased another doll to live with him. *Air Doll*, directed by Kore'eda Hirokazu (Tokyo: Bandai Visual, 2010).

man deprives Nakada of any certainty that he—as Yurako's husband and the filmmaker who "screens" her body—knows her body best, leading in turn to a physical deterioration and eventually his death. A tangible access to the loved body does not guarantee to this film director any authenticity to feel Yurako. Nakada writes, "When thoughts like this well up inside me, no matter how tightly I hold you, it doesn't feel like it's the real, one-of-a-kind 'you.' And, just as you may have become a shadow, I've come to seem like one as well. The love we had, though not utterly destroyed by this, has been turned into something hollow and deceptive [*kūkyo na mono, uso na mono*] and more impermanent than a single film shot."[83] The man who "holds" Yurako from distance seems, for Nakada, to possess the firmer grasp of her. The shadow becomes to take over the lived, turning Nakada shadowy and the obsessive man alive. It is as though full visuality brings a disintegration of the desiring subject, instead of securing him reach to the desired object fully.

The source and drive of pleasure in Tanizaki often arises from the female body, although the seer's relationship to it is never completely settled. In Tanizaki's 1927 "Nihon ni okeru Kurippun Jiken" ["The Crippen Murder"] the masochist enjoys seemingly behaving as the slave of a female master, which seems to him like a theater play. Looking like those men who praise their wives or lovers like goddesses, they use them like dolls or instruments that give them a particular pleasure.[84] And yet, Kōno Taeko, discussing this story, describes it as an instance "where the masochist comes to dislike the sadist other," a theme explored incompletely,[85] as signalled in which a man murders his sadistic wife; he has become bored with her, in another woman. Instead of the male dominating the female body, the latter rules over the play, even when it is the object of desire. Kamei Hideo, reading the female body in Tanizaki from the standpoint of the theory of embodiedness, argues that the women depicted by Tanizaki exist in a kind of confusing maze (*meiro*); the women themselves are a kind of

83. Tanizaki Jun'ichirō, "Mr. Bluemound," trans. Paul McCarthy, in *The Gourmet Club: A Sextet*, 159–160; "Aozuka shi no Hanashi," in *TJZ*, vol. 14 (Tokyo: Chūoh Kōronsha, 2016), 49–50. Originally published in the journal *Kaizō* over four issues in 1926.

84. Tanizaki, "Nihon ni okeru Kurippun Jiken," in *TJZ*, vol. 13 (Tokyo: Chūoh Kōronsha, 2015), 11.

85. Kōno Taeko, *Tanizaki Bungaku to Kōtei no Yokubō* [*The Literature of Tanizaki and Affirmative Desire*] (Tokyo: Chūoh Kōronsha, 1980), 185–186.

maze.[86] Or, as Chiba Shunji puts it, the beloved possesses a dual nature, of being goddesses as well as dolls, tyrants as well as instruments.[87] The object–subject relationship in the above always bears the possibility for overturn. Combined with the cinematic flickering of light from darkness, shadows in light, the presumably seen object "touches" the seeing, with transformative effects.

Tanizaki's attention to visual effects through his active involvement in cinematic production resonates even in his postwar works. His attention to cinematic techniques such as the close-up, the dissolve and the fade in/ out (*yōmei, yōan*), and overlap[88] are observable in *The Key* as a literary technique, especially in his depiction of illusion. Tanizaki prompts a dynamic interaction between characters of the lived body and of the imagined one, attempting to translate cinematic effects on the screen to the literary effects on the page.[89] Often, the characters' transformation in Tanizaki occurs to an idealized female figure, subordinating other characters (including the female character, as Ikuko considers having her daughter Toshiko marry Kimura just for appearance as "sacrifice" in the end of *The Key*[90]), or changing them through illusion. Deleuze considers that the illusion in cinema "is corrected at the same time as the image appears for a spectator without

86. Kamei Hideo, "Shintairon-teki ni mita Tanizani Jun'ichirō: Nyotai to Meikyū" ["Tanizani Jun'ichirō through the Perspectives of Embodiedness: the Female Body and the Maze"], *Kokubungaku: Kaishaku to Kyōzai no Kenkyū* 30: 9 (1985), 41.

87. Chiba, *Tanizaki Jun'ichirō*, 47.

88. Tanizaki, "Eiga no Tekunikku" ["Cinematic Techniques"], *TJZ* vol. 8, 460–466. Originally published in 1921 in *Shakai oyobi Kokka*.

89. See Koide Hiroshi's comaparive analysis on Tanizaki's involvement in cinematic creations and the influence of French cinema (*Les Diaboliques* [*Diabolique*] by Henri-Gorges Clouzot in 1955) on Tanizaki's *The Key*. Koide Hiroshi, " 'Kagi' to Furansu Eiga: Tanizaki Jun'ichirō no Sakuhin Seisakujō no Hitotsu no Patān" ["*The Key* and French Cinema: One Pattern in Tanizaki Jun'ichirō's Fiction"], *Kokubungaku Kenkyū* 30 (1964): 78–84. Satō Mioko also points out that Tanizaki attempted the sharp representation of the flesh in pure film movement in his "Mr. Bluemound"—using a filmic shot of the 1921 film *Jasei no In*, directed by Kurihara Kisaburō, for which Tanizaki had written a script, to light the line of the female body from behind, in his depiction of Yurako's body, which appears to be transparent when dressed in a silk gown. Satō Mioko, "Tanizaki Jun'ichirō 'Aozuka shi no Hanashi' ni okeru Eiga no Isō: Eiga Seisaku/Juyō wo meguru Yokubō no Arika" ["The Position of the Film in Tanizaki Junichiro's 'Aozukashi no Hanashi': The Presence of Desire in Film Production and Reception"], *Nihon Kindai Bungaku* 91 (2014): 50.

90. Tanizaki, *The Key*, 160.

conditions"; cinema gives a movement-image simultaneously, instead of movement following or being "added" to the image.[91] It might be that what Tanizaki pursued in moving images is this unconditionality where images can be animated simultaneously when movements can be visualized. Tanizaki was haunted by distance, suspension, and conditionality, which made it not only difficult to reach the yearned-for object, but also to achieve movement and image simultaneously, much as he desired both light and shadows at the same time.

The Imagined through Touch

In *The Key*, which was written two decades after *In Praise of Shadows*, the relationship between Ikuko and her husband is dependent on their reading each other's diaries. They are prying into each other's sexual life out of suspicion. When the wife discovers the key to the drawer in which her husband hides his diary, and starts to read it, she enjoys a sense of superiority—thinking that he does not know that she also keeps a diary herself. The scopic positions in *The Key* are reciprocal between the protagonist and Ikuko, especially via the existence of Kimura. Kimura becomes "indispensable to our [the narrator-protagonist and Ikuko's] sexual life"— stimulating the protagonist's jealousy for Ikuko.[92] A sexual stimulation is further nurtured through the mediation of contact with a surface—the page of a diary, the photographs inserted in between pages, and the texture of the skin surface of each of the characters. The visibility of the loved one is cultivated via touch, the tangibility via illusion, yet almost without coming to touch the complete body. The convergence of vision and touch, texture and light, also affects reading in *The Key*, in an intricate manner. The mutuality of relationality—a dynamic interaction with a paper-thin distance between the subject and object, vision and touch, light and shadow—changes the relationship between Ikuko and protagonist, too, turning Ikuko into an active subject who views her husband's body at extremely close range while he is in a coma (caused by high blood pressure

---

91. Gilles Deleuze, *Cinema 1: the Movement-Image*, trans. Hugh Tomlinson and Barbara Habberjam (Minneapolis: University of Minnesota Press, 2013), 2.
92. Tanizaki, *The Key*, 21.

and a stroke), instead of only being observed in every detail herself. In *The Key*, the crucial element to make their sexual life a dynamic interaction is the modulation of light to capture or *write* the body—even though ultimately full visibility of the object causes a physical deterioration to the seeing subject. Admittedly, light is not something that is usually visible and "read" as such in a text. However, light in *The Key* regulates, consequently, the reachability of the object for the readers of diaries and of the novel. In effect, reading, seeing, and touching become mutual activities.

One day, Ikuko records the persistency of her husband's gaze under the light. He seems "to pore over my body, as minutely as possible," giving a special attention to her feet, leading her to write in her diary, "Are those gross, sticky, nasty caresses what you have to expect from *all* men?"[93] The husband's persistent gaze takes on a haptic capacity at this point, as he seems to adhere and almost lick her skin as he gazes. The husband, with a fascination for the possibilities of fluorescent lighting and a longstanding fantasy of seeing Ikuko's naked body under the radiance of bright light, takes off her nightgown after she has sunk into a deep sleep as a result of a Vitacamphor injection for her cerebral anemia, and begins to study her body as if it were a map; for the first time, he records, he has an unimpeded view of her nude body in its entirety. The husband writes, "Only by touch have I been able to picture to myself the beauty of her body, which is why I wanted so desperately to look at her under that brilliant light. And what I saw far exceeded my expectations."[94] He used to imagine her body through touch without fully seeing it, but now it has become available as the visible—his gaze caresses it in attending all possible details from her bosom, buttock, legs, ankles, to the surface of her skin, whose purity dazzles him: in his words, "devouring her with my eyes" ("*me wo motte sono shisei wo musabori-kui, tada tansoku shiteiru bakarideatta*").[95] Here, in the protagonist's perception of Ikuko's body, touching precedes seeing; in other words, incomplete visibility gave him the texture and contour of her body through touching. Michael Baxandall, in his discussions of shadows and their role in seers' apprehensions of objects' shapes, writes, "vision is trained by touch to be a more powerful and far-ranging sense

---

93. Tanizaki, *The Key*, 16.
94. Tanizaki, *The Key*, 28.
95. Tanizaki, *The Key*, 30; "Kagi," 108, "uttering sigh after sigh," left untranslated.

than touch itself, all by a process of associated sensations."[96] The protagonist, in desiring light but without actually having it to "see" Ikuko's body, is accustomed to seeing her body in blurred form—by touching—before coming to shape her naked body under radiant light. Much as the strong desire to reach the yearned-for object in Kawabata is conducted through the gaze and words, the husband here contours Ikuko's body after twenty years of only touching it in their married life.

However, soon he is seized with a sudden notion; first, he suspects she is actually awake and merely pretending to be asleep to conceal her embarrassment. Such an idea simply stimulates his fantasy, as he imagines what will happen when she reads his diary entry about what he did to her while she was unconscious. In contrast, when the husband-narrator goes into a coma after a stroke, and his naked body is exposed under the light to Ikuko and her daughter during a doctor's examination, she experiences a kind of revulsion: "He has examined every inch of me [she records], to the very pores of my skin, but I haven't known his body nearly as well as I know Kimura's. I haven't wanted to. I suspected it would only make me detest him all the more. It gave me a queer feeling to think I've been sleeping with such a miserable creature."[97] At a certain point, Dr. Kodama rubs both sides of the narrator-husband's scrotum with chopsticks (in order, as he later explains, to test the reflexes of the suspensory muscles) as he (the narrator-husband) lies there unconscious, and wife and daughter try to avert their eyes. Earlier in the story, Ikuko has noted in her diary the memory of her honeymoon night when her husband removed his thick-lensed glasses, and she winces at the sight of his face. As he leaned down close to look at her, she notes, she saw the texture of his "smooth, slippery, waxy skin" (*kime no komakai, alminium no yō ni tsurutsuru shita hifu*) at close range, which made her feel ill.[98] The natural palpable texture of the skin surface brings startling visual (and indeed corporeal) effects to Ikuko when viewed under artificial conditions. Here the earlier-discussed "artificiality" in Tanizaki's works, which previously helped transform women from natural to created—is given a kind of reverse variation: the bare form of a husband's body is rendered artificially to his wife. The more

---

96. Baxandall, *Shadows and Enlightenment*, 28.
97. Tanizaki, *The Key*, 120.
98. Tanizaki, *The Key*, 15: "Kagi," 98.

closely it is viewed, the more artificial-seeming the male body becomes. It is not only female characters in Tanizaki's stories that undergo transformations. Male characters also transform, as in *The Key* and "A Portrait of Shunkin." Tanizaki enables the characters' transformation through visual-haptic means.

In *The Key*, a variety of artificial stimulants—tablets, injections, camera, and light—gives the husband-narrator the freedom to gaze at Ikuko's naked body as much as he wants, marking a transformative moment for their relationality. Inebriated with brandy and drifting off into a half-sleep, Ikuko has (she writes) the illusion of holding Kimura in her arms. As opposed to the general understanding of "illusion," that might suggest something unstable, transient, and floating, what she saw brought something much more concrete, tangible, and physical. "Even now [she writes] that sensation lingers in the flesh of my arms and thighs," reporting something entirely different from her husband's embrace, the concrete textures of Kimura's body—strength of his young arms, firm and resilient chest, and dazzlingly fair skin.[99] When Ikuko lost her consciousness in the bathtub, her husband asked Kimura to help him wipe her and bring her body into the bedroom; Ikuko assumes that she was in the arms of her husband, and her husband's arms, she writes, only reminded her of Kimura. Her husband's body is not "felt" but rather disappears behind her strong sensations associated with Kimura; "I kept on having that feeling of pressure [*akkaku*], of completion, a feeling I can't associate with him [husband]."[100] Kimura's body, naked shape of which she has yet seen, comes to form both tangible textures and concrete visual images in her illusion; her desire to touch his body is infused with delusion. Here, it is not only the protagonist's shaping of Ikuko's body, as discussed earlier, but also regarding her perception of Kimura's body, touch leads vision; the loved one's naked body is shaped by touching in incomplete visibility, followed by the actual seeing to come. In the mingling of the senses, imagined touch with the loved one starts to press her skin with firmer tangibility and pressure than the husband's body that she knows.

Ikuko imagines and plays with Kimura's body (an extramarital relationship) in place of her husband's body (a feudal marital relationship, in

---

99. Tanizaki, *The Key*, 36–37.
100. Tanizaki, *The Key*, 37; "Kagi," 114.

which she has been a loyal wife) almost in a replaceable mode. She can be loyal to the marriage system by substituting her desired object from husband to the lover and engaging with the latter in her illusion, willing to discover his body not only in her imagined touch but "to find out what he's *really* like."[101] We may remember that, in the postwar dissolution of familial structure as discussed in the introduction, the father, who used to be the central figure in the traditional Japanese family, had become replaceable. At the same time, the replaceability of one figure with another was confirmed in Tanizaki's own life; Tanizaki changed wives multiple times; and, in what is widely known as the "Odawara incident," even engaged in a rather public marital "transfer."[102] Tanizaki, even here, seems to require an oscillatory relationship with the object in approaching but not fully possessing. Tangible textures and (in)visible images, along with the associated chain of stimulations, would aid in constituting the (imaginary) body. Conditions to avoid immediate touch with the desired other in *The Key* thus appears in multiple forms of surface—the diary page, photographic surface, and light that covers the body that reveals parts of partners' bodies in detail, which conversely heightens (for the protagonist), yet decreases (for Ikuko), the desire to touch the other.

In contrast to the earlier-discussed photograph of Shunkin in her mid-thirties, taken in the initial stage of photography assumingly in the late 1860s, that of Ikuko in her mid-forties (born in 1911), supposedly in the mid 1950s in *The Key*, is taken with an American Polaroid camera. A Polaroid camera, Kimura explains, is easy to operate without a tripod, uses a Strobe flash, and produces prints immediately; at the time it was still rare, as was the film it used (printing-paper superimposed on negative), which needed to be imported: Polaroid photography in Japan, explained in the story, was used to make the still pictures shown on television at the

---

101. Tanizaki, *The Key*.
102. This is the case based on Tanizaki's split with his friend, the poet Satō Haruo, over Tanizaki's first wife Chiyo. Tanizaki became attracted to Chiyo's younger syster Seiko (who later became a model of Naomi), had a relationship with Seiko, and began to ponder upon how to break up with Chiyo. Satō's sympathy toward the maltreated Chiyo developed into a relationship between the two. Tanizaki, having decided to remarry Seiko, changed his mind, which resulted in the breakup of Tanizaki and Satō. After a decade of turmoil, when Tanizaki divorced Chiyo (reflected in a dysfunctional marriage life in *Some Prefer Nettles*), Chiyo remarried Satō in 1930.

end of *sumo* wrestling bouts, to immediately explain the winning hold.[103] The point of capturing the body shifted from still figure portraiture as in "A Portrait of Shunkin" to compartmentalizing physical movements as in *The Key*, as if to once again heighten Tanizaki's fetish for partial bodies toward the end of his life. And yet, despite technological advancements over time, the pictures in *The Key* are still often out of focus, taken with a Polaroid camera but with a slow lens, no range finder, and out-of-date old film. Taking some pictures of Ikuko, from the front and back, the protagonist has Kimura develop those photographs with the intention of inducing Kimura and Ikuko to become closer, and even inserts them in his diary so that Ikuko will see them. The daughter Toshiko also has a look at them, and her participation too ultimately stimulates Kimura's and Ikuko's pleasure. The chain of seeing (and being seen) heightens the further desire for tangibility even though, and perhaps precisely because, the images are out of focus: blurred image cultivates touch of the object.

The protagonist in *The Key*, who starts off by hoping to use his jealousy of Ikuko and Kimura as a sensual stimulant for his marital sex life, is taken over by it and, in the end, suffers from high blood pressure and has a stroke. Ikuko loses consciousness for a second time in the bath after an evening spent with Toshiko and Kimura and, in this state, calls Kimura's name deliriously. On the diary entry of this day, the husband-narrator writes:

> In an instant my jealous rage had vanished. I no longer cared whether she was asleep or awake, shaming or not; I didn't even want to distinguish myself from Kimura. At that moment I felt I had burst into another world, soared up to some towering height, to the very zenith of ecstasy. This was reality, the past was only illusion.[104]

Ikuko is now fully acknowledging her love for Kimura, with her desire to see his naked body, which she always dreamed of (in her illusion), "without any interference from my [her] husband."[105] After the husband-narrator realizes that it is Kimura who has turned her wife into a bold, aggressive

---

103. Tanizaki, *The Key*, 41.
104. Tanizaki, *The Key*, 72.
105. Tanizaki, *The Key*, 75.

woman, when she calls Kimura over and over again, even as she bites the husband-narrator's tongue and earlobe, he begins to feel dizzy, and he sees a double outline of Ikuko's body. This is followed by his dream in which the husband-narrator's head is transformed into Kimura's head, both of them growing from a single body; "the entire image was doubled."[106] The narrator-husband's intense jealousy, mediated by Kimura, at the end causes a physical deterioration, allowing Ikuko and Kimura to dispense with the final "paper-thin distance" altogether, as we find out in an entry in Ikuko's diary written after her husband's death to narrate her union with Kimura retrospectively. Although Ikuko once wrote that she identified Kimura with her husband and felt that her husband and Kimura were one, the closer she grew to Kimura, the more independent his body began to feel from her husband's, because of actual touching.

In *The Key*, Tanizaki brings the dualities of writing and reading and of touch and vision altogether, making full use of the diary format. Critic Shibusawa Tatsuhiko, when discussing vision in Tanizaki with reference to his blind stories, writes that the more one requires the other's gaze, the less one requires the gaze onto the self, as it is possible "to enjoy the gaze of another in the world of fantasy" (*kūsō no sekai de aite no shisen wo kyōju suru*), by closing the eyes.[107] When one desires the other, one may manage to, even if only partially, touch it by seeing, contiguously touch it with a shadow, see it by touching, or reach it via reading: the (dis-embodied) written reaches the other. Tanizaki mobilizes the relationship between the subject and object, the tangible and the visible, and writing and reading. In particular, an artificial condition is necessary to produce, sustain, and enrich the imaginary, which is then shared with the reader, who indirectly possesses the other at a distance. Indeed, Akari Chiaki, regarding *The Key*, writes that Tanizaki searched for connection or relationship (*tsunagari*): sexual intercourse as the ultimate form of skinship (*sukinshippu*) to get into inside of the other, as if penetrating a key to keyhole to open and read another's diary.[108] Tanizaki's textual surface prompts readers' imagination to fill in the space with the visual, tactile, or sonic in

---

106. Tanizaki, *The Key*, 79.

107. Shibusawa Tatsuhiko, "Tanizaki Jun'ichirō to Mazohizumu" ["Tanizaki Jun'ichirō and Masochism"], *Kokubungaku: Kaishaku to Kyōzai no Kenkyū* 23: 10 (1978), 11.

108. Akari, "Kyū Dōtoku wo koete," 68.

the story—wishing to join in reaching the searched-for object, who may appear only momentarily as a flickering on the screen. Baxandall notes, "shadow perception is much more about light, atmosphere and distance, and here *tout est relatif*—that is, a matter of differentials."[109] The perception of the object stems from the condition of shadows, the condition of light, and the ambience. As much as Tanizaki was attracted by both shadows and light, the body that Tanizaki desired necessitated the touch of visual perceptions in the mixture of distance, shadow, and light.

Coda

As we have seen, the yearned-for object in Tanizaki remains incomplete, both in touch and vision, fragmented in memory and illusion, nearing and distancing, appearing and disappearing. In *Some Prefer Nettles*, which reflects the time when Tanizaki was contemplating his own divorce, the protagonist Kaname is attracted to the female geisha Koharu in *Love Suicide* of the *bunraku* puppet theater, who is obedient to her husband, a shadowy still doll who kneels submissively with her head bowed. He observes that someone like Koharu would represent the image of "the eternal woman" ("*eien josei" no omokage*) in Japanese tradition.[110] Kaname sees this *bunraku* puppet play in the midst of his preoccupation with his divorce from his wife Misako, who is a Tokyo-raised, modern, educated woman, in contrast to his father's Kyoto-born lover Ohisa, who is considered comparable to a traditional doll. In this situation, however beautiful Kaname finds Misako's skin to be, this does not excite him; the image of the eternal woman in Tanizaki's works rather reflects the woman lost in the character's (and author's) childhood—the mother. As Watanabe Naomi writes, for the one who lost his mother when his memory was still vague, the importance is not the fact that she was the "mother," but rather the promise, or contract, that she might be, taking various forms, closer

---

109. Baxandall, *Shadows and Enlightenment*, 120.
110. Tanizaki, *Some Prefer Nettles*, trans. E. G. Seidensticker (London: Vintage Books, 2001), 25. "Tadekuu Mushi," *TJZ* 14 (Tokyo: Chūoh Kōronsha, 2016), 71. Originally serialized on newspapers *Osaka Mainichi Shimbun* and *Tokyo Nichinichi Shimbun* from 1928 to 1929 and published as *Tadekuu Mushi* in 1929 by Kaizōsha.

through a play of detour, deferral, and anticipation.[111] Even Tanizaki's foot fetish is often discussed in relation to his mother Seki's beautiful skin—as if her skin functioned as a precursor to his later pursuit of the ideal fetish object. The male characters never quite reach this figure; she is blurry, half-seen, amidst a plethora of the senses.

Tanizaki's characters occupy the space in between actuality and illusion, vision and touch, and light and shadow. Touch in Tanizaki's works thus remains incomplete: either due to hindrance or condition to close the distance between one and the other, or due to limited visibility to completely see the object. And yet, this limited reach conversely heighten characters' as well as readers' imagination for reaching the yearned-for object, giving further texture or tangibility to the object. Barthes, contrasting to the Western marionette—that is, a projection of bodily gestures, "fallen from the body to become a fetish"—states that the *bunraku* puppet, without strings and with its impassiveness and subtlety, "converts the body-fetish into a lovable body."[112] For the puppet, the lovable character of the body appears not through a unification of movement and voice that creates "*the one* who acts," but through a detachment of codes of expression.[113] Even in this sense of puppet as an ideal image, the yearned-for object in Tanizaki illuminates the dynamic distance between the part and the whole, approaching and not completely reaching, without the integrated wholeness of the body. The body in Tanizaki, without being gathered into a whole and complete image, necessitates one sense aiding another. The motionless, slightly bowed Koharu, reminiscent of the depictions of the blind Shunkin, is shaped as a yearned-for object, being visible but out of full reach, so as to produce a further imagined touch. Watanabe suggests that men get closer to the women they idealize at the same time that they get farther (*tōzakarinagara chikaduku*) from them.[114] This palpable, oscillatory distance is the source of enjoyment.

---

111. Watanabe, *Tanizaki Jun'ichirō*, 97.

112. Roland Barthes, "Lesson in Writing," in *Image Music Text,* trans. Stephen Heath (London: Fontana Press, 1977), 172.

113. Roland Barthes, "Lesson in Writing," 175.

114. Watanabe Naomi, "Byōsha to Yokubō: Mazohisto (Shōsetsuka) Tanizani Jun'ichirō" ["Description and Desire: Masochist Novelist Tanizaki Jun'ichirō"], *Shinchō* 87: 6 (1990): 203.

The unreachable in Tanizaki, potentially doubling with the lost mother, becomes closer through the mutuality of the senses. Tanizaki signals the potentiality of reaching, even if it may not involve fully embracing the body; and yet the lived elements of the characters—narrated by storytellers or characters, and verbalized by Tanizaki—paradoxically, become disembodied, like a phantom body. The point of touch lies, as Tanizaki manifests, not necessarily in the realization of "touching" itself, but in the mobilization of relationalities—between the subject and object, distance and closeness, touch and vision, and shadow and light. Barthes, when he discusses "the pleasure of the text," recognizes that this pleasure takes the form of a drift driven by language's illusions, seductions, and intimidations; another name for this drifting is, as he suggests, "*the Intractable*—or perhaps even: Stupidity."[115] As discussed in the beginning of this chapter, Isoda Kōichi characterizes Tanizaki's work through a framework of the aesthetics of frivolity, haunted by nothing else but the beautiful. Or, this might be what William Haver associates, in his discussion of Tanizaki, with "an attempted deception, a seduction" in a form of staged parody in the text, stemming from the radical undecidability of veracity; "it may be true, it may be a deception, it may be truth masquerading as deception, and so on, ad infinitum."[116] There is an irresistible force that the senses written in the texts emit: it compels the readers to "feel." This force is sometimes difficult to incarnate when one remains in self-control; in the state of blurriness of vision, consciousness, and reality, one gets in touch with the not-yet-known that transforms one's self-awareness. The seer disappears in front of reader's witnesses. Tanizaki allows partial touch, leaving the sense of incomplete reach; the sense of the incompletely bridgeable—whether it is a distance, luminous shadow, or the imagined—makes his characters find the ever-sustained pleasure in attempting to touch.

---

115. Roland Barthes, *The Pleasure of the Text*, trans. Richard Miller (New York: Hill and Wang, 1975), 19. Originally published as *Le Plaisir du texte* in 1973 by Éditions du Seuil.
116. William Haver, *The Body of This Death: Historicity and Sociality in the Time of AIDS* (Stanford, CA: Stanford University Press, 1996), 173–174.

CHAPTER 3

Mediated Touch

Membrane, Skin, the "I"

The Membrane that Narrates

In Yoshiyuki Junnosuke's *The Dark Room* from 1969, the traces of contact that Natsue feels in relation to her multiple partners are manifested through her bodily habits and the fragments of stories she has to tell. She performs these in ways that the male protagonist Nakata cannot prevent, and this leads him to interrupt the immediate contact between them. The contact traces on the skin become for Nakata an imaginary membrane that mediates and even stimulates his touch: "I won't deny that the men in Natsue's past—who were still there, a membrane [*usui maku*] between us— served as a welcome stimulant. And the desire to find some part of Natsue's body still free of this film [*usui maku*] that seemed to cover it so completely was another factor that kept our relationship going."[1] Jealousy as a sexual stimulant, discussed earlier in the context of Tanizaki's *The Key*, figures also in Yoshiyuki's works, such as "Shūu" ["Sudden Shower"] from 1954 and "Shōfu no Heya" ["In Akiko's Room"] from 1958, even though Yoshiyuki's male characters are less adept at handling their own emotions.[2] Yoshiyuki's protagonists tend to fail at maintaining emotional distance as physical

---

1. Yoshiyuki, *DR*, 149; "Anshitsu," *YJZ* vol. 7, 316.
2. Ayame Hiroharu notes how in contrast to Tanizaki's male characters (such as in *The Key* in the triangular relationships) he depicts, who seem like masters of sensual affairs (*iro*), Yoshiyuki's male characters are unskilled at controlling their emotions or even possibly pure (*junjō*). Ayame Hiroharu, *Hankotsu to Henkaku: Nihon Kindai Bungaku to Josei, Oi, Kakusa* [*Defiance and Transformation: Modern Japanese Literature and Women, Aging, and Disparity*] (Tokyo: Ochanomizu Shobō, 2012), 200–01.

entanglements lead to involvement. Yamamura in "Sudden Shower," has a relationship with a prostitute Michiko, whom he has to accept he cannot monopolize; he comes to the conclusion that spending time with prostitutes will inevitably lead him to experience jealousy. He tells himself, in a seeming attempt to gain distance on that feeling, "Supposing he could tame this jealousy, couldn't it be turned into a wonderful spur for his love affair [*irogoto*]?"[3] Similarly, Nakata in *The Dark Room* cannot cast aside the shadow of Natsue's other men, whose "faces and bodies remained decently obscure."[4] That shadow, as well as the traces of other men, is a strong motivating factor in his pursuit of her body.

Yoshiyuki has received extensive criticism from feminist scholars especially for his strongly heterosexist assumption, his erasure of the otherness of the loved object, and his effacement of female subjectivity. It is also remarkable that so little of the contemporary scene (such as the women's liberation movement and the Japanese students' protests) seem to figure in *The Dark Room*, whose story is set to start around 1968.[5] Especially in his early works, Yoshiyuki describes red-light districts, inns for short stays with call girls, and bars with hostesses, facilities that he himself frequented. It is possible that in this preoccupation he was unconsciously driven by the example of his father Yoshiyuki Eisuke, a briefly noted author who took a prominent role in the Japanese Dada movement and wrote about confusion, prostitution, urban modernity, and the cinema.[6] Anthropologist Anne Allison describes the division between a non-procreative sexuality that positions men "voyeurs, fetishists, and consumers,"[7] and a family-oriented, procreative sexuality in the posteconomic boom of late 1960s, which is also discernible in Yoshiyuki's works where, for both genders, the body is used as a convenient commodity to satisfy sexual desire. The

3. Yoshiyuki, "Sudden Shower," trans. Geoffrey Bownas, *Japan Quarterly* 19: 4 (1972), 457; "Shūu," in *YJZ*, vol. 1 (Tokyo: Shinchōsha, 1997), 118. Originally published in *Bungakukai*.

4. Yoshiyuki, *DR*, 146.

5. See Tsuboi Hideto, *Sei ga Kataru: 20 Seiki Nihon Bungaku no Sei to Shintai* [*Sexuality Narrates: Sexuality and the Body in Twentieth-Century Literature*] (Nagoya: Nagoya Daigaku Shuppankai, 2012), 429.

6. Yoshiyuki comments on the transience of his father Eisuke's literary fame in his essay, "Watashi no Bungaku Hōrō," 8–9.

7. Anne Allison, *Permitted and Prohibited Desires: Mothers, Comics, and Censorship in Japan* (Boulder, CO: Westview Press, 1996), 46.

postwar economic growth as well as the disruption of the kinship system in Japan marked the father's absence from the familial space and rendered the mother's overbearing psychological presence, with low-paying jobs even when working away from their homes.[8] Such a historical context contemporary to the novel itself conveys the dispersed image of the family.

In this context, I would like to draw attention to the fact that the recognition of the self in Yoshiyuki always occurs through the contact with others. Despite the severe criticism, especially regarding the gender dynamics, Yoshiyuki captured subtle physiological changes with his acute awareness of the senses, through layered literary narratives: characters' utterances, narratives told by narrators or authors within the novels, and a recognizable autobiographic voice.

Touch examined in this chapter mainly via Yoshiyuki does not guarantee "reaching" the other; the interstice formed through earlier contact traces in Yoshiyuki mediates relationality, instead of simply conducting sensations, making one aware of the existence of both himself and others. What is felt on or through the surface, perceptions, and characters' narratives concerning their physiological changes are projected onto figures with whom the characters construct a relationality. The skin or membrane herefore serves more as a collection of contact traces than a means of immediate contact. As discussed in the introduction, I define the (imaginary) membrane as an acccumulated layer of contact traces that affects the continual reshaping of the embodied self's relationality; imaginary membrane suggests that there may be some interstice to truly reaching an other, and that forms reflexive consciousness. Touch is a way to reconfigure the self in relation to others, problematizing what is (un)reachable as well as what is not yet verbalized beyond physical and symbolic touch.

Despite the issues of sexual inequality, Yoshiyuki visualizes the mediating "skin" by depicting physiological sensations and their psychological implications for characters in terms of verbal nuances, recognizing their capacity for permeability, or lack thereof. Yoshiyuki makes the function of the skin and membrane in his writing sensible to the readers and probably himself by conveying his experiences through language, to an extent that is quite unparalleled in the work of other writers. One earlier writer, Funabashi Seiichi (1904–1976), also describes the sensual body with

---

8.   Yoda, "The Rise and Fall of Maternal Society," 874–875.

detailed attention to subtle surrounding elements, such as the sound of the friction of a silk-made kimono, the color combination of kimono and skin, and the texture of the skin.[9] Funabashi manifests an aesthetic of touching in not touching, with a certain sense of physicality, involving touching the beloved's shoulder just once or kissing a letter from the loved and madly embracing it[10]; gestures that remind us of the protagonist in Tayama Katai's "Futon" ["Quilt"] in 1907, who smells the quilt and hair ribbon that his beloved has left behind.[11] Yoshiyuki, rather than concealing or suggesting as above writers or earlier-discussed authors Kawabata and Tanizaki, depicts the bodily interaction. Yoshiyuki's writing, in particular, reflects the function of the mediating membrane (in disclosing his gender-unequal depictions) through the double-literary structures of the main and digressive narratives and fictional and autobiographical elements.

Given these elements, I claim, despite his limited portrayal of the female body, touch in Yoshiyuki requires attending to another's response, with an awareness of the fundamental impossibility of understanding the embodied experiences of another. The literary characters in Yoshiyuki, albeit objectified, often "speak" through bodily movement as well as utterance. The male protagonist cannot ignore those utterances and traces of contact: he listens, even if he cannot fully understand them. Building on the analyses of the loved object in Kawabata and incompletely bridgeable distance in Tanizaki in the previous chapters, I analyze in this chapter the mediated nature of touch in Yoshiyuki's texts in conversation with psychoanalytic accounts of the skin-ego and speech and phenomenological accounts of the embodied experience. I hope that my analysis of a reflexively conceived self, a self conceived in relation to the other (via touch,

---

9. In an essay on Funabashi, Yoshiyuki quotes Ōe Kenzaburō's comparing Kawabata and Funabashi who both depicted the female beauty: in Kawabata's works where one finds abnormal sexual consciousness, Ōe said, one only gets a sense of the liquid moving inside the cells of human body. In Funabashi's works one finds a normal person's sexual consciousness in modern and tranditional forms, one gets the sense of the women's skin (Yoshiyuki adding his account that) in Funabashi's depictions of women's clothes as if he were groping their skin and making the clothes perhaps more visceral than the skin). Yoshiyuki, "Funabashi Seiichi Shōron," 238–239.

10. See Funabashi Seiichi, "Gamō" ["Goose Feather"] from 1947 in *Funabashi Seiichi Senshū* [*Selected Works of Funabashi Seiichi*], vol. 2 (Tokyo: Shinchōsha, 1969), 231–277.

11. Tayama Katai, "The Quilt," in *The Quilt and Other Stories by Tayama Katai*, trans. Kenneth G. Henshall (Tokyo: University of Tokyo Press, 1981), 95–96.

but mediated by an interstice or membrane) in Yoshiyuki's writing may serve to show how the impulse in it is always to translate the embodied into words within an interpersonal setting. This chapter, foregrounding the reading of literary texts to raise conceptual questions, explores the mediated nature of touch, through an imaginative membrane in conjunction with language (narrative, speech, voice, and breath beyond language), visuality, and weight.

In my view, the distinctive characteristic of Yoshiyuki's writing lies in how he verbalizes the physiological and psychological interactions of living bodies in a manner that is not completely fictional, but semi-fictional. Maruya Saiichi calls this semi-fictional "genre" *zuihitsu-tai shōsetsu*, meaning a work that is in between an essay and a novel, referring to earlier examples such as Nagai Kafū's 1937 *Bokutō Kitan* [*A Strange Tale from East of the River*].[12] Yoshiyuki studied Laurence Sterne, paying particular attention to the feature of digression—digressive and decentred narratives problematizing awareness of the progression of time—a tendency that he takes further in *The Dark Room*.[13] In his "Shimetta Sora, Kawaita Sora" ["Damp Sky, Dry Sky"], a travel "journal" written in 1971, Yoshiyuki mentioned his desire to try his hand at Sterne's "digression and digression."[14] With his characters often meditating on past experiences with reference to Freud and psychoanalysis,[15] Yoshiyuki employs ways of

---

12. Maruya Saiichi, "Yoshiyuki Junnosuke wo Yomu: Kōshoku to Taikutsu" ["Reading Yoshiyuki Junnosuke: Sensuality and Boredom"], in *YJZ*, vol. 7 (Tokyo: Shinchōsha, 1998), 466.

13. Kawamura Jirō, "'Anshitsu' ni tsuite" ["On *The Dark Room*"] in *Yoshiyuki Junnosuke no Kenkyū*, 41.

14. Yoshiyuki uses the English expression "DIGRESSION AND DIGRESSION," followed by his translation as "Yokomichi mata Yokomichi" [sideways and sideways [detour and again detour]. Yoshiyuki Junnosuke, "Shimetta Sora, Kawaita Sora," in *YJZ*, vol. 8, 131. Originally published in seven installments in *Shinchō*.

15. In "Otoko to Onna no Ko" ["The Man and the Girl"] from 1958, Yoshiyuki refers to the Freudian theory of dreams in the protagonist's witnessing of the vanishing of a neighboring man's umbrella, corresponding to his detumescent penis in a packed train. His penis becomes erect while in contact with a young girl, and the proximity of their bodies is witnessed by the neighboring man (Yoshiyuki, "Otoko to Onna no Ko," in *YJZ*, vol. 5 (Tokyo: Shinchōsha, 1998), 236–237); and in *The Dark Room*, to a Freudian interpretation of his experience with women, tracing back to his first woman, Keiko (Yoshiyuki, *DR*, 114–115).

layering the narratives through his attention to stream of consciousness, psychology, and psychoanalysis. Having escaped conscription during the war due to his sickly constitution, he spent his youth reading and went through a further series of sicknesses including typhus, allergy, dermatitis, and cataracts. This experience with sickness gave him the time and occasion for desultory reading, and later seemed to weigh upon him in an acutely physiological manner.

A semi-fictional narrative focused in part on the narrated perceptions effectively brings out one's attention and relation to the external object. The sensory reflection of the self within the literary structure is sometimes compared to *mise en abyme* in Nagai Kafū, Yoshiyuki, and Marcel Proust.[16] When the protagonist in Proust's *In Search of Lost Time* dips a madeleine biscuit into his cup of tea and carries it to his lips, a chain of involuntary arousal of memory through smell and touch occurs, as if sensations are associated with the mental function of remembering:

> when nothing subsists of an old past, after the death of people, after the destruction of things, alone, frailer but more enduring, more immaterial, more persistent, more faithful, smell and taste still remain for a long time, like souls, remembering, waiting, hoping, on the ruin of all the rest, bearing without giving way, on their almost impalpable droplet, the immense edifice of memory.[17]

Along with the membrane in Yoshiyuki, such literary representations of chains of contacts raise the following questions: Can the experience of touch be stored on the bodily surface and endure as a form of memory lodged there? Can a trace be erased and another mark written on top of it, like a palimpsest? And what would be the effects of this? Characters' physiological and psychological turmoil, captured via the author's language and senses and mapped onto paper, form another "skin" that mediates the direct physical contacts. In her reading of speech act in Molière's *Dom Juan,* Shoshana Felman writes of the mouth as the *"place of mediation*

---

16. See Murayama Noriaki, "'Mise en abyme' ni kansuru Ichi Kōsatsu: Proust, Kafū, Yoshiyuki" ["An Analysis of *Mise en abyme*"], *Senshū Daigaku Hokkaidō Tanki Daigaku Kiyō*, 37 (2004): 51.

17. Proust, *In Search of Lost Time*, vol. 1, 49–50.

between language and the body."[18] In Yoshiyuki, in my view, it is the membrane or alternative skin that mediates between language and the body; it mediates touch physically and metaphorically, further heightens the desire for immediacy, and makes those in contact reflect on how they relate to other bodies.

Touch, when written, requires readers to reread inscribed sensations through their present bodies in a delayed manner; these sensations are alternately repressed by and repeated in the texts. Physiologically speaking, while the skin conducts physical stimuli to the central nervous system and connects them, it is preventative in that, as it mediates, it interrupts direct touch, insofar as one considers the skin to be less the means of the self's full givenness than a bodily frontier. If the surface retains sensations, traces, and memories, touch is always an experience mediated through previous experiences of contact and indeed through what surfaces. In addition to Yoshiyuki's extensive attention to the skin and membrane, the double structure created through his writing style—between fiction and real life, the protagonist as author within the novel and the implied author as Yoshiyuki himself, and the protagonist's relationality with other characters and Yoshiyuki's relation as the narrator to them—weaves another layer of mediation. These layers or surfaces mediating the body and language in Yoshiyuki's writing enables a critical rereading of ways to construct one's relationality to others.

I argue that the interstice or, in Yoshiyuki, the membrane—separate from the living organism of the skin and created in protagonist's mind in conjunction with the partner's bodily and verbal utterances—affects both his perception of her and their relationship. In a range of Yoshiyuki's works, the interstice appearing bears the traces of contact, emotionally affects the toucher, and mediates touch, regulating the reachability to the other. In Yoshiyuki's short story about a chiropractic, "Katsushika" ["Katsushika Ward"] in 1980, the narrator-protagonist is thinking back and remembering a relationship he had in the past. The woman whom he met once a week is not able to completely hide her relationship with another man, whose "signs were there," manifest in her ambiance (*kehai*) when she was

---

18. Shoshana Felman, *The Scandal of the Speaking Body: Don Juan with J. L. Austin, or Seduction in Two Languages*, trans. Catherine Porter (Stanford, CA: Stanford University Press, 2003), 37. Originally published as *Le Scandale du corps parlant: Don Juan avec Austin, ou, la séduction en deux langues* by Editions du Seuil in 1980.

with him. Despite her smooth well-tanned skin, we are told, her body was "wrapped in a gray 'membrane'" (*maku* 膜, which is distinguished from skin, *hifu* 皮膚) touched by another man, and her fingertips felt "tacky" to the male protagonist.[19] However, the stickiness went away when they make love. In both "Katsushika Ward" and *The Dark Room*, the protagonists who aim at being distant from their lovers—a tendency found in a number of Yoshiyuki's works—find their lovers' bodies mediated through *maku*: the membrane.

In his story "Chōjūchūgyo" ["Birds, Beasts, Insects and Fish"] from 1959, the protagonist is in love with his partner Yoko (modeled on the actress Miyagi Mariko, with whom Yoshiyuki had relationship in real life) and is constantly preoccupied with the marks left on her body. Yoko is concerned that her past partner's invisible presence fills her room, and that the protagonist might meet up with "a man you don't [he does not] know"[20]; as well as with the protagonist's potential reaction during sex to her deformed body due to past sickness, which brings her past partner back to her mind. The traces of the man from her past heighten the protagonist's interest in her, with his wish to overwrite his mark onto her touched (and so already marked) skin. This could be read as the "I," of the protagonist, attempting to invade the past man's trace by carving an ecstasy on her body,[21] or rewriting his mark over her skin. The protagonist, who witnessed her lung making a strange sound like a broken accordion when her body moved suddenly, affectionately kisses the large scar on her body, intending to reach a deeper scar within.

Contact traces from the past in Yoshiyuki's works, unconsciously gathered and accumulated on the body, form an interstice, in my view, that interrupts immediate touch, and that plays a recurring role in the male

---

19. Yoshiyuki, "Katsushika Ward," trans. Lawrence Rogers, in *Fair Dalliance: Fifteen Stories by Yoshiyuki Junnosuke*, ed. Lawrence Rogers (Kumamoto: Kurodahan Press, 2011), 162; "Katsushika," in *YJZ* vol. 4 (Tokyo: Shinchōsha, 1998), 263. Originally published in *Gunzō* in 1980.

20. Yoshiyuki, "Birds, Beasts, Insects and Fish," trans. Maryellen Toman Mori, *Japan Quarterly* 28: 1 (1981), 96, 97, 101; "Chōjūchūgyo," in *YJZ*, vol. 2 (Tokyo: Shinchōsha, 1997), 71, 75, 85. Originally published in *Gunzō* in 1959.

21. See Izumi Keishun, "'Kako no Otoko' no Konseki wo Aibu suru Watashi: Yoshiyuki Junnosuke 'Chōjūchūgyo' ron" ["I who Caress the Traces of the 'Past Man': A Reading of Yoshiyuki Junnosuke's 'Chōjūchūgyo'"], *Rikkyō Daigaku Nihon Bungaku*, vol. 116 (2016): 78.

protagonist's perception of his partner and his psychological involvement. Critic Kawamura Jirō argues that the theme of *The Dark Room* is how the mind (including fear, attraction, or subtle changes of emotion) struggles against sexuality (*sei*) as nature[22]; Yoshiyuki perceives the body, the senses, and sexuality as compelling forces set against the mind. Sekine Eiji questions this distinction between mind and "nature" (sexuality), exploring Nakata's cynical attitude toward life; his cynicism, arising from his sense of being betrayed after his wife Keiko's affair with his friend Tsunoki, gives him an overly defensive attitude towards his partners, and makes him empathize with a prostitute when she remarks that she lives her life as circumstances dictate (*tsuide ni ikiteiru*).[23] The sexual imagery in the story tends to be self-absorbed and fruitless. Extant studies of Yoshiyuki's acute attention to the senses related to both psychological and sexual concerns tell us much about the protagonist's interactions with his partners. I would go further and say that in Yoshiyuki the alternative skin, interstice, or membrane formed by contact traces, memories, and imagery moves beyond being just a surface to being at a site where experiences are silently still alive. A surface is a site of confluence, a space that conducts interactions between the body and language, the physiological and the psychological, outside and inside. In my view, a reading of selfhood in Yoshiyuki calls for paying attention to partners' gestures, their unspoken utterances, the spaces in between their words, their sighs, and their silences. The unsaid can be equally expressive as the said.

Didier Anzieu articulates a similar notion of "surface" to Yoshiyuki's membrane through his idea of the skin, called the "Skin-ego." Anzieu claims that previous sensations and emotions stored on the skin affect the formation of identity as skin-ego, after the "common skin" period. Here, the skin, or an interface, is felt to be shared between the mother and the child as "a single screen that resonates with the sensations, affects, mental images, and vital rhythms of both."[24] Anzieu sees this reciprocal skin is nurtured through fantasies related to the mother's body; it is only after

---

22. Kawamura Jirō, *Kankaku no Kagami: Yoshiyuki Junnosuke ron* (Tokyo: Kōdansha, 1979), 185.

23. Sekine Eiji, "Tekusuto no Kōzō Bunseki III: Yoshiyuki Junnosuke 'The Dark Room' – sono Shūkyōsei" ["Structural Analysis of the Text III: Yoshiyuki Junnosuke 'The Dark Room' and its Religiosity"], *Baikō Jogakuin Daigaku Ronshū*, vol. 16 (1983): 19.

24. Anzieu, *The Skin-Ego*, 67.

the child manages to overcome anxieties connected to those fantasies that "it will achieve its own Skin-ego," through the process of interiorizing the interface and the mothering environment.[25] Both Yoshiyuki's membrane and Anzieu's skin are by-products of contact with others that go beyond the biological, serving also as components of touch by conducting and mediating sensations.

Anzieu's skin, especially as of the common-skin period, has similar elements with the dependent mother–infant relationality proposed by Hirai Nobuyoshi and Doi Takeo.[26] Naomi Segal argues that Anzieu's concept of skin, as the "leading organ," allows for psychoanalysis to go beyond the inherently hierarchical assumptions of gender difference based on the primacy of the phallus and castration.[27] In this view, the skin is gender neutral, compared to sexual organs; it may also suggest that the skin is to some extent age neutral. Psychiatrist Hatashita Kazuo notes Yoshiyuki's yearning for skinship with his mother Aguri, who was a busy hairdresser, suggesting that the lack of such skinship led him to search out in prostitutes to identify with his unattainable "mother" and may have driven him to a search for supplemental physicality.[28] This account suggests the certain continuity of one's relation to the other, that arose from skin-based relationship, from childhood to adulthood. And yet, it seems that the membrane in *The Dark Room* only allows for a one-way flow. Nakata creates an imaginary membrane at the confluence of bodily stimulations and psychological

---

25. Anzieu, *The Skin-Ego*, 68.

26. As discussed in my introduction, Japanese pediatrician Hirai promoted the wide use of *skinship* in the Japanese context in the 1970s, warning about the increasingly less tactile communication between mother and infant. Psychiatrist/psychoanalyst Doi, with his theory of *amae* (dependence), emphasizes a particular form of dependent intimacy, starting with the mother–child relationship, as a model for other subsequent relationships (thereby particularlizing the Japanese psyche through the concept of *amae*). See Hirai's *Ushinawareta Boseiai*; Doi Takeo, *"Amae" no Kōzō* (translated as *The Anatomy of Dependence* in 1973) (Tokyo: Kōbundō, 2007).

27. Naomi Segal, *Consensuality: Didier Anzieu, Gender and the Sense of Touch* (Amsterdam and New York: Rodopi, 2009), 56, 72.

28. Hatashita Kazuo, "Sakka ron kara no Rinshō Shindan: Yoshiyuki Junnosuke" ["Clinical Disgnosis through the Discussion of the Author"], *Kokubungaku: Kaishaku to Kanshō* 39: 14 (1974): 135. This special volume was titled, "Sakka no Sei ishiki: Seishinkai ni yoru Sakka ron kara no Rinshō Shindan" ["The Authors' Sexual Consciousnesses: Clinical Diagnosis by a Psychiatrist through the Discussions of Authors"].

excitations; but Natsue is unaware of it. The fact that Natsue contributes to the membrane but may not recognize it (it is perceived predominantly by Nakata), demonstrates the one-sided reachability of the membrane.

The first thing to note here in the literary analyses of the skin and imaginary membrane in Yoshiyuki is the distance between the author's real-life experience as a writer and his character's experiences, even if his novels are written in the I-novel style. Secondly, the mother–infant relationship may not be always as readily available as one might assume. Thirdly, the skin, the widest and most ubiquitous sense receptor on the body, is inseparable from sexual desires and activities; indeed, Matsuura Rieko, whom I discuss in the next chapter, aims to displace the locas of sensuality from the sexual organs to the whole-body skin. The yearning for transparent, ummediated form of touch that it involves persists in relationships, beyond the relationship to the mother, onto which it is projected.

The Imaginary Membrane to Mediate the Body and Language

In *The Dark Room*, the perspectives of the female characters are not revealed until Nakata comments on them or they "speak" themselves. For Nakata, a shadow of Natsue's other invisible partners that emerges through her bodily and verbal utterances plays a significant role in the creation of an imaginary membrane: "She would deliberately say this sort of thing [discussing experiences with other men] as we made love. The words would turn to moans, and she would arch her back, and move her body about ...."[29] Whereas Anzieu's concept of skin seems more neutral regarding gender assumptions, Natsue lacks the transparent access that Nakata has to this imaginary membrane. Nakata considers ideal a woman who is "all sex organ without any brain,"[30] and treats the female characters as if their role is to accommodate his desire and fantasy. At the same time, however, the detailed attention given to describing bodily stimuli and the female bodily responses to which Nakata inevitably "listens" complicates any reading of the story as one of males simply consuming females. The literary characters speak through their bodies, which is captured by Yoshiyuki's language

---

29. Yoshiyuki, *DR*, 145.
30. Yoshiyuki, *DR*, 43.

that gives attention to physiological manifestations and their psychological influences. In my reading of Yoshiyuki's works, the physical affecting the psychological and vice versa, is often articulated through a double structure involving a story within the story, and a going back and forth between them especially in cases where Yoshiyuki makes his protagonist a novelist. Bodily movements and verbal utterances develop the imaginary interstice and the relationality of the corresponding characters. Below, I further analyze the interstice, the membrane, as the mediatory intersection of body and language, with a particular attention to utterance.

The analysis of accessibility and touch in *The Dark Room* reveals an ironic twist. Natsue is the only one who knows her past, which Nakata "knows" only through her narrative and bodily performance, which then affect his interpretation of and relationship to her. She implies the presence of other men through her speech. In his contact with her body, he is then concerned whether his touch is the first one on the clean film of her skin or whether it has already been mediated by an earlier touch. This echoes certain features illuminated by Kawabata in pursuing the untouched girl, and Yoshiyuki in his earlier works. In Yoshiyuki's short story, "In Akiko's Room," about the male protagonist's relationship to the prostitute Akiko in the red-light district of Tokyo, he is preoccupied by the delusion that an unknown man's body is "pressing deeper and deeper into her" ("*oshiwakete hairikondeyuku*"),[31] only a few parts of which still remain unknown to him. The imagined expansion of those unknown parts provokes in him a fit of jealousy, after which he no longer finds her room the restful place it once was, and he tries to verify that he is the one who has caused her physical tiredness. Likewise, Nakata in *The Dark Room* tries to find something in his physical relations with Natsue that would be a "first."[32] Nakata feels an imaginary surface on which traces from the past cast a shadow, but Natsue alone knows her past.

The unsaid, or the combination of said and unsaid, does also shape convincing narratives, which Nakata cannot ignore. Nakata is actively

31. Yoshiyuki, "In Akiko's Room," trans. Howard Hibbett, *Contemporary Japanese Literature: An Anthology of Fiction, Film, and Other Writing since 1945*, ed. Howard Hibbett (Boston, MA: Cheng & Tsui Company, 2005 [1977]), 405; "Shōfu no Heya," in *YJZ*, vol. 2, 15. Originally published in *Chūoh Kōron* in 1958.
32. Yoshiyuki, *DR*, 149.

searching for an inscription left on the skin or the membrane, which retained the memory of previous touch, despite his tendency to decline full transparency with others because of his hesitation to allow himself to be "taken hold" of by women. The interstice and the phantasmatic traces perplex Nakata, in conjunction with Natsue's relevant verbal narrative and bodily movement, his active search for a clean "film," his reluctance to be bound by anyone, and his recognition of the impossibility of either transparency or a full grasp of the other. Natsue's verbal narrative is often entangled with a certain somatic excitement. Nakata says: "I could feel her breath coming faster even as she spoke. Whenever I asked her about the other men she'd had, she would answer immediately. In time, she began to tell me about them of her own accord, and made herself excited in the process."[33] Despite the uncertain believability of what she tells him, he cannot be indifferent to her voice as uttered through her body. The combination of words, bodily movements, and traces form for Nakata an imaginary interstice, crossing time and space, possibly with greater effects on him than facts.

The dialogue I create here with psychoanalytic theories to think about the function of skin, membrane, and interstice in Yoshiyuki's fiction serves two purposes in my reading, involving the use of confessional language in place of bodily experience on the one hand, and Yoshiyuki's own suffering from depression on the other. There are fundamental tactile and visual prohibitions in the psychoanalytic setting of undressing, showing one's naked body, touching the psychoanalyst's body, or being touched. Psychoanalysis, Anzieu claims, is only possible when touch is prohibited, although as a hypnotherapist, Freud, "a man of the eye and the hand rather than a man of words," initially employed the pressure technique without a clear-cut distinction between hypnotherapy and psychoanalysis.[34] In problematizing the gender imbalance wherein men are encouraged to touch

---

33. Yoshiyuki, *DR*, 145.

34. Anzieu, *The Skin-Ego*, 151. Freud gradually shifted from hypnotherapy to psychical analysis in his realization, through the phenomenon of transference, of the necessity of denying physical intimacy with patients and abandoning the capricious results of hypnotherapy. See the cases of Lucy (106–24) and Elisabeth von R. (135–81) in Josef Breuer and Sigmund Freud, "Studies on Hysteria," in *SE*, vol. 2, trans. James Strachey et al. (London: Hogarth Press, 1964), and "Resistance and Repression," in *SE*, vol. 16.

and women not, with reference to the Gospel story of Thomas and Mary Magdalene—although Nancy recognizes care and benediction in Jesus blessing Mary Magdalene by keeping her at a distance[35]—Anzieu also suggests the superiority or favor of communication through language—"Do not touch me" implies "Only listen and speak."[36] Anzieu suggests that verbal or symbolic touch takes the place of a bodily touch, yet foregrounds the role of skin in identity formation, with further cultural specificity and contradictions regarding the taboo on touching in its Christian formulation. Communication by language is given greater importance than communication between bodies, while involving relics, the shroud, anointing, the washing of another's feet, and miracles through touch.

In contrast to the Catholic writer Endō Shūsaku, who meditates on the absence of guilt feelings in the Japanese psyche,[37] in Yoshiyuki's novels there is no moral struggle in the sexual relationships with multiple partners in both sides of male and female characters. As much as Nakata maintains simultaneous relationships with Takako, Maki, and Natsue, and calls a prostitute when he needs a female body, all of them being placed "on the same level,"[38] Natsue also has simultaneous relationships with Nakata and another man, regarding this lover as "a sexual convenience."[39] Yoshiyuki depicts as indispensable the interaction between the psychological and sensual. One set of questions here concerns the extent to which

---

35. Nancy, *Noli Me Tangere*, 36.

36. Anzieu, *The Skin-Ego*, 157.

37. Earlier, Akutagawa Ryūnosuke depicted a Jesuit missionary's difficulties in Japan due to the "power to recreate" (*tsukurikaeru chikara*), that is, the tendency to recreate deities in Japanese forms, in his 1922 short story, "The Faint Smiles of the Gods" (trans. Tomoyoshi Genkawa and Bernard Susser, in *The Essential Akutagawa: Rashomon, Hell Screen, Cogwheels, A Fool's Life and Other Short Fiction*, ed. Seiji Lippit (New York: Marsilio, 1999), 126–127). Karatani Kōjin argues however that such difficulties were simply evidence of the violence of the shogunate (Karatani, *Nihon Seishinbunseki*, 85–86). In the Meiji period, modern writers adopted Christian ideas such as a love that emphasizes spirituality over carnality, even though Christian morality conflicted with established understanding of the world. Mori Ōgai's "Kanoyōni" ["As if"] from 1912 explains that, in order to make the illogical logical, in discussing the substance of things, God, evolution, freedom, spirit, duty, one had to treat them as if they existed (Mori Ōgai, "Kanoyōni," in *Ōgai Zenshū* [*The Complete Works of Ōgai*] (Tokyo: Iwanami Shoten, 1972), vol. 10, 70–76).

38. Yoshiyuki, *DR*, 47.

39. Yoshiyuki, *DR*, 126.

language can represent touch, sensations, and bodily experiences, and the extent to which language and the body intertwine. When symbolic contact "touches" others over the divides of language, space, and time—as psychoanalysts symbolically "touch" analysands in the form of their verbal interpretations, or as the protagonist author in Yoshiyuki's 1966 novel, "Hoshi to Tsuki ha Ten no Ana" ["The Star and the Moon, Holes of the Sky"], confirms the existence of his literary character's body as depicted in the novel within the novel with a touch of his finger in his mind[40]—what is at stake concerning mediated touch and texture?

Yoshiyuki details characters' psychology and mental imagery, but he himself experienced depression, including during the time when he wrote *The Dark Room* in his mid-forties. This includes: a melancholy temporality in Yoshiyuki's writing that generates alienated feelings, powerlessness, and nihilistic thoughts (*sogai kan*, *muryoku kan*, and *kyomu kan*) as pointed out by critic Miura Masashi;[41] and depression triggered by Yoshiyuki's psychological independence from his dead father Eisuke in his story "Suna no Ue no Shokubutsu gun" ["Flora on Sand"] in 1963, when he had passed the age of thirty-four at which Eisuke had died, as pointed out by psychiatrist Ohtaki Kazuo.[42] In a recent psychopathological study, Saitō Shinnosuke rereads Yoshiyuki's depression as involving a schizoid tendency; frightened of devouring others (as well as being devoured by others) in intimate relationships, such persons withdraw from object relations, in maintaining a safe distance from feared others but abandoning emotional relationships with them.[43] W. R. D. Fairbairn, whom Saitō refers to in his work, establishes the term "object relations" and highlights object libido instead of sexual libido in the oral stage, experiences with which can lead to certain

40. Yoshiyuki Junnosuke, "Hoshi to Tsuki ha Ten no Ana," in *YJZ*, vol. 7 (Tokyo: Shinchōsha, 1998), 82. Originally serialized in *Gunzō* and published by Kōdansha in 1966.

41. Miura Masashi, *Merankorī no Suimyaku* [*A Water Vein of Melancholy*] (Tokyo: Fukutake Shoten, 1984), 7–8.

42. Ohtaki Kazuo, "Yoshiyuki Junnosuke no Byōseki: Utsu no Imi ni tsuite" ["Psychopathology of Junnosuke Yoshiyuki: On the Meaning of his Depressive Experience"], *Byōseki shi* 37 (1989): 53.

43. Saitō Shinnosuke, "Yoshiyuki Junnosuke no Yūutsu: Utsu byō ni yoru Sōzō to Sōshitsu ni tsuite" ["Melancholy in Junnosuke Yoshiyuki: The Creation and Forfeiture by Depression"], *Byōseki shi* 91 (2016): 14–15.

psychological states in later life—for example, "defence against emotional loss gives rise to *repression of affect* and an attitude of detachment"[44]—recognizing its artistic creativity as a substitute of immediate revelation of one's internality. Saitō and Kobayashi analyze Yoshiyuki's "Genshoku no Machi" ["Street of Primary Colors"] from 1956 (1951), suggesting that the schizoid creates fissures (*sakeme*) in the space between himself and the world, and in between himself, as a defense against an outer terrifying world; those with a schizoid structure tend to withdraw out of the fear of "mutual devouring," as the fear of devouring others out of love makes them concerned about others devouring them.[45] This account suggests, somewhat similar to Kawabata's instance, that one withdraws from contact due to fear—not out of indifference, but rather out of heightened interest in the object, which then becomes fear.

While my reading of the loved object in Kawabata (articulated in chapter 1) focused on fear of devouring the incorporated loved object, the analysis here illuminates the fear of a "double" devouring that provokes the schizoid person to withdraw, in response to the very pursuit of affection. The protagonist in "The Star and the Moon, Holes of the Sky" wonders whether his callous treatment of Noriko is born of a misogyny arising out of a fear of deep entanglements with women. But his callous treatment paradoxically deepens his tie to her. Yoshiyuki's men feel themselves on the verge of being devoured by their partners in direct measure to how much they become emotionally involved with them. Because of this, they often distance themselves from others before this happens, which leads to failure of some sort.

As one way of consciously removing his protagonists (and himself) from deep entanglement with partners, Yoshiyuki uses women characters who exist outside the familial context, often in red-light districts. The exception to this is Sugiko in "Yūgure made" ["Toward Dusk"] in 1978, who keeps her virginity and never allows penetration: as critic Kawamoto

---

44. W. R. D. Fairbairn, *Psychoanalytic Studies of the Personality* (London: Routledge, 2001), 15.

45. Saitō Shinnosuke and Kobayashi Toshiyuki, "Yoshiyuki Junnosuke no Byōseki: Schizoid Pāsonaritī no Chiryō no Ba toshite no Bungaku" ["Pathography of Junnosuke Yoshiyuki: His Literary Activities as a Therapeutic Space for Schizoid Personality"], *Byōseki shi* 89 (2015): 40–41. Kimura Bin, who has extensively worked on schizophrenia in a Japanese context, offers a consideration of the self as an internal difference with itself, while advancing the concept of in-between-ness (*aida*). See Kimura, *Bunretsubyō to Tasha*.

Saburō notes, "a sexual taboo" artificially created by Yoshiyuki at a time when sexual taboos had become loosened.[46] It is also the time, since the late 1960s, when postwar economic growth intensified sexual commodification, a version of which was still observable in the late 1980, based upon a clear distinction between a woman obtained with money and a wife obtained through marriage; the former is the place where the husband might visit but where "he would never stay."[47] This can be read as an artificially necessitated withdrawal by Yoshiyuki from the possibility of jealousy on the part of the protagonist in relation to experienced women with the physical presence of men. With such a carefully layered manner of shaping one's relationality to the desired other, the notion that the otherness of female bodies or characters is being ignored or erased is surely far too simplistic.

In Yoshiyuki's writing, the imaginary membrane, or invisible interstice, plays a key role to develop protagonists' relationality to their partners. It is the membrane that lies on the partners' bodies, for the protagonists, the trace of an earlier touch functioning as metaphor, applied to both experienced and inexperienced women. In "Street of Primary Colors," Akemi's carnal interactions with various men cancel the immaturity of her actual body, and instead give the fullness of a mature flesh. Akemi later becomes conscious of a membrane (*maku*) between her and a man, associated with the illusion of her loved one Motoki—a frontier, which blocks her body from some sort of union with a man—got rid of, and her body directly merges into Motoki's body.[48] In "In Akiko's Room," Akiko's body, after one year, has begun to accumulate the dirt of the district, which forms "a layer of grime" deposited ("*sou wo nashite chinden shiteiru*") beneath her skin.[49] In *The Dark Room* and "Katsushika Ward," such a membrane (*maku*) on the woman's body, formed through contact with the unknown, seems to

46. Kawamoto Saburō, "'Ren'ai Shōsetsu' no Fukanōsei: Yoshiyuki Junnosuke, Yūgure made" ["The Impossibility of the Romantic Novel: Yoshiyuki Junnosuke, *Toward Dusk*"], *Kaie*, November issue (1978): 20.

47. Anne Allison, *Nightwork: Sexuality, Pleasure, and Corporate Masculinity in a Tokyo Hostess Club* (Chicago, IL & London: University of Chicago Press, 1994), 130.

48. Yoshiyuki Junnosuke, "Genshoku no Machi," in *YJZ*, vol. 5 (Tokyo: Shinchōsha, 1998), 78. The first version of this story was published in *Sedai* in 1951; adding the version from 1952, the revised version was published by Shinchōsha in 1956.

49. Yoshiyuki, "In Akiko's Room," 406; "Shōfu no Heya," 18.

the protagonist to have vanished through his physical interactions with her. The membrane or interstice also appears in the case of young Noriko in "The Star and the Moon, Holes of the Sky," whose naked body is "thinly wrapped in a young mist" (*wakasa no moya no youna mono ni usuku tsutsumareteiru*), although it is absent from the body of the prostitute Chieko, from whom the protagonist is emotionally disengaged, customers having "shaved [it] away" from Chieko's body.[50] Also, in Yoshiyuki, images of virginity do not necessarily correspond to immediacy or a purity free from contact; the critic and translator Shibusawa Tatsuhiko sees the figure of the virgins as equivalent to that of the prostitute, suggesting that the term "prostitute" indicates the state in which the "female erotic principle" is most fully realized.[51] In Yoshiyuki, the virginity represented through Sugiko in "Toward Dusk" is not particularly appreciated, though his prostitutes are not voiceless. Nor are Yoshiyuki's virgins necessarily placed higher or desired more than his sexual partners.

In Yoshiyuki's works, I would argue, the membrane is formed through interactions over time, with contact traces appearing and disappearing beneath current contacts as in a palimpsest that is being rewritten and over-written. The idea of the imaginary membrane thus is a metaphor for the way relationships between bodies are continuously mediated through unconscious behaviors, repeated gestures, whispered words, and mental imagery. For Yoshiyuki, the body is unknowable, no matter how much one is engaged with the other, and no matter how much contact with her has already been made. Yoshiyuki's writing above all suggests that the verbal and bodily are intertwined. Concerned about Natsue's relationships with other men past and present, Nakata tries to convince himself: "*The one thing you need is Natsue's body*, I reassured myself. *And you've got it here, now*. I felt the tiredness ebbing from my own body at the thought."[52] Occasionally, the body itself even attempts to pre-empt conversations, as when Natsue evades the suspicion of her partner by immediately making love with him as a form of bodily concealment.[53] The body is used in place

---

50. Yoshiyuki, "Hoshi to Tsuki," 101.
51. Shibusawa Tatsuhiko, "Watashi no Shojo Sūhai" ["My Worship of Virgins"] (1966), in *Homo Erotikusu* [Homo Eroticus] (Tokyo: Gendai Shichōsha, 1967), 322.
52. Yoshiyuki, *DR*, 163.
53. Yoshiyuki, *DR*, 146.

of words that she wants to avoid using: the body "does" for words and narrates its experiences.

With Natsue, it is as if her fragmentary narratives, voices, and breath shape Nakata as the listener who cannot ignore them. All of this affects Nakata's perceptions of and relationship to Natsue. Felman explains about speech as in the very realm of eroticism, in combining psychoanalytic and J. L. Austin's speech act theories: "To seduce is to produce language that enjoys, language that takes pleasure in having 'no more to say.' To seduce is thus to prolong, within desiring speech, the pleasure-taking performance of the very production of that speech."[54] This "speech," in my view, or at least in my reading of Yoshiyuki, includes in addition to utterances things like voices, moans, and breath. Distinguishing between performative utterances that accomplish an action and constative utterances that merely make a statement, Austin argues for what the language does: "There is something which is *at the moment of uttering being done by the person uttering*."[55] Although Austin's theory does not highlight the role of the listener as much as the emergence of the speaking subject, the element of speech is still suggestive in the analysis of Yoshiyuki's writing; insofar as the speech act not only lets the speaking subject perform but also lets the listener appear. Or, even, insofar as it lets the silent speak. Part of the reason why Yoshiyuki's protagonists become entangled with their partners physically and psychologically is their attentiveness to the various and subtle ways their partners communicate. In this regard, I claim, through my analyses of interstice membrane in Yoshiyuki, that not only speaking but also listening to voiceless speech marks the emergence of the attentive subjects that are affected by others' utterances.

And yet the features of the membrane in *The Dark Room* are not entirely captured in translation. In the Japanese text, the word most often translated as "membrane" is *maku* (膜), which generally means a surface or tissue, and *nenmaku* (粘膜), a mucous membrane, is also translated as "membrane."[56] In addition, two different terms are both translated as

---

54. Felman, *The Scandal of the Speaking Body*, 15.
55. J. L. Austin, *How to Do Things with Words* (Cambridge, MA: Harvard University Press, 1975), 60. Originally delivered as the William James Lectures at Harvard University in 1955.
56. Yoshiyuki, "Anshitsu," 341; *DR*, 168.

"skin"—*hifu* (皮膚), normally used in a biological or medical context, and *hada* (肌), a term used in daily life that also has the connotation of something more abstract and intrinsic, more akin to human nature.[57] Yoshiyuki uses the term *hada* less frequently than *hifu*, though he uses it in relation to the lesbian Maki at a particular moment when Nakata is not viewing her as an intimate partner, and *hifu* when Nakata sleeps with her, equally translated as "skin."[58] Yoshiyuki's depictions of subtle changes to the environment, including smells and air pressure, suggest the unknowability of the other and the untranslatability of another's embodied experience, prior to the question of translatability between different languages. The unknowability figures and heightens the desire of protagonists and readers alike. Touch in Yoshiyuki is in part a repetitive attempt to "reach" the other that never quite succeeds.

A fantasy of transparent touch stems from the infant's primary touch with the mother through something like a common skin. In operation, it involves the body as already in relationship to, and mediated through, previous touches, sensations, imaginings, and language; and the construction of new relationships necessarily evokes sediments of previous bodily experiences, even more so when we discuss the cases of adults. Mediation necessarily arouses the fantasy of immediate contact precisely because of the rupture, gap, or space between them in which the contact takes place and the fantasy is heightened. Yoshiyuki's protagonist senses the shadow of other men that seems to remain on his partner's body. Touch is mediated through past contact traces, embodied experience, and utterances, which form an imaginative membrane. Therefore, Yoshiyuki thematizes the mediation between the body and language in writing the interstice. To describe the skin or thin membrane that generally defines one's corporeal boundary is at the same time to question how one can reach the other—the unknowable yet indivisible body of another.

---

57. As an example of the general use of *hada*, "I can get along with him" can be expressed as "*Kareto to wa* [with him] *hada ga* [skin] *au* [get along]." "*Hada* [skin] *wo yurusu* [allow]" implies allowing somebody to have a physical relationship. In both of these cases, *hada* is not replaceable with *hifu*.

58. Yoshiyuki, *DR*, 20, "Anshitsu," 155; *DR*, 103, "Anshitsu," 258.

Mediated Construction of the Self

Yoshiyuki shows that touch does not necessarily guarantee immediacy but reveals a mediated manner of reaching the other via previous contact traces, memory, and the work of interpretation. My further examination of mediated touch asks how vision and touch are interrelated, and—taking the earlier discussion regarding the duality of touch and vision through Tanizaki—how elements of light and darkness may affect touch in considering the original title of *The Dark Room*, *Anshitsu*, which literally means a darkroom for developing photographic images. The correlation between touch and vision has been discussed earlier, but with regard to the Yoshiyuki's cases, as Miura Masashi puts it, the visual is depicted haptically and the sonic described visually,[59] the process of mediation convoluting the multiple senses, depictions of the senses become necessarily intersensorial. Concerning the sexual affairs in a closed room with dim light depicted in Yoshiyuki, Yamazaki Masakazu also writes that vision, lacking a sense of distance, functions like the haptic.[60] Stimuli emitted via an imagined body part or mental scenery contribute to the construction of relationality as much as haptic. Not only touch itself, but other sensory effects such as through vision (light, shadow, color) and smell and air come together to affect one's consciousness, when contact is made. Yoshiyuki brings these multisensory effects as "touch" to reflect the self, in relation to the other.

In *The Dark Room*, Yoshiyuki inserts various short memories into his narrative descriptions of the present. Between passages about Nakata's initial interaction with Natsue, their subsequent relationship, and Nakata's depression, Yoshiyuki inserts Nakata's observations of a collection of monochrome photographs titled *Onna* [*Woman*]. Because Nakata is too exhausted to examine the photographs at the time, most of the collection remains untouched on his desk. However, at one point his relation to them changes:

> This time, I had a feeling that some unseen hand must have deposited the book unnoticed on my desk. I went through it thoroughly,

---

59. Miura, *Merankori no Suimyaku*, 116.
60. Yamazaki Masakazu, "Kōritsuita Waisetsu: Rekishi no Kiretsu II:" ["Frozen Obscenity: Fissure of History II"], *Shinchō* 76: 9 (1979): 180.

page by page. That done, I was to open it again only occasionally, as the fancy took me, but each time I found it as gripping as ever. For a whole year, in fact, it was as though I was shuttling to and fro between the book of photos and Natsue's body.[61]

When he returns to the collection of photographs to find a single white woman clinging to a black man's bare torso from behind, their fingers tangled together on his shoulder, Nakata begins to feel that the woman's face resembled Natsue's. After this realization, he shifts from narrating his thoughts about Natsue, whose words, when they are lying together, start to "blur, and melt, till only a sound [*koe*, voice] remained," through the repetitive process of Nakata asking and Natsue replying about her past partners.[62] Around the time when he starts opening himself to Natsue nearly two years after their initial meeting, "the change in my own mind had modified the image of Natsue projected on it,"[63] this change being narrated through his interaction with Natsue, narrative digressions, visual imageries, and his self-reflection. Correspondingly, Nakata gradually notices the changes in Natsue's body: her skin color, which turns from amber to white "behind a colorless, semitransparent film" ("*han tōmei no mushoku no maku*")[64] and her body odor, which used to have a characteristic scent but has now become odorless. The mode of communication for contact between the two here is much wider than literal sense of the "haptic."

Nakata's association of Natsue with the photographed woman grips and ties Nakata to the image. Yet, because there is no further communication between the photographed woman itself and Nakata, his particular relationship to this photo is created through his image of Natsue. For Roland Barthes, the photograph is an "emanation of the referent." "From a real body, which was there, proceed radiations which ultimately touch me, who am here."[65] Barthes's idea of light as a carnal medium is the point where touch and vision become entwined, bridging the body of the photographed and the onlooker's gaze. "A sort of umbilical cord links the body

---

61. Yoshiyuki, *DR*, 129.
62. Yoshiyuki, *DR*, 134; "Anshitsu," 297.
63. Yoshiyuki, *DR*, 135.
64. Yoshiyuki, *DR*, 135; "Anshitsu," 298.
65. Barthes, *Camera Lucida*, 80.

of the photographed thing to my gaze: light, though impalpable, is here a carnal medium, a skin I share with anyone who has been photographed."[66] Light as carnal medium resonates the idea of haptic visuality, while also bringing its surface texture as the skin to the fore in linking the seer to the photographed figure, even when this figure itself is foreign. In recovering from his depression, Nakata's consciousness and bodily states change, with intermitted narrative digressions about his interaction with the imagined Natsue via the photographed woman and her actual physicality. A ray emitted by the woman (Natsue as imagined by Nakata) reaches Nakata. Natsue further pulls Nakata toward herself through a visual, cutaneous, and verbal exchange. Nakata is supposed to be the seer in this novel— the seer of the photograph and of Natsue's body—but he might be also reflected through Natsue's functioning as subject of the look in his reading of the photograph. Miura Masashi points out a turnabout between the seer and the seen in his reading of Yoshiyuki's other short story, "Bara Hanbai nin" ["Rose Selling Man"] from 1950; the seer, once recognized as seen, comes back to being the seer, to find himself both seeing and being seen.[67] The anonymous woman is the relativized shape of Natsue, which causes Nakata to become self-reflexive.

Nakata's image of Natsue is reflected through his fantasy, as conjured up by her imagined body. Jacques Lacan regards the gaze as a necessary element in constituting the subject in his account of mirror stage, but when he discusses the gaze in relation to light, there is a moment where light plays a corporeal function: "It is through the gaze that I enter light and it is from the gaze that I receive its effects. Hence it comes about that the gaze is the instrument through which light is embodied and through which … I am *photo-graphed*."[68] The gaze for Lacan is the point through which light is embodied, and this external light captures the individual. As visual perception is projected onto external objects here, self-consciousness is already mediated and partly mis-recognized. Light as well as the gaze reaches the body; in this sense, the imagined Natsue is not the seen but rather, potentially, an active subject who touches Nakata. Despite the photographed

---

66. Barthes, *Camera Lucida*, 81.
67. Miura, *Merankorī no Suimyaku*, 122.
68. Jacques Lacan, *The Four Fundamental Concepts of Psycho-analysis*, trans. Alan Sheridan and ed. Jacques-Alain Miller (Harmondsworth: Penguin Books, 1986), 106.

figures' orientation toward death in Barthes ("the photograph tells me death in the future" as the photographed is going to die or is no longer there),[69] Natsue's image begins as a living entity through this process of bodily and visual interactions. She used to be merely a physical existence to Nakata. He begins to drop the barriers he has erected toward getting close to her and, gradually, Natsue starts to have a different meaning to him. The effect on Nakata of Natsue's image is such that eventually she becomes for him more fully realized both psychologically and physically.

The visual further possesses haptic functions in Yoshiyuki. In "Street of Primary Colors," set in a red-light district in 1950, Akemi is uncomfortable about the doubtful gaze of the man, which seems to her wet, as if he were licking her all over (*"namemawasu youna, utaguribukai shimetta me"*).[70] While taking her colleague Ranko's photos with her boyfriend as a memento of their love, Akemi finds that her apathetic eyes excite those lovers by the fact of their being seen. With an unknown customer who has bought the photo by chance, Akemi feels a repetition of the gaze. Unlike Ranko, who, aware that her photo is being sold to a random buyer, finds herself excited by the man's anonymous gaze, Akemi feels a hatred for the insidious gaze that seems to fill the air and assault her like sharp glass pressing into her skin.[71] When taken outside the district by one of her customers, a firewood dealer who wishes to marry her, Akemi, feeling his big shoulder pressing against her body, finds herself unavoidably accepting his proposal. As this firewood dealer attempts to hide the traces of her prostitution, Akemi asks Ranko's boyfriend to take a photo of her naked too, and imagines this photo being scattered in the air. She feels a sensation of piercing her skin, tingling (onomatopoeic *hirihiri* in the original),[72] imagining the faces of firewood dealer, as well as her beloved Motoki, with his cold eyes. Imagining this photo scattered outside the district, she decides to return to it. The imagined gaze, manifested in multisensory manners, directs, perplexes, and unsettles Akemi's life.

Needless to say, Yoshiyuki's depiction of the gaze is gendered, illuminating the limit of one's capacity to understand the emotional and physical

---

69. Barthes, *Camera Lucida*, 96.
70. Yoshiyuki, "Genshoku no Machi," 26.
71. Yoshiyuki, "Genshoku no Machi," 60.
72. Yoshiyuki, "Genshoku no Machi," 95.

conditions of the gendered other. The gaze as an extra excitation in the shape of voyeurism especially in "Suna no Ue no Shokubutsu gun" ["Flora on Sand"]—the title borrowing from Paul Klee's abstract watercolor painting "Flora auf Sand" ["Flora on Sand"] in 1927—illuminates the mosaic of manifold desire of looking subjects. The protagonist Iki, who sells cosmetics but also develops an idea for a detective story, is taken to a show by two friends. They witness a female performer standing in the next room, removing her clothes, touching her naked body, arching her back on the tatami mat, and directing her eyes to the customers, as if confirming their gaze upon her in the ill-lit room. The narrator remarks: "The woman is not in need of another body being attached to her body. Yet, it was clear that she needs other's eyes glittering in the dark room," men's stares directly invisible to her eyes, such as the congested blood vessels around their eyes, secreted yet ceaseless saliva, their dried mouths, coming up to her retina and stimulating her.[73] Written in the early 1960s of the rising consumer entertainment culture, this narrative seems to confirm the recreational desire, outside the familial system amid the rapid economic expansion of the time. Author Ikezawa Natsuki, writing about this story by Yoshiyuki, highlights that such a pleasure-seeking relationship tells us that in the end seeing, or gazing, is all that men can do; seeking pleasure with prostitutes via money, or heightening another's pleasure in seeing by participating a game via money—they can only see, without understanding, what is incomprehensible.[74] In the economy of seeing and being seen, one receives excitement and pleasure yet without quite being able to share it.

The function of female partners in Yoshiyuki's works is primarily to excite, soothe, and comfort the male protagonists, through the assurance provided by their physical presence, although the protagonists realize that it is impossible to be fully comforted by or know their partners. Ueno Chizuko, in discussion with Ogura Chikako and Tomioka Taeko, explains that, in Yoshiyuki, the protagonist is anxious about the passive responses his female partner gives to his stimuli. She, no matter how deeply he relates

---

73. Yoshiyuki, "Suna no Ue no Shokubutsu gun," in *Yoshiyuki Junnosuke Zenshū*, vol. 6 (Tokyo: Shinchōsha, 1998), 258. Originally published in *Bungakukai* in 1963.

74. Ikezawa Natsuki, "Yoshiyuki Junnosuke wo Yomu:'Suna no Ue no Shokubutsu gun' to Seiteki Jikken" ["Reading Yoshiyuki Junnosuke: *Flora on the Sand* and Sexual Experimentation"], in *YJZ*, vol. 6, 453.

to her physically, is supposed to leave him, for him "to wander around in the solitary wilderness."[75] Furthermore, in his descriptions of lesbian interaction, Yoshiyuki replicates the conventional image of lesbianism associated with the butch/femme identity pair, narrated in *The Dark Room* as "wretched and pathetic," while connecting lesbians "dressing up as men" with "penis envy."[76] Yoshiyuki's characters also pursue a non-reproductive sexuality, often with anxiety about reproduction; Sekine Eiji points out that, around the time that Natsue tells Nakata that she has become infertile, Nakata's health improves.[77] The protagonist's realization of impossibility of fully knowing someone and fully being comforted by someone is inseparable from his withdrawal from the friction of human relationship and his flight from family responsibility.

Barthes's "the bright room" figures the seen as captured in exactitude, which is reminiscent of the optical device known as a "camera lucida" that was once used as an aid in drawing accurate images. But the darkroom always shuts out external light with a thick curtain; the "camera obscura" produces an upside-down image via the direction of light through a pinhole in a dark space. Most of the interactions between Yoshiyuki's protagonists and their partners (regardless of whether they involve money or not) occur in a closed, shady, dark room. Once they are in the room together, the internal exploration—spatially and bodily—exceeds their communication with external others. Jonathan Crary, in his discussion of the observer's role in vision related to camera obscura, writes, "The secure positioning of the self within this empty interior space was a precondition for knowing the outer world."[78] But the spatial positioning of the self within the dark room itself becomes the site for physical experiment in Yoshiyuki. Natsue in *The Dark Room* was previously careless about light, but when she comes to have different meanings to Nakata, it begins to disturb her: "she hadn't objected to the light in the room, so it wasn't as if it was dark. Come to think of it, it was only recently that I'd begun noticing her new signs of modesty, too."[79] Subsequently, Natsue prefers to make love in the dim

---

75. Ueno et al., *Danryū Bungakuron*, 52–53.
76. Yoshiyuki, *DR*, 89.
77. Sekine, *"Tasha" no Shōkyo*, 95.
78. Jonathan Crary, "Modernizing Vision," in *Vision and Visuality*, ed. Hal Foster (New York: New Press, 1999), 32.
79. Yoshiyuki, *DR*, 135.

light coming from the slit of the curtains or with a small amount of electric light.

Nakata becomes conscious of the changes between him and Natsue, through his move between the imagined Natsue in a photo book, her image in his mind, and her actual physicality. Natsue later becomes ashamed as she becomes conscious of being seen. For these individuals, their consciousness of being seen is bound up with their reflexively finding themselves, and then being seen by the readers. Such a system of seeing forms a chain of contact that connects yet separates the physical distance between subject and object. The mediated nature of touch permeates the bodily interactions, while further problematizing the gender politics.

Giving through the Surface

The function in Yoshiyuki's works of the membrane, the skin, and the surface raises the question of whether bodies really encounter each other through mediation. An "encounter" is surely constituted by the presence of a witness, through thinking, sensing, and touching, and with the play of weight—pushing against each other, leaning on the other, and entrusting one's body to the other. The issue of weight, despite the lack of general attention to it, is a focal point for the further discussion of touch, affecting how surface permeates or conveys pressure, friction, and the materiality of those in contact. In *The Dark Room*, Nakata comments on one of his lovers Takako: "Takako's body would dwindle and melt away in your arms like a snowflake in the palm of your hand"; while of Natsue, who remains with him until the end, he comments "Natsue's body got more and more supple, with a kind of inner resilience, and faintly damp all over with sweat."[80] Although other women have left Nakata for various reasons, the one with resilience, Natsue, eventually develops a deeper engagement with Nakata, which leads to questions about the role of weight, and pressure on the surface, in touch.

In this final section on mediated touch through Yoshiyuki, I will consider surface pressure, both ideological and physical, in the bodily interactions depicted by Yoshiyuki. While Anzieu and Merleau-Ponty do not

---

80. Yoshiyuki, *DR*, 47.

articulate the importance of weight, it is the pressure on the surface and the subsequent giving (as in "bending" or "altering" under such pressure) that offer those in contact a recognition of the other as well as the self. Jean-Luc Nancy—raising questions about Heidegger's distinction of touch between the stone lying on the path, a lizard lying on the stone, and a human hand resting on the head of another, that the stone has no access to the other—claims that Heidegger fails "to weigh precisely the weight of the stone."[81] Recognizing the weight of contact, he writes, "The body *is* weight. Laws of gravity involve *bodies* in space. But first and foremost, the body itself weighs."[82] The skin and the membrane are the frontline of separation, connection, and mediation of one person with another, but the physical realization of touch also lies in how much one weighs and how much support the other gives. Although the discussion of touch tends to focus on distance and dislocation, I would like to call attention to weight and pressure as crucial to realize what it is to be in contact with the other.

Yoshiyuki often describes the pressure on the body metaphorically, and in terms of assumptions of gender: his female characters tend not to press back firmly, which again raises the question of an occlusion in his writings of female agency. Although Yoshiyuki depicts the role of pressure in touch, it is not always a body with a clear identity as such that presses. In *The Dark Room*, Nakata and Natsue engage in a sadomasochistic play based on the inspiration of Pauline Réage's 1954 *Story of O* and an essay by Jean Paulhan on a slave revolt in Barbados in which, after freeing themselves from slavery, the former slaves approach the master asking to return to bondage, having now realized the supposed happiness of the state of being slaves.[83] Fundamentally not particularly disposed towards such games, Nakata gets bored with beating Natsue with his belt. He starts feeling foolish, and throws the belt aside.

---

81. Jean-Luc Nancy, *The Sense of the World*, trans. Jeffrey S. Librett (Minneapolis: University of Minnesota Press, 1997), 61.

82. Nancy, *Corpus*, 7.

83. Yoshiyuki, *DR*, 139–140; See Jean Paulhan, "A Slave's Revolt: An Essay on *The Story of O*," in Pauline Réage, *Story of O* (London: Corgi Book, 1972), 265–287. *Story of O* (*Histoire d'O*) was translated into Japanese in 1966 by Shibusawa Tatsuhiko as *Ô jyou no monogatari* with Paulhan's essay as an introduction, and renamed into a current title *O jyou no monogatari* in 1973.

"I'm the sucker here," I thought to myself. I'd used the word lightly in a similar situation before, but now it carried a new weight.

But that thought too was swept aside in its turn. A bundle of extremely fine, subtly intertwined threads attached themselves to my skin and began to exert pressure on it. Sometimes, quite suddenly, they changed into a single thick thread and came forcing their way into my senses.[84]

Immediately after this, the narrative shows Nakata finding himself unable to help asking her whether he can see her the day after. The pressure is present, but the clear identity of the pressing is absent. Similar to the membrane, this thread is an abstract image, associated with or arising from concrete elements of Natsue's physicality.

At the end of the story, when Nakata arrives at the building where Natsue lives, he senses her smell:

Nowadays, Natsue's body hadn't any real smell to speak of. Yet a faint odor hung about it, an odor that both stimulated the senses and induced a faint melancholy. I climbed the stairs and walked along the long concrete corridor. The smell grew steadily stronger: the smell that I was sure no one but I could detect. Soon it filled my nostrils, stiflingly oppressive.[85]

Sensory pressure reaching the body takes various forms, often metaphorical, unlike the singular form of the body. In "Rose Selling Man," too, the rigid resistance the protagonist feels on his finger in attempting to cover the partner's nipple, an obstacle separating the two, consists of a fine hair around her nipple,[86] with a symbolic presence in the story.

The question of "weight" in Yoshiyuki might be further effectively read in relation to support into a family context; it seems that not only how Yoshiyuki constructs male protagonists' relation to female characters but also to parental roles needs some attention. The earlier-mentioned "Flora on Sand," considered as a work that marks Yoshiyuki's separation from his father Eisuke and

---

84. Yoshiyuki, *DR*, 165.
85. Yoshiyuki, *DR*, 170.
86. Yoshiyuki, "Bara Hanbai nin," in *Yoshiyuki Junnosuke Zenshū*, vol. 1 (Tokyo: Shinchōsha, 1997), 32.

subsequent depression, is clearly concerned with non-reproductive sexuality. The story concerns itself with the intimate experience that the male protagonist Iki has with plural women, alongside snatches of overlying memories of his father. It depicts concurrent sexual affairs, imagined incestuous relationships, a groper on the train, Iki's father's extramarital affair, and the pursuit of sexual excitation through bonding, sexual stimulations felt via eighteen-year-old Akiko with her school-girl uniforms, and Iki's jealousy of other men. A background shadow seemingly present throughout the story is that of Iki's father, whose voice at the end of the story says, "Don't misunderstand. I am letting you continue my life that ended at the age of thirty-four," and "I am getting inside of you." Iki replies, "You'd get in trouble if you were inside me," and "That's the revenge."[87]

Yamazaki Masakazu writes that boys attain maturity by (mentally) killing off their fathers, their subsequent regret about this giving them their subsequent maturity. Yoshiyuki's protagonists, however, due to their early maturity, pass through a moment of becoming mature; they relativize their desire and insistence, recognizing ludicrousness of themselves whenever they try to take any action.[88] It is not only due to early maturity, but there is no father image supporting his family and taking care of children in Yoshiyuki to begin with. Yoshiyuki's relationship to his farther Eisuke was rather unaffectionate; most of his memories of his father involve being shouted (at) or hit in a form of educational slap, hardly remembering of his body odor. Literary critic Kawashima Itaru claims that Eisuke became a significant figure for Yoshiyuki for the fact that he, Eisuke, had a reputation for being dissolute.[89] Eisuke rarely comes home and, as soon as he does, he is already preparing for the next time he will go out. Eisuke's image seemingly lasted long on Yoshiyuki until he reaches middle age, yet with the memory of father's physical absence.

Motherhood is defined by ties that are both physical and psychological, and deeply related to female physical attributes such the womb, milk, and the breast. But literary works such as those of Yoshiyuki and Kawabata reveal the radical absence of the father in early tactile scenes. Object

---

87. Yoshiyuki, "Suna no Ue no Shokubutsu gun," 284–285.
88. Yamazaki, "Kōritsuita Waisetsu," 193–194.
89. Kawashima Itaru, "Sei no Genfūkei" ["The Original Scenery of Sexuality"], in *Yoshiyuki Junnosuke no Kenkyū*, 105.

relations theorists such as Klein and Winnicott focus on the infant–mother relationship and W. R. Bion, who underwent training with Klein, further suggests that the fantasies of the mother's body are conceivably present even in group dynamics.[90] While, French psychoanalysis, especially that of André Green, examines the more negative aspect of the mother's presence through the concept of the dead mother and highlights the father's delayed role in Kleinian view. Green states, "The important thing is that the father in their [i.e., Kleinians'] view comes *afterwards!* … the father comes as the second poor chap who is nearly a replica of the mother, with some distinctive traits, oh yes, but of minor importance."[91] The mother's figure is more empirically verifiable especially in observation-based analysis, compared to the father's symbolic role. But the absence of the father figure in literary texts further illuminates the specific social context at that time.

The erasure of the mother figure in Yoshiyuki drives his pursuit of non-reproductive sexuality, though Etō Jun suggests that there is also an erasure of the father when, in "The Star and the Moon, Holes of the Sky," the protagonist compares himself with Noriko's father. Her father cannot sleep with her, but the protagonist can take on his role, creating an artificial world that denies both the mother as symbol of nature and the father as a position in a cultural order so as to construct what to the protagonist is an artificial world.[92] Yamazaki Masakazu also points out the thinness or weakness of adherence (*shūchaku ga amarinimo yowai*); Yoshiyuki's protagonists know that they do not have anything in particular to protect, nor much attachment to any reality, causing a deficiency both in their basic requests and their commitment to any beliefs or even preferences for how to live, not knowing what to ask for.[93] This artificial construction of the world may involve the uncertain age of the characters in Yoshiyuki's works; his protagonists, who are often of middle age, sometimes seem older than their actual age and mentally exhausted. They occasionally seem to be behaving like boys, experimenting with and observing how women react, and escaping their responsibilities when actually pursued. Kōno Taeko, a contemporary

---

90. He writes, "The more disturbed the group, the more easily discernible are these primitive phantasies [about the mother's body] and mechanisms." W. R. Bion, *Experiences in Groups and Other Papers* (London: Routledge, 1989), 165.

91. Gregorio Kohon, "The Greening of Psychoanalysis," 35.

92. Etō, *Seijuku to Sōshitsu*, 196.

93. Yamazaki, "Kōritsuita Waisetsu," 190.

of Yoshiyuki's, notes that the question of age brings a certain (loss of) tangibility (*tezawari*) to his sentiments; when Yoshiyuki passed the age at which Eisuke died, he may have felt as if this death had been brought to life by his father beginning to inhabit him internally, contributing to a loss of the sense of his own age.[94]

Yoshiyuki describes a hesitancy toward reproduction, child-rearing, and familial bonds—the protagonist in "Yami no Naka no Shukusai" ["Festival in Darkness"] in 1961 escaping from the baby's smell permeating his clothes and referring to familial intimacy as sticky and unclean.[95] Along with the protagonists' cynical attitudes toward life and childbirth as evidenced above, descriptions of abortion in *The Dark Room* suggest a disavowal and even hatred in Nakata toward childbirth. As Margaret Hillenbrand points out, techniques practiced in Japan for infanticide and abortion are described in *The Dark Room*, including *tsubushi,* in which a woman intentionally closes her thighs while giving birth,[96] often without a moral constraint on having an abortion. However, as Miyoshi Yukio recognizes, a challenge to the "motherhood myth" ("*bosei shinwa*") seen in the negation of the mother's role and denial of her child is more radically manifested by women writers contemporary to Yoshiyuki, as after-effects of the women's movement of the late 1960s.[97] As discussed in introduction, authors such as Kōno Taeko and Takahashi Takako represented female characters who decide, act, and touch from themselves, with clear agency, denying motherly love.

Yoshiyuki is careful about the thickness and surface of the body in relation to physiological states and accumulated traces as already shown; the male protagonist in "In Akiko's Room" has "a long intricate conversation"

---

94. Kōno Taeko, "Yoshiyuki Bungaku ni okeru Nenrei no Imi" ["The Meaning of Age in the Writings of Yoshiyuki"], in *Yoshiyuki Junnosuke no Kenkyū*, 136.

95. Yoshiyuki, "Yami no Naka no Shukusai," in *YJZ*, vol. 6, 84. This story depicts the psychological struggle of the protagonist, a low-paid author modeled after Yoshiyuki, in a triangular relationship with his wife and his lover, who is a star modeled on Miyagi.

96. Hillenbrand, *Literature, Modernity, and the Practice of Resistance*, footnote in 215. See Yoshiyuki, *The Dark Room*, 63. Legal prohibition was only introduced after the Meiji period, with the crackdown on *mabiki* in 1831, but laws outlawing both abortion and infanticide were enforced in 1868, aiming to increase births for centrally defined goals such as industrialization. See William R. LaFleur, *Liquid Life: Abortion and Buddhism in Japan* (Princeton, NJ: Princeton University Press, 1992).

97. Miyoshi, *Nihon Bungaku Zenshi*, 445–446.

with Akiko's body, which "conveyed all sorts of meanings," without words, "that had been lost to me [protagonist] when I was merely forcing myself on her."[98] Unlike male characters in the literature of the flesh (*nikutai bungaku*), the protagonist's carnality in Yoshiyuki is neither strong enough to oppose the state body nor powerful enough to penetrate the other, partly because of sickness, the insufficient fullness of the body, and a lack of confidence, having belief neither in the body nor in any ideological weight that is placed on it. Yoshiyuki's protagonist is therefore attentive to the subtle elements such as moisture, air, and smell in the surrounding environment and inevitably "listens" to the other.

Nevertheless, Yoshiyuki rarely depicts any tangible "giving" from the touched female, though he depicts a rigid response on the part of the touched male. In "Nedai no Fune" ["My Bed is a Boat"] from 1958, the protagonist, a schoolteacher, unexpectedly has an interaction with a man in drag called Misako. When Misako presses her body (described with female pronouns) against that of the protagonist, he is surprised to find her masculine sexual organ touching him, which he describes in masculine terms: "Her hard sexual organ had bumped knife-like against the relaxed expanse of my stomach. I had assumed an asexuality in her, so I was caught off guard."[99] Although Yoshiyuki does not represent prostitutes as an underclass but treats them equally as normal persons,[100] he hardly writes about women characters that push back the male protagonists or fulfilled relationships with them. As he becomes entangled with Natsue, Nakata observes, "It wasn't just the feel of her sex that attracted me; gradually, my whole body cleaved to hers" ("*karada zentai ga sono karada ni haritsuiteyuku*").[101] The word used for this cleaving, *haritsuiteyuku*, literally means "getting [infinitely] stuck to" or "becoming [infinitely] attached to," without space or friction between the two touching objects or weight felt

---

98. Yoshiyuki, "In Akiko's Room," 403.

99. Yoshiyuki Junnosuke, "My Bed is a Boat," trans. Lawrence Rogers, in *Fair Dalliance*, 5; "Nedai no Fune," in *YJZ*, vol. 2, 35–36. Originally published in *Bungakukai*.

100. Shirakawa Masayoshi, "Yoshiyuki Junnosuke: Sei no Dandism" ["Yoshiyuki Junnosuke: Sexual Dandism"], *Kokubungaku*, 39: 14 (1974): 131. See Heather Bowen-Struyk, "Sexing Class: 'The Prostitute' in Japanese Proletarian Literature," for the depiction of prostitutes in modern literature in *Gender and Labour in Korea and Japan: Sexing Class*, ed. Ruth Barraclough and Elyssa Faison (Abingdon: Routledge, 2009), 10–26.

101. Yoshiyuki, *DR*, 159; "Anshitsu," 329.

pushing against between them. Regardless of the fact that touching and its effects on a surface seem to bring to bear on each body the weight and fullness of presence of the other, with a sense of pushing and being pushed back or of touching and giving as well as being touched and given to, here gender and reproduction seem to mark a limit of this.

In Yoshiyuki, without any reliable "stake"—national, familial, or ideological—the body is depicted as a phenomenon that can be the object of experimentation and observation thereof. The male protagonist's body is unreliable and weak and does not represent physical strength. Murakami Haruki, in analyzing Yoshiyuki's short story "Mizu no Hotori" ["By the Water"] from 1955, which is about the writer's recuperation for lung desease at a hospital, argues that at the center of Yoshiyuki's works there is an "artificial move" (*gikōteki idō*) in which the self is equally pressured by the internal ego and the external world; fleeing from face-to-face confrontation with the world as well as with the ego, Yoshiyuki's characters continue to dislocate themselves, and the dislocation of the self or "I" is a fundamental feature of his novelistic worlds and their fleeting trajectory away from the self.[102] Yoshiyuki writes extensively about carnality, but this does not mean that he believes in the body in the same way as did the writers of the flesh. Without returning home—to the familial body whether it is of individual or of national, the self is continuously adrift. It is in flight; although given the difficulties of being indifferent to Japan's wartime militaristic nationalism, Ayame Hiroharu recognizes Yoshiyuki's strength in weakness, or strength to recognize his own weakness, by being both mobile and durable.[103] Yoshiyuki wrote seemingly "light," erotic fiction, or recalling "soft literature" of the late Edo period,[104] almost always involving sexual affairs but extensively exploring bodies and psychology via sex. Yoshiyuki, in my view, illuminates the struggles involved in being close to someone and at the same time acknowledges the impossibility of ever knowing for sure whether one ever truly knows the other person fully.

In Yoshiyuki, while touch shows the existence of bodies that are in contact through surface sensibility, the subject–object relation is interrogated.

---

102. Murakami, *Wakai Dokusha no tame no Tanpen Shōsetsu Annai*, 60–61.

103. Ayame, *Hankotsu to Henkaku*, 215.

104. Howard Hibbett, "Yoshiyuki Junnosuke" (as an introduction to "In Akiko's Room"), *Contemporary Japanese Literature*, 401.

The sensation of being touched by touching appears frequently in depicting touch: "Natsue was lying on her belly, her face buried in a large pillow. As I laid a hand on her shoulder blade, she shrank away. 'I'm embarrassed,' she said in a small voice, her body wriggling. The smooth skin, faintly damp with sweat, moved beneath my palm."[105] In this case, Nakata is touching and the one being touched is Natsue; but Natsue's movement also expresses an agency. This relation throws into question Merleau-Ponty's veritable touch where one's right hand touches its left hand, the touching subject becoming the thing to be touched and recognizing oneself reflexively.[106] In Yoshiyuki, touch clearly involves the two parties of the touched and the touching, rather than touching the things as passive sentiment or solipsistic touch. The toucher feels the movement of the touched, which is how he recognizes his contact with the other. And yet, in touching, there is not always a clear line between the toucher and the touched; touch is exchanged between the two bodies, and the subject–object relation dissolves in that moment, even with the fundamental unknowability of the other. When Nakata feels Natsue's skin move, this makes him realize that he is once again in touch with her; Natsue provides the movement, awareness, and confirmation of his touching.

All of this surely brings into question some issues lying in feminist critiques of Yoshiyuki and his depictions of the male ego, as literary scholar Tsuboi Hideto, for example, sees judgmental aspects in those feminist critiques of the male ego.[107] Yoshiyuki started writing novels to express his sensibility and sensual experiences, which Yoshiyuki himself felt were not in line with society at the time.[108] Shirakawa Masayoshi also points out that Yoshiyuki, writing about sex, makes the reader understand that he is touching human existence through sex.[109] Feminist critiques focus on how the protagonist—whom they often assume to be Yoshiyuki—uses and indeed exploits the female body, but they may not pay enough attention to how Yoshiyuki "writes" about and at least tries to see the body. Despite Nakata's lack of attribution to female bodies of an equal subjectivity that

---

105. Yoshiyuki, *DR*, 155.
106. Merleau-Ponty, *The Visible and Invisible*, 133–134.
107. Tsuboi, *Sei ga Kataru*, 428.
108. Yoshiyuki, "Watashi ha Naze Kakuka?" ["Why do I Write?"], in *Yoshiyuki Junnosuke Zenshū*, vol. 8 (Tokyo: Kōdansha, 1971), 252. Originally published in *Gunzō* in 1966.
109. Shirakawa, "Yoshiyuki Junnosuke," 132.

might make a mutual dialogue, Tsuboi re-evaluates the awareness of this lack: "Nakata and the narrator cannot see Natsue's naked shape; additionally, this awareness of 'being unable to see' should be valued," given that Nakata tries to examine her and Maki's origin, which results in all a fruitless effort.[110] Not seeing and not being able to see are different matters. Despite Yoshiyuki's limited understanding in portraying the female body, he also shows an awareness of the fundamental impossibility of understanding the embodied experiences of another. This awareness conversely indicates the attention of the body and its embodied experience in Yoshiyuki's works.

In this regard, Yoshiyuki's treatment of touch contributes to rethinking the reflexivity in touch wherein Merleau-Ponty mediates the self-reflexivity of touch in relation to oneself, instead of the self as reflected by the other. The reflexivity of touch is not limited to the self but also involves an opening to those in contact, even if this awareness is not depicted from the point of view of the other. Yoshiyuki's writing shows that touch requires attending to another's response, as the protagonist cannot completely disregard the female subject with whom he is in contact. He concerns himself with the existence of other men through contact traces or in the air (*kehai*), and so that are fundamentally invisible, and often struggles with illnesses (which in the case of Nakata may be a motivating factor). Touched and pushed by a male character escaping from the external and retreating into himself, the female body is not oppressed to the extent that her subjectivity is effaced and ignored by him. The protagonist in "In Akiko's Room" realizes that Akiko's body does not respond as usual and interprets this as a sign of tiredness. She is hesitant to sleep with him but gives no clear reasons for the refusal, only smiling ambiguously. However, "when I touched her I realized that she was physically exhausted. Her body was mute."[111] This triggers the protagonist's irritation and jealousy of the unknown man who has made her tired. The protagonist discovers changes in her body through touch. This is not an erasure of the other, although the question remains of the extent to which he trusts the other's response.

In his short essay "Sasai na Koto" ["Trivial Things"], Yoshiyuki writes about how easy it is to traverse the bridge between man and woman via sex; "The fear of piling up a body over another's body becomes stronger,

---

110. Tsuboi, *Sei ga Kataru*, 435.
111. Yoshiyuki, "In Akiko's Room," 404.

while its personality remains clueless despite its face. Driven by such a fear, one tries to confirm having had at least a physical connection with someone, but the energy put into this person is absorbed without resistance, like pouring water in a bottomless hole."[112] Considering the observations thus far, this sense of absorption into a bottomless abyss is related to anxiety about, or the lack of solid ground, for giving. Resistance by the touched female is rarely perceived by the male protagonist and rarely described by the narrator. However, the reciprocal nature of touch suggests that the man's body does not properly weigh on hers and may even not be firmly perceived by her. Such anxiety may come from the energy absorbed without resistance: my weight being absorbed in pushing, another's energy is absorbed in not pushing back. This absorption, on the one hand, heightens the sense of impotence in the male protagonist as he is not able to accept the female's response without suspicion. On the other hand, the absorption shows the absence of a solid weighty mass to touch, push, and lean against, resulting in uncertainty about what to rely on.

When there is a rupture on the ground, without physical and psychological stability, ways of thinking change. Confronted by an abyss, one is uncertain whether one can even touch the ground without the risk of falling into a bottomless hole. One also needs gravity even to rise. Falling down consists of two forces pulling and resisting each other, as if to say, "we do not *want* to fall," which Hélène Cixous posits as the human condition in her reading of Heinrich von Kleist's "On the Marionette Theater"; we cannot fall freely as puppets do.[113] In Yoshiyuki, the ground is not a default for touch to be potentially absorbed. Similarly, Felman sees the loss

---

112. Yoshiyuki Junnosuke, "Sasai na Koto," in *YJZ* vol. 8 (Tokyo: Kōdansha, 1971), 251. Originally published in in *Warera no Bungaku* in 1966.

113. Hélène Cixous, "Grace and Innocence: Heinrich von Kleist," in *Readings: The Poetics of Blanchot, Joyce, Kafka, Kleist, Lispector, and Tsvetayeva*, ed. and trans. Verena A. Conley (Minneapolis, University of Minnesota Press, 1991), 37. In Kleist's "On the Marionette Theater," the principal dancer, who is trained to remain upright against the pull of gravity, talks about the grace (in falling) of marionettes, who prepare for their next ascent and the renewal of their bodily momentum by touching the ground lightly, which contrasts with the human need to rest on the ground. Heinrich von Kleist, "On the Marionette Theater," trans. Christian-Albrecht Gollub, in *German Romantic Criticism*, ed. A. Leslie Wilson (New York: Continuum, 1982), 238–244. Originally published as "Über das Marionetten Theater" in *Berliner Abendblätter* in December 1810.

of the ground in performative speech: "Austin, however deconstructing—like Don Juan—the founding, originary value of the 'first', is conscious in his turn of the fact that the very performance of the performative consists precisely in performing the loss of footing: it is the performance of the *loss of the ground*."[114] Neither being able to touch another's fresh skin nor to rely on another's surface to rest one's bodily weight fully, Yoshiyuki does not start with a trustworthy, reliable ground. His characters check, test, and question others as well as themselves, paying attention to the others' responses. Instead of presuming that he understands others, Yoshiyuki depicts the otherness of the other. In acknowledging the impossibility of knowing others fully, he pays attention to external and internal stimuli and situates his characters in relation to others to reflect the self.

In Yoshiyuki, no rival force rarely arises between touching bodies; one's force and weight often dissolve into another. Touch mainly consists of surface contact, and communication is felt and built on the (one-sidedly-recognized) surface membrane. It rarely includes "pushing-giving," but more often "touching-absorbing" or "pushing-melting." The protagonist touches another to identify the past embedded in her physical responses. To find a "clue" in a bodily encounter, which he strives for but never quite attains, one seeks a response in mutual pressing—another's touch to be properly weighed and received. This chapter has shown how touch on the skin is already mediated by previous touches, most likely by different persons, arguing against the general assumption that one can reach others simply through physical contact. Yoshiyuki shows how complicated (or almost unattainable) it is to have a transparent relationship with intimate objects. It is also not always easy to get a solid response from the one with whom one is in contact, or to find a reliable ground to base a weighing. Previous contact connects the present touch with another, while interrupting direct, fresh tactile experience with another, thereby reflecting the self. Mediated touch woven in Yoshiyuki's texts invites those in the past, beyond those who are present in a solipsistic circle of intimate communication, thereby reflecting the self to come.

---

114. Felman, *The Scandal of the Speaking Body*, 44.

CHAPTER 4

Renewing Relationship through the Skin

Skinship

Matsuura Rieko, in her 1987 "Nachuraru Ūman" ["Natural Woman"], a story about a same-sex relationship between two manga artists Yoko and Hanayo who contribute to the same coterie magazine (*dōjinshi*), brings reader's attention to the sensations arising from the skin:

> Our breasts touched softly and a pleasant feeling of numbness spread out through my body almost to put it to sleep. My mind, about to be awakened, again goes into a haze. Then all the actions from the first kiss to falling to sleep last night were resurrected. I pushed my hot chin against Hanayo's cold chin. Hanayo held me even tighter. I was almost moved to tears.
>
> I came to know last night for the first time in my life that a bare skin and another bare skin moistly breathe in together. When we cast off our clothes, leaving nothing, and layered our bodies together, I was struck by a wave of feeling far greater than I had expected and, all of a sudden, the thought welled up in my mind that it might be good to die here, just as we are.[1]

---

1. Matsuura Rieko, "Nachuraru Ūman," in *Nachuraru Ūman* (Tokyo: Kawade Shobō Shinsha, 2007), 133. This work has been translated into French by Karine Chesneau in 1996 as *Natural Woman*.

The protagonist/first-person narrator Yoko's naïve attitude and in-between sexuality eventually makes Hanayo suffer in their sadomasochistic relationship, changing the meaning of one object and corresponding emotional responses of those involved. Matsuura in the above quotation illustrates how deep engagement with a person's loved object cultivates and develops intimate feelings, which simultaneously develops a language with which to express them. Matsuura's literary depictions capture what the subject may be feeling about, but what the sensing subject might not have yet recognized and "verbalized" as such—something preverbal from the standpoint of the subject. Matsuura encourages the reader to question the intersection of touch and language, including the ways in which the sensual created by the use of language leads to awareness of one's relationship to the other, that is, how touch may prompt the formation of the subject as well as the object.

In earlier chapters, I showed the ambivalent feeling toward the loved object in Kawabata, the incomplete touch over distance with the yearned-for object in Tanizaki, the mediation and accumulation of touch in Yoshiyuki, which culminates in a reading of Matsuura. In the writing of Kawabata, the loved object is experienced as inevitably unreachable while being shaped in the attempt at touching it; Kawabata marks an eternal attempt to touch the unreachable. In Tanizaki, touch is conducted partially with a space in between and attempted under certain contrived conditions. Tanizaki mobilizes the relationships between vision and touch, light and darkness, and reading and writing, which heighten the desire for unimpeded touch—Tanizaki's seductive invitation for touch. In Yoshiyuki, touch is characterized by its mediated nature, revealing the unknowability of the embodied experience of another. This then arouses the awareness of self, with characters' psychological shifts and interruptions. Yoshiyuki's characters are never certain about their understanding of the other in touching. These accounts altogether illuminate the complexities in reaching another's existence, turning the visually constructed assumption about touch in that one can reach another by closing the distance, while questioning the extent to which the felt experience can be verbalized.

Matsuura demonstrates the sensations (which I here consider as pre-verbal and pre-rational) layered on the characters' bodies via their multivalent forms of relationality and sexuality, such as the homo-/hetero-/bi-sexual, friendship, romantic relationship, and pseudo-family relationship, characters' physical transformations and disabilities. Kawabata and Tanizaki, pursuing the unreachable or no-longer-available idealized woman, recognize the same-sex intimacy especially in the adolescent developmental process. Yoshiyuki depicts bodies through the male protagonist's psychological and physiological states, based on a male heterosexist viewpoint. In contrast, the loved ones who function as the source of the protagonists' primary memory in Matsuura's writing orientate both their sexual awareness and their later relationships. When the primary object is unreachable, her characters project their feelings—including fondness, love, hate, and envy—onto the third or alternative object; they continuously search for and regenerate the loved one. Intimate interactions in Matsuura, with a variety of sexual orientations and species, thus translate the binary understanding of relationality to the other, including the mature and immature and the controlling and controlled.

Readings of Matsuura's writing have tended to argue that she is interrogating heteronormativity and the primacy in relationships given to genitalia and sexuality in general. Critical works on Matsuura often highlight issues, corresponding to the topics Matsuura has extensively written about, such as phallocentrism and lesbianism. Matsuura herself considers, at least in the mid-1990s, that relationality based on the mother–child model has been over-worked.[2] *Oyayubi P no Shugyō Jidai* in 1993 (originally published in *Bungei* from 1991 to 1993 in ten installments, and awarded *Joryū Bungaku shō* / Women's Literary Award in 1994)—Matsuura's fiction available in English, translated as *The Apprenticeship of Big Toe P* in 2009—is a Bildungsroman story written in an almost "picaresque" style, about a young woman named Kazumi and her experiences, meeting a number of characters of diverse sexualities and who have various disabilities. Kazumi's own "disability" is that her big toe one day suddenly turned into a penis.[3]

---

2. Matsuura Rieko and Shōno Yoriko, *Okaruto Odokumi Teishoku* [*Occult Taster Special*] (Tokyo: Kawade Shobō Shinsha, 1997), 159.

3. Matsuura Rieko, *Oyayubi P no Shugyō Jidai* (Tokyo: Kawade Shobō Shinsha, 1993); *The Apprenticeship of Big Toe P*, trans. Michael Emmerich (Tokyo: Kōdansha International, 2009). Ikoma Natsumi discusses Matsuura's *Big Toe P* in terms of the grotesque and abnormal body that Kazumi becomes through the possession of a "big toe penis," which for Matsuura expresses both the organ of male social bonding possessed by a female character and opposition to the authoritative character of the phallus in a patriarchal society (Ikoma Natsumi, *Yokubō suru Bungaku: Odoru Kyōjo de Yomitoku Nichiei Gendā Hihyō* [*Literature that Desires: Japanese-English Gender Criticism through Dancing Madwoman*] (Tokyo: Eihōsha, 2007), 328–330).

The protagonist of the novel, Kazumi, is a naïve, girl-like woman, who appears to have grown up with scant knowledge of societally enforced norms, while being oblivious to the possibility that her feelings for her friend Yoko are homosexual. Yoshiko Yokochi Samuel notes that the story "challenges the notion that heterosexual union is the only socially acceptable form of sexual activity and suggests as its alternative 'skinship,' sexual intimacy by means of body contact of all sorts."[4] Kazumi Nagaike, in her discussion of Matsuura's following work, *Uravājon* [*The Reverse Version*] in 2000, argues the idea of non-girls (*hi-shōjo*), those who deviate from her social conditions through "knowledge outside the process of coquetry"— as the boys without a penis.[5] Both analyses illuminate Matsuura's works that disturb the importance placed upon genitals and instead diversify intimate relations. While accepting these analyses against phallocentrism, yet also calling attention to the (lack of) critical reading on skinship and the object relationship in Matsuura, I argue that skinship in Matsuura is neither merely the mother–child relationship nor the sexual intimacy surging onto the surface, without creating clear divisions among the types of relationality. Skinship advances the conceptualization of the intimate relationship with its regenerative nature.

Matsuura has been continuously attentive to what is felt surrounding the body, particularly pleasure through the skin sensuality (*hifu kankaku teki na kairaku*), specifically using the notion of "skinship."[6] As I outlined in my introduction, the coined term skinship has been in use in Japan since the 1970s, referring to the intimate communication (primarily between the mother or other caretaker and a child), involving various types of contact, including co-sleeping, breast-feeding, co-bathing, and non-verbal communication. Hirai Nobuyoshi advocated skinship, by which he meant not only a way to communicate the mother's warmth and thereby develop the child's feelings of assurance, but also a way to nurture thoughtfulness,

---

4. Yoshiko Yokochi Samuel, "The Apprenticeship of Big Toe P," *World Literature Today* 84: 4 (2010): 64.

5. Kazumi Nagaike, "Matsuura Rieko's *The Reverse Version*: The Theme of 'Girl-Addressing-Girl' and Male Homosexual Fantasies," in *Girl Reading Girl in Japan*, ed. Tomoko Aoyama and Barbara Hartley (Abingdon: Oxon, 2010), 115.

6. Matsuura Rieko, "Oyayubi Penisu toha Nanika?" ["What is an Oyayubi Penis?"], in *Oyayubi P no Shugyō Jidai* vol. 2, 329. Originally delivered as a lecture at Waseda University and published in *Waseda Bungaku* in 1994.

consideration, and compassion, all of which form the basis for later social relations like friendship.[7] In Matsuura's writing, however, various types of skin-to-skin relationships, often making her characters self-conscious, occupies a visible place more than the parental skinship. A familial touch that is rather rare in Matsuura appears in *The Apprenticeship of Big Toe P* between the blind pianist Shunji and his uncle; his uncle's hesitant hug, which made him happy, makes him comment, "'No one ever hugged me that way again'."[8] For the blind Shunji, the touch he remembers from his childhood is now allowing him to communicate love and natural affection, while allowing a smooth transition between the intimate touch in childhood and the more erotic touch he experiences in adulthood. He enjoys the physical contact with another human being, like a child holding hands with a classmate. The intimate relationship through the skin regenerates as one's life progresses.

The disintegration of the traditional family and the gradual hollowing out of the nuclear family in the postwar period in the absence of father and mother contributed to a paradoxical reconsideration of close bonds and intimacy. Matsuura debuted in 1978 with her "Sōgi no Hi" ["The Day of the Funeral"], which won the *Bungakukai Shinjin shō* (Bungakukai New Writers' Award), while still enrolled at Aoyama Gakuin University in Tokyo to major in French. During this decade, a range of feminist writings spread and depictions of same-sex intimacies were open in Japanese manga and popular representations in the 1970s. Having read the works of Kōno Taeko and Kurahashi Yumiko (1935–2005) since her teenage years on the one hand and Jean Genet and Marquis de Sade on the other, as well as being exposed to girl's manga, such as of Yashiro Masako (1947–) and Yamagishi Ryōko (1947–), it seems the climate for sexual liberation was embedded in Matsuura's creations. Julia Bullock, in her reading of feminist development before the women's liberation movement in the 1970s via Kōno Taeko, Takahashi Takako, and Kurahashi Yumiko, claims that against the common assumptions of woman's "natural" role to be wives and mothers, these authors "identified women's bodies as the site of gender oppression and thus attempted to trouble facile linkages between body and

---

7. Hirai Nobuyoshi, *Sukinshippu de Kokoro ga Sodatsu* [*Nurturing the Heart through Skinship*] (Tokyo: Kikakushitsu, 1999), 37–38, 122–124.
8. Matsuura, *The Apprenticeship of Big Toe P*, 115.

gender, biology and destiny."[9] If such an assumed "naturalness" of women's role was a prime contestation in feminism movements in postwar Japan, Matsuura went a step further to question naturalness between women in the post-family era, a time when the family was shaped beyond blood relation.

Matsuura herself shows the extent of sympathy toward feminism in its desire for new femininity, but Matsuura tries to criticize the patriarchy and male society in a manner other than trying to break them via a direct opposition or binary structure; as she explains herself, Matsuura intends to move to a different level and pass them through.[10] Bullock observes the "projection" of negative qualities associated with the corporeal from men to women as in the literature of the flesh depicted by male authors during the Occupation period.[11] Matsuura's strategy not to confront directly but to bring it to a different level of critique, I argue, also means shifting the orientation of "projection"—that from men to women to that from female character to another female character. Projective identification, discussed in Kleinian object relation theories as identifying oneself from the other onto which the subject projects negative feelings, bears a new meaning here; the projection in Matsuura functions not between oppressive

---

9. Julia C. Bullock, *The Other Women's Lib: Gender and Body in Japanese Women's Fiction* (Honolulu: University of Hawai'i Press, 2010), 5.

10. See "Kikei kara no Manazashi" ["The Gaze from Deformity"], Matsuura Rieko and Tomioka Kōichirō, in Matsuura Rieko, *Sebasuchan [Sebastian]* (Tokyo: Kawade Shobō Shinsha, 2007), 206–08. Ichimura Takako discusses lesbianism in Matsuura's writing, with particular attention paid to disabilities or deformities, neither as an opposition to heterosexual love nor as an extension of feminism to employ idealized lesbianism as a force of feminism (Ichimura Takako, "Judith Butler to Matsuura Rieko: Shisen no Kōsa" ["Judith Butler and Matsuura Rieko: Intersecting Views"], *Artes Liberales* 66 (2000): 33–34). See also Tsujimoto Chizu's discussion of "Natural Woman" with an attention to the construction of human relationship through the mind, the body, and language beyond lesbianism (Tsujimoto Chizu, "*Nachuraru Ūman* Shiron" ["An Essay on Nachuraru Ūman"], *Gengobunka Ronsō* 6 (2012): 85–87). Izutani Shun, through the comparative reading of the novel and filmic adaptation of *Natural Woman*, emphasizes the continuous redefinition of the female homosexual relationship in everyday life, instead of prioritizing sexuality. Izutani Shun, "Hōi sareru/Shōtotsu suru Josei Dōseiai—Matsuura Rieko 'Nachuraru Ūman' ni okeru Yokubō to Kankeisei" ["Circumscribed, Crushing Female Homosexuality—Desire and Relationality in Matsuura Rieko's *Natural Woman*"], *Ronkyū Nihon Bungaku* 99 (2013): 49.

11. Bullock, *The Other Women's Lib*, 36.

males and gendered others (women), but between undifferentiated self and others, gender-wise. Minoritarian female subjects who possess indefinable sexuality[12]—such as Yoko in "Natural Woman," Kazumi in *The Apprenticeship of Big Toe P,* or other key characters in Matsuura's works—question the way relationships are constructed through binary terms and instead cultivate the ways we think of recognition and love of the self.

This final chapter is a response or counter-response to the previous chapters on touch that broadly manifest hesitancy, fantasy, and unknowability to reach the other in touching, depicted by the male authors' hands. In this chapter, I focus on the relationality developed by means of contact through the skin, skinship, through a reading of Matsuura's works. As a female writer who has continuously written about the relationship beyond the divides of relationality, whether it be family, romantic, or erotic relationship or friendship, she offers an account of touch, different from the male authors above, as the site of bodily encounters and the source of affective, erotic, and sexual developmental processes. My reading of touch through Matsuura's work, while in dialogue with object relations, performativity, and affect, altogether demonstrates that, I contend, skinship as the site of encounter nurses both emotional and physical awareness and the development of those involved; it orientates or renews the relationship to others, while cultivating a language to express such a feeling called love.

Writing Intimate Relationships through Alternative Sensualities

Beginning with her first work, "The Day of the Funeral," which was originally published in *Bungakukai* in December 1978, Matsuura has

---

12. For the range of signification to conceive the term "sexuality," instead of focusing exclusively on sexual drive, sexual orientation, and sexual acts, see Miki Yoshiko, Hohashi Naohiro, and Maekawa Atsuko, "Wagakuni no Hoken Iryō Ryōiki ni okeru Sekushuaritī no Gainen Bunseki" ["A Concept Analysis of Sexuality in Japan's Health and Medical Care Domain"], *Nihon Kangokagaku kaishi* [*Japan Journal of Nursing Science*] 33: 2 (2013): 76. For skin-to-skin touch in forming attachments in relationships, with the hormone oxytocin having positive effects on both the one touched and the one touching, see Yamaguchi Hajime, *Hifu Kankaku no Fushigi: "Hifu" to "Kokoro" no Shintai Shinri gaku* [*The Mystery of the Skin Sensuality: Somato-Psychology of the "Skin" and "Heart"*]) (Tokyo: Kōdansha, 2016), 182–185.

continually written about self-love and love of the other, considered by contemporaneous critics to be this work's main theme.[13] "The Day of the Funeral" is a story about women who professionally perform crying and laughing, with their tears and laughter creating a dramatic atmosphere for funerals and serving as sites for communion, feeling each other's presence not through physical union but through such things as the thickness of air and trembling. Feeling ashamed of such an intimate encounter being observed by a funeral attendee, the narrator-protagonist (crier) considers killing her counterpart and herself together. With their hands strangling each other to the extent that the narrator-protagonist's consciousness goes far away to be freed from gravity (*"kankaku ga tōnoku. jyūryoku kara kaihō sareru"*),[14] her counterpart leaves on her neck a fingermark, which is then touched and kissed by a boy who loves her. His attempt at erasing another's mark on her neck with his own lip mark is painful for her. The heterosexual act with this boy is seen by the narrator as nothing more than a replacement of a relationship that she deems more important but feels difficult to express in any concrete way, except continuously thinking: "The only way to keep the balance is to pretend [*kyōgen suru*]."[15] Matsuura has depicted nuanced forms of intimate relationships that are focused neither exclusively on carnal union nor heterosexual relationship. Does this, however, immediately mean that she is trying to write about intimacies via same-sex relationships against heteronormativity and phallocentrism?

Takahashi Takako especially considers laughter in "The Day of the Funeral" as an expression of a "primitive" femininity located in-between a womb-like darkness and the world considered in its luminosity.[16] This, on the one hand, suggests an inhabitation of the boundary of the pre-verbal and symbolic orders. Matsuura, on the other hand, suggests in this story the impossibility of complete unification with the loved one; one desires their counterpart to love the other as well as oneself, only to realize the incomplete unification of their respective departures. The

---

13. Takahashi Takako, Kawamura Jirō, and Ōhashi Kenzaburō, "Dai 37kai Sōsaku Gappyō" ["The 37th Collected Reviews on Creative Writing"], *Gunzō* 34: 1 (1979): 353.
14. Matsuura Rieko, "Sōgi no Hi," in *Sōgi no Hi* (Tokyo: Kawade Shobō Shinsha, 1993), 56.
15. Matsuura Rieko, "Sōgi no Hi," 64.
16. "Dai 37kai Sōsaku Gappyō," 355.

protagonist, when faced with a situation in which she has to perform her crier role at her counterpart laugher's funeral, comments at the end of the story: "Unification [*Ketsugō*]! The word that all at once makes me feel tired. It was all she and I pursued. From our first meeting, we tried again and again in vain. We got attached to each other. But she died yesterday. Our wish left unrealized."[17] The unification both through heterosexual physical unity and same-sex psychological unity in this story does not reach any end point, suggesting the fundamental loneliness of individuals, despite the deep intimate feelings among them.

One noticeable feature of much of Matsuura's fiction is that intimate relationships are pursued outside the purview of the family. Matsuura depicts intimate relationships without the family image in short stories, published together as a single volume with "Natural Woman" in 1987—"Ichiban Nagai Gogo" ["The Longest Afternoon"] and "Binetsu Kyūka" ["Vacation with a Slight Fever"], published in May and November 1985, respectively, in *Bungei*. In "The Longest Afternoon," Matsuura depicts the relationship between Yoko and the flight attendant Yukiko, and in "Vacation with a Slight Fever," she features Yoko, who has experienced separations with Hanayo and with Yukiko, and Yuriko who studies fashion design. These stories all deal with the same protagonist, Yoko, and her intimate relationships with a series of women, in particular Hanayo. Yoko projects her relationship with Hanayo onto others, as if Hanayo was her primary love object. Yoko's sadomasochistic relationship with Yukiko remains physical with no emotional involvement, but Hanayo triggers in Yoko recurring memories of pleasure and pain. Yoko's platonic feelings toward Yuriko, on the other hand, surge on the surface of her body as an extra-verbal bodily response. "Natural Woman" imbues touch with extremes of love and violence between Yoko and Hanayo; touch as an unavoidable expression of love turns violent as loved ones are beaten, hit, and injured, and the relationship between sadistic Hanayo and masochistic Yoko changes. For Hanayo, the beloved Yoko becomes a source of emotional suffering even when her lovable features remain the same. In the end, it becomes difficult for these characters to maintain their relationship, with inability to see the end of same-sex relationality. "Natural Woman," which ends with Yoko and Hanayo's separating as the only way to escape

17. Matsuura, "Sōgi no Hi," 70.

from their endless search for love, marks, in my view, an ongoing process of departure from the primary loved object.[18]

The preoccupation with intimate relationships that are not reducible to a clear-cut structure and that cultivate the intersection of touch and language is present in the more recent work *Kenshin* [*The Dogbody*]. In this story, the female protagonist Fusae finally realizes her longstanding wish to become a dog and communicates with her female owner, Azusa, through touching and licking, conveying sensual nature arising from the skin. When dog Fusa first meets Azusa, Fusa feels joy more than simply comfort through Azusa's touch: feeling, by Fusa, ticklish and thrilling touch and sometimes gentle stroking as if being invited for play.[19] The now-canine Fusa and another character, Akeo—who has navigated Fusae to become a dog with the condition that he receives Fusae's soul (*tamashii*) if she enjoys happily her canine life—communicate via consciousness (*ishiki*) instead of words. Azusa's thought, verbalized as the language of consciousness, is shared with Fusa. Verbalization here deepens the significance of non-verbal skinship,[20] instead of taking away the affective features irreducible to language. Involving the sense of affections demonstrated neither merely through words nor gestures, but through consciousness, the intimate relationship cultivates the multivalent ways of expressing feelings.

Furthermore, Matsuura's writing dislocates the locus of sensuality from genitals to the skin and widens the threshold of erotic experience from sexual relationship to friendship or fellowship (*yūai*), toward a proliferation

---

18. On the primary object relation, Michael Balint, from Sándor Ferenczi's proposition of passive object-love, sees later psychological developments such as feelings of hate and narcissism as a response to the primary object relationship to be unconditionally loved, although later he recognizes active aspects of the primary object-love. Harold Stewart, *Michael Balint: Object Relations Pure and Applied* (London: Routledge, 1996), 19–20.

19. Matsuura Rieko, *Kenshin*, vol. 1 (Tokyo: Asahi Shimbun Shuppan, 2010), 176; it was originally serialized online, "Timebook Town," from April 2004 to June 2007.

20. See Momose Natsumi, "'Kenshin'-ron 2: Seiai-kan to Ningen-kankei no Tōtatsuten" ["Analysis of *Kenshin* II: The Purpose of its Views of Sexual Love and Human Relationships"], *Gesuto Hausu*, additional vol. IV (2012): 39. Momose argues that the characters in Matsuura's works tend to be indifferent about their own sex and sexual acts, and ambiguous about their recognition of the sex of the other, so that they are excluded from various "isms" such as phallocentrism and the unification of eroticism through the genitals (Momose Natsumi, "'Kenshin'-ron 1: Senkō Sakuhin Kōsatsu" ["Analysis of *Kenshin*: A Study of Earlier Works"], *Gesuto Hausu*, vol. IV (2012), 36–37).

of normativity. In Matsuura's recent work *Saiai no Kodomo* [*The Most Beloved Child*], first published in *Bungakukai* in February 2017, school-girls' friendship takes the shape of pseudo-family over the real family, with Mashio who plays the mother role, Hinatsu who plays the father role, and the main character Utsuho who is treated like a child. Utsuho's (real) mother Itsuko beats and castigates Utsuho, on whose body bruises are found by the girls who are the plural narrators, referred to as "us." The girls imagine a scene where the pseudo-father Hinatsu checks the bruises on Utsuho: "Hinatsu, stroking the back of Utsuho's head, is unable to take her eyes away from the yellow bruise. She wants to stroke the bruise, too, but hesitates, thinking it might hurt, but wants to heal this scar. She kisses and licks the bruise as her desire leads her to do, as an animal mother does for its child."[21] The familial relationship is taken rather disparagingly by the girls with elements of *boshi yuchaku* (like *boshi micchaku*; an adherence between mother and infant) between Hinatsu's sister and her mother, as well as between Itsuko and Utsuho. That is, the possibility of replacing even the child–parent relationship. Through some extent of politicization of the skin, Matsuura opens possibilities for an alternative relationality toward a renewable skinship, constructed in relation to the new object/ person, while reforming the self.

Writing about skinship in the age of post-familial relationships, Matsuura shows that the relationship is renewable to the extent that it replaces the familial intimacy and that skinship cultivates beyond the mother. In an interview on the self-realization of sexuality, Matsuura proposes the idea of shuffling the parents; blood relations are not absolute, she argues, and parent and child are interchangeable (*kōkan kanō*).[22] Matsuura further notes in the interview with a contemporary female writer Tsumura Kikuko when discussing *The Most Beloved Child*: "I have thought for a long time that even parent and child might be a replaceable relationship. It might be terrible if they feel secure just by having a blood link or having given birth, as if one possesses another."[23] Matsuura places no limits on the

21. Matsuura, *Saiai no Kodomo*, 124.
22. Matsuura, "Intabyū Matsuura Rieko: Sekushuaritī no Jiko Jitsugen no tameni" ["Inter-view Matsuura Rieko: For the Self- realization of Sexuality"], *Subaru*, 37: 10 (2015), 197.
23. Discussion between Tsumura Kikuko and Matsuura Rieko, "Taidan: Mainā na Kyōdōtai no Romansu" ["Conversation: The Romance in a Minor Community"], *Bunga-kukai* 71: 6 (2017): 156.

type or form of relationship in which her protagonists engage: concerning what, with whom, or how they play with, or "touch" one another. This is the point where my reading expands the existing analyses on sexuality and eroticism in Matsuura by the nature of renewable relationality through the skin. My reading aims to develop what we conceive, sense, and love through the skin, expanding our understanding of and capability for relationality in the fluid space Matsuura creates by going into the skin, inverting polarities, and making the body independent of categories appear.

Asking post-Freudian questions about object (transference), including the links between different kinds of love (for example, self-love, friendship, and sensuality), André Green writes: "The main feature of love is a feeling of irresistible attraction, experienced in exaltation, and the desire to be as close as possible to the loved object."[24] One continuously searches for the object to love and to be loved due to the impermanence of and unavoidable separation with the primary loved object. Moreover, as discussed thus far in this book, one tactile experience can refer back, or forward, to another, touching the other at different life phases and sites. One could return to the "position" that one occupied earlier in the developmental process, as in the Kleinian sense, and experience variations of the similar relationship in search of the primary object or renew on the basis of the loved object(s). Here, the term "position" comes to bear a dual function in my reading as to characters' positionality in the text as well as developmental process to be further discussed below. It is not possible to completely separate what is, respectively, sexual, infantile, or familial touch, as they each complement one another, with longstanding effects. The relationality is never fixed; it is dynamic and performative.[25]

---

24. André Green, "To Love or Not to Love: Eros and Eris," in André Green and Gregorio Kohon, *Love and its Vicissitudes* (London and New York: Routledge, 2005), 11.

25. The term "performative" has been employed in philosophical, anthropological, and rhetorical analyses, including: J. L. Austin's investigation of a performative statement as "doing" as opposed to a constative one as "saying" [J. L. Austin, *How to Do Things with Words*]; Shoshana Felman's rereading of performative theory through Austin and psychoanalysis, in stressing the inherent possibility of misfire, self-subversion, and untranslatability in itself [Felman, *The Scandal of the Speaking Body*]; Richard Schechner's notion of performance as a "twice-behaved behaviour" or "restored behaviour," always being subject to revision and never the same again, in conversation with anthropological studies of rituals such as those of Victor Turner [Richard Schechner, *The Future of Ritual: Writings on Culture and Performance* (London: Routledge, 1993)]; and Joseph Roach's "genealogies of performance" that contextualize culturally specific memory [Joseph Roach, *Cities of the Dead: Circum-Atlantic Performance* (New York: Columbia University Press, 1996)].

Ambivalent Feelings about Love

Matsuura's "Himantai Kyōfushō" ["Obese Phobia" or, literally, "Obese Body Phobia"], originally published in *Bungakukai* in June 1980,[26] brings the mother into the discussion on touch and skinship through a different path from the mother as a reliably warm giver of love. In "Obese Phobia," told in a third-person narrative, the female protagonist Yuiko is depicted as naïve and docile enough to be teased by her three roommates at her college residence. Yuiko's obese upper-level roommates oblige her to perform unreasonable tasks due to her obedient attitude, the subordinate role attributed to her as a first-year student, and her hatred for obesity. One day, Yuiko starts stealing insignificant things from her roommates—hand cream, stationery, and cigarettes—as a way of exacting revenge on them. Their fat bodies signify more to her than mere corpulence; she realizes that the only naked, obese bodies she can recall are that of her mother in her childhood and those of her three roommates, whom she inevitably sees naked in the bathroom at her residence, recognizing the source of her phobia in her mother's obesity. The thought of her obese mother unconsciously lingers in Yuiko's mind throughout the story, wondering whether she took her mother's breast when she learned of her mother's mastectomy due to cancer and feeling hateful of herself for being unable to forgive her mother's obesity. When Yuiko puts stolen scissors in her drawer later in the story, she suddenly has the thought that what she has gathered from her roommates is her own mother's lost breast. In the end, Yuiko is physically oppressed by a roommate's fat body, causing her to imagine becoming herself fat. Only then does the obese body become lovable for Yuiko.

"Obese Phobia" was written, Izutani Shun argues, when interests in dieting, low-calorie eating, bodybuilding, and exercising were heightened to achieve a healthy body in the 1970s consuming society.[27] Matsuura feels a body with strengthened muscle without fat, as in bodybuilding, is unfavorable, and she instead favors soft and superfluous flesh, as that of her

---

26. It was collected together in 1980 with "The Day of the Funeral" and "Kawaku Natsu" ["Dry Summer"], which was originally published in October 1979 in *Bungakukai*, as *Sōgi no Hi*.

27. Izutani Shun, "Jikai suru Teikoku, Sekai ni Nosabaru Shintai: Matsuura Rieko, 'Himantai Kyōfushō' ron" ["An Empire to Self-Destruct, a Body to the World: On Matsuura Rieko's 'Himantai Kyōfushō'"], *Ritsumeikan Bungaku* 652 (2017), 109–10.

favorite female wrestler, Bull Nakano. She writes of sex appeal in child-like sensuality (*kodomo no kannō sei*) in her 1987 essay "Seiki kara no Kaihō wo" ["Liberation from Genitals"]; finding Bull Nakano's attraction in her innocent fatness—not obesity—as if a child has gotten fat in the middle of growing up, Matsuura names such a child-like sensuality without genitals as "sex gang child" (*sekkusu gyangu chairudo*), inspired by the British punk band, Sex Gang Children.[28] Matsuura's aim in the liberation from genitals here is to recognize genitals simply as organs without any special meaning to be discussed at length.

While it is rare in the story by Matsuura that the mother has an underlying presence throughout the story, she is narrated as psychologically killed or dead from breast cancer. Through the character Yuiko, who experiences a yearning for the dead mother whom she once repudiated by replacing the mother's "meat" with other stolen materials, Matsuura depicts ambivalent feelings, that are the elements to shape her characters. In my chapter on Kawabata I explained how Sándor Ferenczi, a member of Freud's psychoanalytic circle and Melanie Klein's mentor, theorized introjection (as an extension of the ego and autoerotic interests to the external world, taking the loved object in) and exteriorization in such a way as to bring attention to the inside/outside, pleasure/unpleasure, and love/hate polarities.[29] In Kleinian analysis, the logic is that the good object is incorporated, and the bad feeling is projected onto the other or expelled in a form of projective identification. André Green, who separated from the Lacanian school and integrated the ideas of members of the British psychoanalysis into his work, notes the pleasure perceived when the good object is cruelly lacking and a subsequent attempt is made to recover the lost or absent pleasure, in the cycle of "incorporation, loss, desire, frustration, aggression, and excorporation."[30] What is at stake in these discussions of self–other relationality

---

28. Matsuura Rieko, "Seiki kara no Kaihō wo" ["Liberation from the Genitals"] in *Yasashii Kyosei no tameni* [*For Gentle Castration*], 82–86 (Tokyo: Chikuma Shobō, 1997, 85–86. "Seiki kara no Kaihō wo" was originally published in the Japanese pop culture magazine *BRUTUS* in January 1987.

29. The Swiss psychiatrist Alphonse Maeder considered Ferenczi's exteriorization as a form of "projection" whereby one's body becomes identified with external things. However, Ferenczi considered it as involving displacement and transference, and as a special case of introjection in which the object of interest is displaced from one to another. Ferenczi, *Final Contributions to the Problems & Methods of Psycho-analysis*, 316–318.

30. André Green, *On Private Madness* (London and New York: Karnac, 2005), 88.

is how one negotiates with one's own ambivalent feelings toward the same object, the awareness of which is marked through language in the text.

In "Obese Phobia," the mother is a gentle woman whose slow-witted demeanor makes her daughter, Yuiko, feel depressed. Yuiko was not aware of her mother's obesity until she went to elementary school: until that point, "the mother was not yet even the mother; she was a part of the self's body."[31] Yuiko realized her mother's obesity for the first time on parents' day at the school, when she saw that her mother's body was three times as big as that of any of the other parents. This caused her to feel hatred for her mother, and she began to distance herself from her. She refuses her mother's arm when her mother offers to hold her or to bathe together, and she withdraws into her room. She asks her mother not to come to the next parents' day. Only after the comparison to other mothers did her mother's body become for Yuiko a marker of shame: obesity as a form of the disliked.[32] Further, Yuiko is uncomfortable at the thought that her father ever touched her mother and that she herself once accepted her mother's body by sucking her breasts. While this story illuminates Yuiko's fear of female reproductive sexuality as Yonaha Keiko discusses,[33] I argue that it also marks Yuiko's departure from the primary loved object. The cut of the mother's breast, recognized as the "other" instead of part of "me," is the departure from it and the beginning of her search for the alternative loved object.

Having repudiated the mother's body, Yuiko now realizes that she has unknowingly committed herself to collecting unimportant objects as unnecessary "meats"—things whose substance, animal flesh, is nourishing though no longer alive—to replace her mother's breast. When Julia Kristeva explains her concept of the "abject" in distinction from the "I," she focuses on radical exclusion from the "me": "Not me. Not that. But not nothing, either."[34] Especially on food loathing—here, it could be

---

31. Matsuura Rieko, "Himantai Kyōfushō," in *Sōgi no Hi*, 191.

32. Obesity is connected to abnormality in Matsuura's "Dry Summer," in which a character called Ayako refers to "himanji" (obese child) as an "abnormal fat child." Matsuura, "Kawaku Natsu," in *Sōgi no Hi,* 117.

33. Yonaha Keiko, "Matsuura Rieko: Ekkyō suru Sei" ["Matsuura Rieko: A Sexuality that Crosses the Frontier"], *Kokubungaku: Kaishaku to Kyōzai no Kenkyū* 37: 13 (1992): 129.

34. Julia Kristeva, *Powers of Horror: An Essay on Abjection*, trans. Leon S. Roudiez (New York: Columbia University Press, 1982), 2. Originally published as *Pouvoirs de l'horreur* in 1980 by Éditions du Seuil.

conceived as the mother's milk for Yuiko, retrospectively—Kristeva writes of expelling of the disliked as expelling of part "me":

> Along with sight-clouding dizziness, *nausea* makes me balk at that milk cream, separates me from the mother and father who proffer it. "I" want none of that element, sign of their desire; "I" do not want to listen, "I" do not assimilate it, "I" expel it. But since the food is not an "other" for "me," who am only in their desire, I expel *myself*, I spit *myself* out, I abject *myself* within the same motion through which "I" claim to establish *myself*.[35]

Yuiko finds herself haunted by her mother's breast, even though she has repudiated it; accepting its replacement in the form of stolen items therefore may well also be to her a form of self-negation. Yuiko has unconsciously sought to replace her mother's breast, which is a form of disavowal of herself. In this sequence, however, the mother's breast, which is transformed into the objects representing the roommates' "meat," is re-transformed into the image of a breast. The negated object—being projected, transformed, and re-transformed through the mediation of third parties—returns as the mother's breast, causing feelings different from phobia.

In a discussion with the female writer Shōno Yoriko (1956–) on this mother–child relationship in "Obese Phobia," Matsuura notes a particular kind of relationality in which the capacity for oppression works both ways. Considering also her own childhood memory of depending on the loved mother, Matsuura explains that a child's emotions toward the mother are necessarily ambivalent ("*ryōgiteki*").[36] Freud recognizes widespread mixed feelings in the mother–daughter relationship in that the daughter feels a mixture of compassion, contempt, and envy toward the mother; the mother feels her daughter is a rival of the sons that the mother wants to favor at the daughter's expense.[37] Klein further articulates the ambivalence felt by the child toward the mother's breast, where the breast that the child sucks serves at first as the loved object, while projecting the bad feelings

---

35. Julia Kristeva, *Powers of Horror: An Essay on Abjection*, 3.
36. Matsuura and Shōno, *Okaruto Odokumi Teishoku*, 157–158.
37. Sigmund Freud, "The Psychogenesis of a Case of Homosexuality in a Woman," *SE*, vol. 18 (London: Hogarth Press, 1955), 157.

out, but becomes a source of anxiety once incorporated; ultimately, the breast will inevitably be lost. For Yuiko in "Obese Phobia," the mother's breast is negated and then is repeated through others (in a form of objects associated with the meat of disliked roommates). Matsuura presents a chain of relationality that involves the regeneration of a relationship to the primary object, and this goes beyond the original negation. In this sense, here too (as with Yoshiyuki), touch is the site of an accumulation and of a continuous "othering" with individuals that differ from the primary object. For one person to relate to (or to negate) another necessitates a renewal, bringing the alternative object and regenerating the primary, to rewrite the relationality.

This relation to the object also questions the agency of the touched or incorporated object. In writing about skin-to-skin communication irrespective of categories by age, gender, or species, Matsuura recognizes that a person's sensual stimulations in childhood can affect his or her sense of shame in adulthood, and that the mother's touch can even become the basis for a kind of fetish. The mother may take pleasure from the sensual attraction of the feel (*hadazawari*) of the child's skin, not from motherly love but as of an indecent fetish. Witnessing the image of the mother's hand stroking the baby's naked bottom, such as one sees often in TV advertisements, Matsuura feels like shouting, "Don't touch," considering it almost like a mother–infant sexual harassment, where the child becomes "the fetish object [*mono = fetisshu*]."[38] For Matsuura, the mother's touch is not necessarily always the source of warm love. The mother–infant skinship is a site of possible oppression and violence, for both mother and child. The mother might caress her child, heedless of how the child feels about it, based on the assumption that a mother's touch is welcome no matter what. As discussed in an earlier chapter, Klein's observation of the child–object relation is focused on animated figures, such as children, and incorporated objects, such as the breast, cannot say "No!" to be incorporated, neglecting the agency of the object. As much as the touched infant might not necessarily welcome the mother's touch, the touched and incorporated object, likewise, might not be in a state where touch is welcomed. Such possibilities point to a limitation of observation-based analysis, conceiving the child's feelings in the realm of fantasy.

---

38. Matsuura Rieko, "Asobareru Kodomo tachi" ["The Played Children"]. In *Poketto Fetisshu* [*Pocket Fetish*] (Tokyo: Hakusuisha, 2000), 22–23.

The mother–infant relationship bears the extent of an erotic compo-
nent, as Cristina Traina relates childbirth and breastfeeding to the progression of orgasm where, bodies bearing the memories of other pleasures,
"child can feel not so different from lover"[39]; "she [the mother] is already
having sex with her infant."[40] While it can also involve a cannibalistic fantasy if we recall the child's relationship to its mother in the Kleinian framework, in which the child seeks to devour the mother's breast. Ambivalent
feelings between mother and infant in the Japanese literary texts were earlier expressed by such writers as Kōno Taeko and Takahashi Takako in the
form of maternal child abuse and infanticide in the 1960s and 1970s as a
resistance to the then common gender norm. Matsuura further considers
the works of Japanese poet Itō Hiromi (1955–), such as *Teritori-ron [On
Territory]* in 1985 and 1987, as a distinctive case of female demonstration
(*onna no sonzai shōmei*) amid abundant gender-related discourse in mid-
1980s Japan, which felt, for Matsuura, "wet with coquetry [*kobi ni nure-
teiru*]."[41] With reference to the Kleinian idea of the good and bad breast,
Itō Hiromi in the 1980s writes of a baby biting off its mother's breast, as
well as a mother killing her child.[42] Her own experience of giving birth
to her first child, Kanoko, drove her to ponder upon the infant–mother
relationship and its psychological effects, from the child's perspective, with
its colloquial language. Jeffrey Angles writes, "Her [Itō's] willingness to
deal with touchy subjects such as post-partum depression, infanticide, and
queer sexual desire shocked Japan—a nation that was until that time more
used to images of women as proud wives, mothers, and quiet care-givers."[43]

---

39. Cristina L. H. Traina, *Erotic Attunement: Parenthood and the Ethics of Sensuality between
Unequals* (Chicago, IL and London: University of Chicago Press, 2011), 17.
40. Cristina L. H. Traina, *Erotic Attunement: Parenthood and the Ethics of Sensuality between
Unequals*, 31.
41. Matsuura, "Seiki kara no Kaihō wo," 82.
42. Itō's *Teritori-ron I* and *II [On Territory]* were published by Shichōsha in 1987 and 1985,
respectively, and child-rearing essay *Yoi Oppai Warui Oppai [Good Breast, Bad Breast]* by
Tōjusha in 1985. Tsuboi Hideto discusses Itō's shift from the mother's throwing away or
killing her child to the infant's destroying and killing its mother in relation to the child's
ambivalent feelings toward the mother's breast in Klein, with reference to Itō's "citation" of
(or reference to) Klein's chapter, "A Study of Envy and Gratitude" (1956) in her *Teritori-ron I*.
Tsuboi Hideto, "Itō Hiromi ron (ge)" ["Discussion on Itō Hiromi, 3"], *Nihon Bungaku*
39: 4 (1990): 24; *Sei ga Kataru*, 569.
43. Jeffrey Angles, "Translator's Introduction," in Itō Hiromi, *Killing Kanoko / Wild Grass
on the Riverbank*, trans. Jeffrey Angles (Sheffield: Tilted Axis Press, 2020), 6.

With the killing or absence of the mother, feeling toward motherhood (*bosei*), Matsuura writes, is mixed with love and hatred ("*aizō irimajiru*"),[44] with further envy and jealousy. Intimate relationship, as much as one holds affectionate feeling towards the other, necessarily generates non-lovable or even hostile sentiments. It is not possible to take only the good aspect of the loved object.

The ambivalence (in the sense of the above-mentioned *ryōgisei*) concerning the object, however, relates not only to one's feeling but also to temporality. Juliet Mitchell writes of the Kleinian position as "a mental space in which one is sometimes lodged," speaking to a "different, earlier, prehistorical sense of time"[45]; adults may revisit a mental state experienced in childhood, as opposed to Freudian libidinal stages through which one passes—of oral, anal, phallic, and genital developmental stages. Kleinian theory focuses on the early childhood relationship with the mother's breast within the realm of psychic fantasy, without paying much attention to the inanimate object, as well as instincts and vicissitudes. And yet, Klein's idea of position is useful in the literary analysis of adult psychology focused on the loved object, in that it connects child anxieties and adult psychosis via the "change-over that occurs from a persecution anxiety or depressed feeling to a normal attitude."[46] In developing Klein's idea of position as "provisional and flexible demarcations, practices of being,"[47] José Esteban Muñoz articulates the racial performativity of "feeling brown" or doing brownness, which is enabled by "practices of self-knowing" as neither white, nor black, nor anything simply

---

44. Matsuura Rieko, "<Bosei> Shinwa wa Tsumi tsukuri: Nishi Masahiko, Itō Hiromi 'Papa wa Gokigen Naname'" ["Sin Making of Motherhood Myth: on Nishi Masahiko and Itō Hiromi, 'Dad in a Bad Temper'"], in *Yasashii Kyosei no tameni*, 201. The essay was originally published in *Misu Katei Gahō* in July 1989.

45. Juliet Mitchell, "Introduction," in *SMK*, 28. Mitchell writes on her short introduction to Klein's 1935 "A Controbution to the Psychogenesis of Manic-Depressive States" that this essay marks the actual deployment of the notion of position, originally used by Klein in 1930. Making "a connection between adult psychosis and infant development - a 'position' is an always available state, not something one passes through" (116).

46. Klein, notes to "A Contribution to the Psychogenesis of Manic-Depressive States," *SMK*, 235.

47. José Esteban Muñoz, "Feeling Brown, Feeling Down: Latina Affect, The Performativity of Race, and Depressive Position," in *Signs* 31: 3 (2006), 681. Muñoz, in his analyses of Nao Bustamante's artwork, considers this discussion of the Kleinian position together with another position proposed by Antonio Gramsci as a mode of resistance.

in between.[48] This sense of positions as a continuous process of knowing oneself and a practice of being oneself parallels, I argue, the characters' "doing" to take a positionality within the text.

Responses to objects amid various feelings shape the "character" of the depicted subjects; moreover, the flip-over of relationship is practiced in the form of "positions" taken by literary characters. Matsuura's obedient female characters sometimes resist the oppressive others—as Yuiko resists her roommates in "Obese Phobia" or as Yoko resists Hanayo in "Natural Woman"—thereby positioning the oppressed in the center of the story and turning the relationality to the oppressing. One's responses, actions, and gestures in the face of others shape its own literary character. Describing what she sees as the divides, differences, and pluralism in the category of "women," literary scholar Iida Yūko argues for a "response-ability" (*ohtoh-sei*) that joins together the fissured subject and writing; as much as in a speech act, the act of writing is a way of responding to a call, bearing additional responsibilities to concern a minoritarian subject.[49] One's response to the other, arising from its body and described in the text, shapes the body of character. Their gestures, poses, or physical features in Matsuura, however, *initiate* interactions between characters, instead of waiting to *respond* to the other.

One person's pose, behavior, and features speak to the other, motivating the latter's response, as well as the reader's engagement with the literary characters. In "Obese Phobia," Yuiko boldly makes use of her demure appearance and weaker position in relation to her older roommates to steal from them. Working part-time at a supermarket, where she offers people samples and promotes sweets, Yuiko knows that she can sell a lot to customers who express sympathetic feelings as she stands there day after day with her bored, sad face. Hanayo in "Natural Woman" resents Yoko for her wiliness in presenting herself as ignorant, innocent, and pure; this becomes a source of irritation for Hanayo. Kazumi, in *The Apprenticeship of Big Toe P*, is depicted, Ogura Chikako argues, as too naïve to wonder about her homosexual feelings for her friend Yoko,[50] while such a naïveté

---

48. José Esteban Muñoz, "Feeling Brown, Feeling Down: Latina Affect, The Performativity of Race, and Depressive Position," 680.

49. Iida Yūko, *Kanojo tachi no Bungaku: Katarinikusa to Yomareru koto* [*Their Literatures: Narratival Difficulty and Being Read*] (Nagoya: Nagoya Daigaku Shuppankai, 2016), 10–17.

50. Ogura Chikako, "Neotenī no Fukushū" ["The Revenge of Neoteny"], *Bungei* 32: 4 [1993]: 95.

gives her a dynamic sexual awareness once she possesses a big toe P. In *The Most Beloved Child*, to the girls' question whether father-role Hinatsu and mother-role Mashio have carnal relations, Hinatsu responds with a smile, "It's too important to tell you [*mottainai kara oshienai*]"[51]; this interaction, Hasumi Shigehiko writes, places Hinatsu at the invisible center of this story, through her relaxed response which neither denies nor affirms.[52] This is even truer when the literary language captures the physical stimuli of the characters' bodily interactions, prompting bodily effects on the reader. Hélène Cixous—among texts that directly make us feel joy or pain and those that are distanced or disembodied, made of style and structure—writes that the latter texts "don't touch us."[53] Affective aspects of (disembodied) language can reactivate the experience felt by literary characters, as discussed in the introduction, which can also prompt the reader's response. Matsuura, indeed, in her postscript for *The Apprenticeship of Big Toe P*, writes, "I would like to seduce readers not through the genitals, but through the skin [*hifu de dokusha wo yūwaku shitai*]."[54] It is as though her language narrating tactile sensations reaches the readers.

In the context of "Obese Phobia," where Yuiko repudiates the mother that was once a part of her, there is also the question of to what extent language marks a recognition of bodily separation from the primary object; what Kristeva calls "abjection" has both linguistic and non-linguistic, or originally pre-linguistic, components, as it involves an instability of the subject–object relation of the symbolic order. The repudiation of the primary love object enables the subject's formation, which also cultivates its language. The negation of the mother[55] correlates with Yuiko's fat phobia,

---

51. Matsuura, *Saiai no Kodomo*, 17.

52. Hasumi Shigehiko, "Toritomenonai Namamekashisa ni tsuite: Matsuura Rieko, 'Saiai no Kodomo'" ["About Ceaseless Sensuality: Matsuura Rieko, 'The Most Beloved Child'"], *Bungakukai* 71: 6 (2017): 167.

53. Hélène Cixous, "Difficult Joys," in *The Body and the Text: Hélène Cixous, Reading and Teaching*, ed. Helen Wilcox, et al. (New York: St Martin's Press, 1990), 27.

54. Matsuura, "Oyayubi Penisu toha Nanika," in *Oyayubi P no Shugyō Jidai*, vol. 2, 329.

55. Unlike the replaceable dead father, manifesting ancestors and functioning symbolically as a kind of introjected psychic apparatus—which is also a significant trope in the postwar Japanese imagination for reasons having to do with the postwar economic miracle—"the dead mother," conceived by André Green, who is depressed and emotionally dead, functions as a psychical blank: "the presence with an absent mother." Kohon, "The Greening of Psychoanalysis," 55. In his discussion of negation, Green avoids using "absence," which indicates a hope of the return of presence, and "loss," which can be mourned. André Green, "The Intuition of the Negative in *Playing and Reality*," in *The Dead Mother*, 218.

especially given that Yuiko has refused to touch her mother and asked her not to come to the school, some time before the symbolic death that is represented by her breast being cut off. And yet, it is regenerative of a relationship with plural others, instead of being simply lost. Stemming from Winnicott's concept of the transitional object as a "not-me," recognized by the infant as other than the omnipotent self, André Green's notion of negation expands on the "objectualising function," through which an extra object between the self and other is created, with our "infinite capacity to create objects."[56] One seeks and learns both to love and to be loved through its relation to the other—of necessary negation, split, or separation in life. Physical responses—such as not touching, cutting, and separating the other—when verbalized in the text render those characters' pre-verbal feelings readable. As much as one relates to the new object, the corresponding feeling of the character relating to it emerges in the texts.

At the very end of "Obese Phobia," one of Yuiko's roommates Mizuki, who has apparently been aware of Yuiko's stealing from early on, starts criticizing Yuiko for her self-centeredness. Yuiko confirms with her stealing her hatred of the obese and its role in confirming her own sense of self. Here the reformulation of the mother–daughter tie is based on its projection onto other individuals with whom the daughter later comes into contact; she finds herself in the other as in her mother through her hatred of the obese—hence Mizuki's criticism that Yuiko is engaged in a narcissistic self-confirmation. Yet, this is not only a rejection of obese bodies, but also an act of forming a new relationship by transferring her hatred onto the obese, which comes back to herself in the form of self-recognition. Muñoz writes of his concept of disidentification as "the survival strategies the minority subject practices in order to negotiate a phobic majoritarian public sphere that continuously elides or punishes the existence of subjects who do not conform to the phantasm of normative citizenship."[57] It is a way to activate their sense of self, in not assimilating into the public but rather restructuring the cultural form by partial disavowal. Yuiko, in order to act against the oppressive obesity that forms majority power in her dorm context, collects alternative meats. This disavowal is a way of continually searching for an object in constructing a new relationality, rather than

---

56. Green, "The Intuition of the Negative in *Playing and Reality*," 219.
57. José Esteban Muñoz, *Disidentifications: Queers of Color and the Performance of Politics* (Minneapolis: University of Minnesota Press, 1999), 4.

completely neglecting reality; this is the reason why the story marks the departure from the primary object.

A dramatic transformation of relationality occurs at the very end of "Obese Phobia," where Mizuki brings Yuiko a comfort that she has never before imagined. As Mizuki lies upon her, Yuiko trusts this weight and gives herself over to it. Whereas previously she felt only hatred for obese bodies, she now becomes trusting. Yuiko imagines that her "I" is becoming bigger and bigger while swallowing another body as "meat," like her mother, like Mizuki, and like her obese friend, through a subjectivity that is moving towards another form of relationality. Due to an inescapable feeling of pressure, Yuiko needs to incorporate what she has hated, which is now felt as compulsive (as opposed to a desired incorporation, as in Kawabata's "One Arm"). Then, moving away from her disliked obesity that is now a part of her own body, "me" that is not "me," Yuiko thinks that she will start loving the obese body: "That is what I have long wished. Ever since I let my mother die."[58] Here, Hasumi Shigehiko implies the possibility for another form of sex, sex without the genitals: Yuiko was breathing through her skin and incorporating the other's obesity through her pores.[59] The physical interaction of bodies in Yoshiyuki with such things as dampness and smell do not always bring the (bodily) pressure associated with the other, trying to withdraw from an emotionally engaged relationship. In Matsuura this unavoidable pressure leads to the recognition of the other, which can in turn facilitate a greater recognition for the protagonist of the need for self-love.

Relationships like this are continuously regenerative partly because the loved—or hated—object rarely stays as it is and one's relationality to it is unfixed. The object relation and object formation involve how one forms an object in desiring it, and how the loved object can be engaged with while signaling its impermanence and thus the sadness at being unable to fully "be with" the other. In Matsuura, the object plays further dynamic roles, by prompting characters' negation, replacement, and regeneration of the other and their relationality to it. The loved becomes dubitable, hated, expelled, and loved again, or it is re-incorporated; the mother who was a part of me, not yet separated from "me," is split, such a hatred for

58. Matsuura, "Himantai Kyōfushō," 235.
59. Hasumi Shigehiko, interview with Watanabe Naomi, "[Shōtokushū Intavyū] Hajirai no Secushuaritī" ["The Sexuality of Shyness"], *Bungei* 32: 4 (1993): 80.

obesity being projected onto other characters, replaced meat of mother being incorporated as a substitute. The hated obesity, now being turned to oneself, becomes lovable. Yuiko ultimately implores in an almost sound-less voice: "Please forgive me. I'll return everything I've stolen from you, I'll give you everything I have. I no longer need anything. So, please be gentle. Love me."[60] One leaves and replaces the primary object in contin-uous search for the other to love the self.

The Unsaid Performative

The ambivalent feelings toward the loved object in "Natural Woman" bears further complicated questions around intentionality, affect, and performativ-ity. While Hanayo continues to be the loved one throughout the volume *Natural Woman* for the protagonist/first-person narrator Yoko, Hanayo also starts giving her pain. Everything that is associated with Hanayo excites Yoko: her eyes, face, straightforwardness, obstinacy, coolness, proud attitude, and her ability to draw highly detailed manga. Hanayo's slightest touch moves and enchants Yoko with seemingly effortless grace, even the way she pats her hair. Hanayo is Yoko's consciously loved object, and provides Yoko with her representative and irreplaceable memory of touch, one that repeatedly returns as if it is the primary object. Yoko is depicted as mostly passive, being touched, excited, soothed, and enchanted by Hanayo, and continuing to enjoy the sen-sations afterwards. Pain feels sweet to Yoko when she is faced with Hanayo's smile. And yet, patting Yoko's forehead, the tip of her nose, and her cheek with one hand while holding a slipper in her other, Hanayo starts slapping Yoko's cheek with the slipper. Welcoming anything that Hanayo gives her, whether it be pain or pleasure, Yoko also starts slapping Hanayo back. Here, the loved object/person who gives the pleasure turns into the one who gives pain, while the exchange of love gradually becomes something for them to suffer from.

Hanayo, upon the termination of their relationship, describes Yoko, who is freed from the social norms and assumptions, as "free almost about to fly in the air" ("*Sora wo tobikanenai hodo jiyū*").[61] While Matsuura's works undo ranges of binary framing from sadomasochism, male–female

---

60. Matsuura, "Himantai Kyōfushō," 235.
61. Matsuura, "Nachuraru Ūman," 205.

gender binaries based on genitals, to hetero–homosexual polarity, Hasumi Shigehiko comments that Matsuura, throughout "Natural Woman," focuses on the anus as a site of contact undifferentiated by gender, instead of the explicit exposure of their genitals, invoking such shyness.[62] Hanayo does not let Yoko touch her genitals, which have been over-touched and, Hanayo thinks, given dirt (*aka*) by men to maintain Yoko's purity.[63] When Yoko later refuses to let her subsequent partner Yukiko touch her there, it is out of fidelity to Hanayo. Hanayo's fingering of Yoko's anus proves a suitable form of intercourse; this couple discovers a "sexual activity that suits us."[64] Yonaha Keiko further analyzes in "Natural Woman" the disappearance of the binaries of sadism and masochism, and pleasure and pain, through Yoko's complicity in welcoming the active counterparts of the terms she starts with.[65] This story in particular marks, through the three layers of short stories in the same volume revolving around the one loved object Hanayo, the process of nurturing a relationship, negotiating with the ambivalent feelings, and making a departure from the primary object. The progression of the story, overlapped with Yoko's gradual awareness of her relation to others, demonstrates constructing the story around characters' doing: the unsaid but performed. Thus, the undoing of binaries in Matsuura, I argue, is intrinsically connected to bodily expressions, reflected by the author's language to capture the characters' pre-verbal felt sensations and gestures.

From a certain point in the story, Hanayo regularly insert her fingers and various objects (ranging from a pen, to the plug of a pair of headphones, to a lit cigarette) into Yoko's anus. Hanayo beats Yoko's bottom, cheek, and breasts with the palm of her hand, an ashtray, and slippers. Yoko sometimes beats her in return. Yoko's innocent look seems to Hanayo to be calculating, although she also recognizes that it in fact reflects Yoko's natural attitude. Hanayo's frustration culminates to say, "You are just absorbed in your own feelings, not me. You don't even have a right to say

62. Hasumi, "Hajirai no Secushuariti," 91.

63. Matsuura, "Nachuraru Ūman," 140–141.

64. Matsuura, "Nachuraru Ūman," 162.

65. Yonaha Keiko, "Sakka Gaido: Matsuura Rieko" ["Author's Guide: Matsuura Rieko"], in *Josei Sakka Sirīzu 21 Yamada Eimi, Masuda Mizuko, Matsuura Rieko, Shōno Yoriko*, edited by Kōno Taeko, Ōba Minako, Satō Aiko, and Tsumura Setsuko (Tokyo: Kadokawa Shoten, 1999), 461.

you like me. For someone like you who is just passionately self-absorbed, without paying attention to anything else whatsoever."[66] Hanayo begins to suffer, as she cannot enjoy pleasure as Yoko does due to her role of controlling and giving pleasure. Hanayo at one point gently places slippers on Yoko's cheek and asks, "Do you like me?" Yoko responds, "I like you," and then Hanayo slaps her, saying, "You are a liar!"[67] Hanayo beats Yoko, whose expression of love (directed to Hayano) seems to her narcissistic. Yet, in beating Yoko and trying to confirm her obedient love, Hanayo herself is also being beaten. Maeda Rui recognizes a subtle yet non-negligible crack between the verbal statement "I like you" and the actual state of "liking" as a necessary gap between sadist and masochist, including that between Hanayo and Yoko,[68] separating the word and the reality it names. The wish to confirm being loved fails; the loved object "you" (Hanayo) in the phrase "I like you" said to Hanayo appears to suggest "me" (Yoko) for Hanayo. The different perceptions arising from the phrase "I like you" do not form any consensus. The love of the other reflected in self-love I discussed earlier is possible here insofar as both parties can believe in such a reciprocity in object love. If Hanayo cannot believe that she is loved, the statement of "I like you" directed to her and the act of love-making separates them farther, the more they physically unite.

In order to depict these characters' relationality, Matsuura borrows the docility associated with animals to express facets of her characters. Maeda Rui identifies "Sebasuchan" ["Sebastian"] written in 1981 as an early example that refers to a dog associated with masochism in Matsuura,[69] where the protagonist Makiko, who is not yet fully aware of her sexual identity, gradually builds one through her sadomasochistic relationships with her female friend Seri and a disabled younger boy, Kōya: Saeki Shōichi puts it, "artificial creation of play [*asobi*] and a world of role play ['*gokko' no sekai*]."[70] When Yoko finds the mark of a kiss placed by someone

66. Matsuura, "Nachuraru Ūman," 189–90.

67. Matsuura, "Nachuraru Ūman," 199–200.

68. Maeda Rui, "Hyakunen no Kōdoku: Matsuura Rieko, '*Kenshin*' wo megutte" ["One Hundred Years of Solitary Dog: Matsuura Rieko, through '*Kenshin*'"], *Gunzō*, 63: 2 (2008): 213.

69. Maeda Rui, "Hyakunen no Kōdoku: Matsuura Rieko, 208.

70. Kōno Taeko and Saeki Shōichi, "Joryū Shinjin no Genzai: Taidan Jihyō" ["New Female Writers Today: Review Discussion"], *Bungakukai* 35: 3 (1981): 195.

else on Hanayo's chest, Hanayo says, "Why don't you put another mark on top of it?" Yoko responds, "We're not dogs competing over marking," to which Hanayo replies by slapping Yoko with her hand on the cheek.[71] Their relationship, however, complicates the division between active and passive and controlling and controlled, as Yoko's body expresses her wish to be touched without saying. She never directly says, "Please touch me," but does so through a bodily posturing designed to get others to touch her. Yoko says that when her friend Keiko strokes her, Keiko is aware of Yoko's wish for her to do so. When the relationship between Hanayo and Yoko involves repeated beatings, Yoko says to Hanayo, "You shouldn't have touched me, even with a single finger touch, if you weren't interested in me from the beginning." Hanayo's suppressed voice reaches her: "It was you who appealed to be touched throughout your entire body."[72] Yoko unconsciously yet compellingly invites others to touch her, involving bodily expressions rather than words.

In comparison to her relationship with Hanayo, Yoko's feeling toward Yuriko in "Vacation with a Slight Fever," compiled in *Natural Woman*, is based on an attraction that develops more as a kind of friendship. Yoko finds something sensually appreciable even in the noise Yuriko makes in eating, which Yoko wants to cherish. She doubts that she can keep hiding her liking for Yuriko from seeming to surge up to the surface of her skin. Eye contact with Yuriko makes her feel shy and she wants to direct her eyes away from her. Yuriko's question, "What's happened?" sounds to Yoko more like, "I am OK about sleeping with you" ["*Yattemo iiwayo*"], although Yoko does not actually feel like having a physical relationship with Yuriko.[73] Yoko cannot hide her intimate feelings for Hanayo, either. Initially, she is satisfied with the fact that Hanayo treats her better than her other female friends, and this gives her relationship to Hanayo an importance for her even though she also has a boyfriend. Feeling dissatisfied, yet not knowing what she actually wants, Yoko pursues Hanayo in the manner of obtaining from her a kiss, feeling her heart beat as she observes Hanayo's features in detail. Yoko's feelings for Hanayo are fully discernible to Keiko, who notices Yoko easily agitated by Hanayo, blushing or freezing at every

71. Matsuura, "Nachuraru Ūman," 185.
72. Matsuura, "Nachuraru Ūman," 198.
73. Matsuura, "Binetsu Kyūka" in *Nachuraru Ūman*, 84.

move. Without intending to, Yoko's intimate feelings for her beloved surge irresistibly onto and through her body.

In my chapter on the loved object in Kawabata, I argued for a reading based on object relations and even creation as if one shapes the object through a strong desire to reach it: one's self confirmation is also verified by the object one tries to reach. The object as well as the body are shaped by whatever is reached for in an attempted approach. As Sarah Ahmed puts it, the "surfaces of bodies are shaped by what is reachable."[74] The reachable object yet changes depending on how one approaches it, what one wants in it, and how one relates to it. By witnessing all and any details of the loved one, wishing to be in contact and desiring a further relationship with it, Yoko is silently expressing her wish. Such a feature is captured in Yoko's own account: "For some reason, if I desire to be touched by others, mostly I have them carried out as I wish. I don't intend to appeal through vocal requests or silent signals, but it seems to be transmitted through a certain ambiance [*kehai*]."[75] This awareness causes Yoko to feel uncomfortable as if she is somehow indecent about herself. Undefinable indications in the air around her (*kehai*), together with characters' gestures and poses, also conveys the not-(yet)-verbalized but desired.

The body, seen as having intentionality as the source of its movements, as in Merleau-Ponty, affects others, even in silence and without "conscious" actions. In a discussion of sexuality that moves in the direction of Freudian psychoanalysis, Merleau-Ponty writes, "Affectivity is usually conceived as a mosaic of affective states, self-contained pleasures and pains, which are not immediately understood and can only be explained through our bodily organization."[76] Here, Merleau-Ponty analyzes our "affective milieu," such as desire and love, to understand "how an object or a being begins to exist for us."[77] The way we relate to and experience the object with affectivity shapes how it exists for us. Writing against reintroducing the dichotomy of soul and body—for which Merleau-Ponty draws attention to how Freudianism contests it by explaining "the psychological meaning of the body"[78]—Merleau-Ponty puts it, "The body is enigmatic: a part of the

---

74. Ahmed, *Queer Phenomenology*, 55.
75. Matsuura, "Nachuraru Ūman," 121–122.
76. Merleau-Ponty, *Phenomenology of Perception*, 156–157.
77. Merleau-Ponty, *Phenomenology of Perception*, 156.
78. Merleau-Ponty, "Man and Adversity," in *The Merleau-Ponty Reader*, 193.

world certainly, but offered in a bizarre way, as its dwelling, to an absolute desire to draw near the other person and meet him in his body too, animated and animating, the natural face of the mind."[79] The desire of reaching displaces the body closer to the other as in whole-body touching, just like Yoko appears to be moving without noticing toward the loved object, with her body, as it were, taking her there. Without being conscious, the method of contacting the other affects how we conceive both ourselves and, indiscernibly, the other. Ahmed thus emphasizes the object relation instead of mere object choice, by saying, "the sex of one's object choice is not simply *about* the object even when desire is 'directed' toward that object: it affects what we can do, where we can go, how we are perceived."[80] By desiring the object, one shapes relationality to it, while shaping its ways of inhabiting space. Matsuura's language, acute to pre-verbal sensations that are yet to be fully recognized by characters, illuminates unnamed feeling as a bodily response that yet makes its own feeling be expressed.

Such silent expressions of intimate feelings are convoluted especially with the development of visual manga creations, allowing the depictions of same-sex relationship to appear in such venues as postwar popular culture, furthering the interwar same-sex intimacy among youth discussed in my chapter on Kawabata. Matsuura, exposed to manga since she was young, considers that girls' manga have functioned as a sort of emotional education (*kanjō kyōiku*) since the 1970s not as a resistance to the mainstream but naturally dealing with homosexuality.[81] This also overlaps with a time when, according to Bullock, "awareness of 'lesbianism' as a politicized sexual identity permeated mainstream Japanese consciousness."[82] While contemporary novels, manga, and popular culture brought the emergence of new types of language[83] arising from everyday life, they did so without

---

79. Merleau-Ponty, *The Merleau-Ponty Reader*, 193–194.
80. Amhed, *Queer Phenomenology*, 101.
81. Matsuura, "Intabyū Matsuura Rieko: Sekushuaritī no Jiko Jitsugen no tameni," 195.
82. Bullock, *The Other Women's Lib*, 129.
83. In reading Yoshimoto Banana (1964–), a contemporary of Matsuura's, John Whittier Treat discusses the break from earlier "pure" fiction, considered "intellectual," toward a fiction targeted at teenage woman and cohorts. Yoshimoto's writing speaks privately to a reader, a fellow girl, to the extent that sometimes her language is discussed to signal the emergence of new *genbun itchi*—the unification of the spoken and written that first occurred in the Meiji period—in the congruence of Yoshimoto's writing with the language

creating a neat category of type of sexuality. Matsuura, for example, read Yashiro Masako's manga *Shīkuretto Rabu* [*Secret Love*], published in 1970, in which the female protagonist Atsushi realizes her homosexual intimacy with her friend Fuyuko within a triangular relationship between herself, a male character Makio who likes Atsushi, and Fuyuko who likes Makio. In witnessing Fuyuko's suicide attempt, Atsushi regrets her own affection for Fuyuko, which she later recollects as "an episode created by reversing the dislike of the other gender by a freakish girl" ["*byōteki ni keppekina shōjo no isei wo imikirau kanjō ga uragaeshi nisarete tsukurareta episōdo*"], as Atsushi's first love.[84] While the motif of same-sex intimacy in Matsuura's stories has been adapted into manga and film more recently,[85] its theme has been expressed through a combined media since the 1970s. This intermediary form of expression, permeated in girls' culture both as creator and reader, made same-sex intimacy a part of their everyday consciousness, while at the same time shaping the language to express it.

In "Natural Woman," the relation to the loved object holds not just for the object choice or relationality, but also for gender performativity. Yoko describes herself: "being born as a woman at random and incidentally doing

---

of popular culture and the sensibility of contemporary everyday life that reflects it. John Whittier Treat, "Yoshimoto Banana Writes Home: Shojo Culture and the Nostalgic Subject," *Journal of Japanese Studies* 19: 2 (1993), 361. Futabatei Shimei's (1864–1910) novel *Ukigumo* [*Floating Clouds*], published in 1887, is known as the first modern Japanese work of fiction, written in *genbun itchi* style. The *genbun itchi* movement, which was promoted by Mozume Takami (1849–1928) for fiction writing, aimed at a greater ease of communication through a simplification of the written language, a choice of conjunctions and tenses, and the abandonment of regional boundaries for dialects. Yamada Bimyō (1868–1910) also wrote novels in the *genbun itchi* style, experimenting with colloquial language, metaphors, objective descriptions, pivot words (*kakekotoba*), and puns. Traditional and new writing styles co-existed for some years after the movement ended. Indeed, Karatani Kōjin writes of Mori Ōgai's 1890 *Maihime* that its use of old literary (*bungo*) style made it much more readily translatable into English. Karatani, *Origins of Modern Japanese Literature*, 50.
84. Yashiro Masako, "Shīkuretto Rabu," in *Yashiro Masako Meisaku Shirīzu 3 Shīkuretto Rabu* [*Selected Works of Yashiro Masako 3: Secret Love*] (Tokyo: Asahi Sonorama, 1978), 33. Originally published in 1970 in *Derakkusu Māgaret* [*Deluxe Magaret*] November issue.
85. Matsuura's *Nachuraru Ūman* was made into a film by Sasaki Hirohisa in 1994 and by Nomura Seiichi in 2010. "Kawaku Natsu," collected together with "Himantai Kyōfushō," was made into a manga in 2003 by Yamaii Ebine under the title "Yoru wo Koeru" ["Beyond the Night"].

a woman" ("*Tamatama onna ni umarete tsuideni onna wo yatteru dake*").[86] Hanayo, having sex with men even though she would not enjoy it, thinks that being a woman means that she has to play the part of being a woman; she realizes that she has sexual desire at all only after sleeping with Yoko, leading her to feel "reborn" as a woman. Hanayo, whose manga focuses on African-Americans around the time of the Emancipation Proclamation, refers to American singer-songwriter Aretha Franklin's 1967 song "(You Make Me Feel Like) A Natural Woman." She projects herself onto the woman in the lyrics, feeling like "having begun to live and become a natural woman only after I met you."[87] Here, encountering "you" and its otherness makes "me" realize the feeling of being a "natural" woman: the construction of the natural woman consisting of the recognition of and differentiation from the other. Judith Butler, on Franklin's contestation about the naturalization of gender, recognizes Franklin's "invocation of the defining Other,"[88] and notes, " 'Like a natural woman' is a phrase that suggests that 'naturalness' is only accomplished through analogy or metaphor. In other words, 'You make me feel like a metaphor of the natural,' and without 'you,' some denaturalized ground would be revealed."[89] Hanayo "becomes" a woman through her hugging and kissing with Yoko; naturalness is felt after being freed from her practice of a female role in a heterosexual relationship. This form of compulsive practices also appears in *The Most Beloved Child*, where Mashio finds it too uncomfortable to write an assigned composition, "What is Like the Perfect Female High School Student" ("*joshi kōkōsei rashisa toha nanika*").[90] Characters repeat, doubt, or resist the practices they are supposed to perform in society.

However, the reason that this relationship does not last long lies in the fact that Yoko, whom Hanayo has thought of as a lovable, passive, obedient boy-like object, leaves her sphere of control, and thus is no longer purely lovable: the perfect balance is always impermanent. Hanayo

---

86. Matsuura, "Nachuraru Ūman," 136.

87. Matsuura, "Nachuraru Ūman," 159. "(You Make Me Feel Like) A Natural Woman" is a single released by Aretha Franklin on the Atlantic label in 1967, lyrics co-written by Carole King and Gerry Goffin.

88. Judith Butler, *Gender Trouble: Feminism and the Subversion of Identity* (New York: Routledge, 2007 [1990]), 30.

89. Matsuura, "Nachuraru Ūman," 212.

90. Matsuura, *Saiai no Kodomo*, 8–9.

generally takes the lead in intimate interaction, though sometimes Yoko wants to lead herself; Hanayo finds this unconvincing, due to Yoko's boyish appearance and the undefined sexuality suggested by her behavior. While Hanayo tries to avoid performing roles that could give their relationship something of the character of house play (*mamagoto*), she is bothered by Yoko's naïveté and spontaneity, perhaps due to, as Yonaha Keiko points out, Yoko looking self-absorbed and heedless of responsibilities.[91] In the end, while Hanayo's recognition of herself as natural necessitates Yoko's in-betweenness, the "otherness" provided by Yoko attests to a limit to this; Yoko is freed from such thinking. Butler attributes some of the terror and anxiety of "becoming gay" to "the fear of losing one's place in gender or of not knowing who one will be if one sleeps with someone of the ostensibly 'same' gender."[92] While Hanayo recognizes herself as a woman through her homosexual relationship with Yoko, the latter is neither particularly bothered nor scared about not knowing who she is gender-wise: standing in-between boy and girl, and child and adult, with the appearance of an "apprentice boy" (*kozō*), described as looking like a child who has failed to return home at dusk, and is unable to find the appropriate gender to belong to.[93] What changes their skinship from a liberating sensual one into a repetitive violent one is Hanayo's ambivalent feeling toward Yoko's sexual in-between-ness, as well as her endless self-absorption and pleasure-seeking.

Yoko's free-floating sexuality and innocent attitude, freed from "how things should be" ('norms'), turns her, as Hanayo's love object, into a source of irritation and threats. Sianne Ngai, in her analysis of envy, problematizes the feminist psychoanalytic approach to envy itself, which "treats it [envy] as a term describing a *subject* who lacks, rather than the subject's affective *response* to a perceived inequality,"[94] thus overlooking the subject's relation to the external world. Instead of the subject lacking some feature, envy arises through a sequence, or relay, of interpersonal communication—how one responds to the call, and how then the other responds back, or how one talks to the other. Melanie Klein defines envy as "the angry

---

91. Yonaha, "Matsuura Rieko," 131. Ogura Chikako sees Matsuura's story as allowing her to enact a personal revenge against her female characters, including Hanayo, who believe themselves to be sensitive to others who seem less so (Ogura, "Neotenī no Fukushū," 98).

92. Butler, "Preface (1999)," *Gender Trouble*, xi.

93. Matsuura, "Nachuraru Ūman," 158.

94. Ngai, *Ugly Feelings*, 126.

feeling that another person possesses and enjoys something desirable—the envious impulse being to take it away or to spoil it,"[95] bound up with projection ultimately directed at the mother in an effort to destroy her creativity. With Hanayo and Yoko, it is more the "child" that Yoko partly is to Hanayo that is envied, in a way that extends beyond their respective sexualities to include their artistic creativity, with Hanayo envying Yoko for her uninhibited and unconventional approach to manga. In this sense, the emotional turmoil arising between them relates to Hanayo's response to Yoko's free-floating sexuality, in-between appearance, and innocence, connected to her creative attitudes. It is not that there is a stable lack; rather, the development of unfixed relationality between them creates a crack in which conflicting feelings emerge. The loved object/person, as much as one's body, is never fixed, as it appears different as the loving changes. The loved also transforms—such that interpersonal relationality is always on the move. One cannot hold the other as it is even if one can momentarily reach its existence. The moment of "perfect" contact that Yoko and Hanayo seem to have found—in their communication through the anus, excitement in fingering, and stimuli through the skin—does not stay as it is.

Envy, generally thought to be directed from one person to another, in Matsuura, also involves a third entity, especially when it develops into jealousy. When being beaten and receiving pain, Yoko feels a certain assurance that they love each other—until she finds a kiss mark on Hanayo's chest left by someone else. On seeing this, she simply asks, "Do you like that person?" Hanayo answers, "I think so. Should I choose?" "Does that person like you, too?" Hanayo answers, "It seems something like that was said."[96] At this point Yoko then hits herself in the forehead with her fist, trying not to burst into tears. Yoko's submissive and continual liking of Hanayo causes Hanayo to suffer from this very thing—being loved. Hanayo then turns away from this relationship for another in order to escape from the endless and extreme nature of this one, which makes Yoko suffer. Yonaha Keiko suggests that, unlike in a heterosexual relationship where pleasure often ends in the man's ejaculation, Hanayo comes to fear her female partner's endless pleasure-seeking, as if she were a slave serving another's pleasure,

---

95. Klein, "A Study of Envy and Gratitude" (1956), *SMK*, 212.
96. Matsuura, "Nachuraru Ūman," 183.

horrified by Yoko's endless needs.[97] The double suffering felt by both sides marks the termination of their relationship. In a sense, the mediation via a third person or third object (in the form of a slipper) becomes a necessary element, not to stimulate or heighten the desire for another as in Tanizaki and Yoshiyuki, but to terminate the endless love seeking.

Matsuura consistently revises fixed understanding of sexual norms, through which she also writes about the very nature of love. Towards the end of "Natural Woman," Hanayo can no longer totally love Yoko, and cannot be swayed even with the help of a third person, despite continuing to function as Yoko's primary love object. At the same time, Yoko comes to be perceived as threatening to Hanayo, as Yoko's naïveté unsettles Hanayo emotionally. The ashtray and the slipper afford them a means of communication and contact, yet also preserve a kind of distance. At this point the feelings arising from skin-to-skin interaction between the two are much more convoluted with love and hate, envy and jealousy, than with securing love, as if to suggest that it is still difficult to understand the other and settle down in any relationship. Moreover, the sense of intimacy in Matsuura, even when she writes of skinship as affective and caring, is not rooted in any sense of familial relationship. Yoshiyuki, in writing about various forms of sexual relationship that are seemingly anti-familial, is haunted by forms of sexuality that are tied to familial structures; as much as his male protagonists proceed in a kind of centrifugal movement away from the family, his female characters shy away from reproduction. The intimate relationships in Matsuura's writing, on the other hand, unsettle or replace the traditional sense of family, with her characters departing from it and thereby performing new roles often shaped not by a fixed element but by the set of unspoken and not-yet-articulated behaviors, feelings, and responses. This continuous unsettling makes her characters appear as individuals, untied and floating, in need of tethering but fearful of its constraints in continual search of relationality.

Renewing Relationality

Touch is an act of encountering various others and registering felt sensations. In Matsuura's fiction, the skin is a site through which one reveals

---

97. Yonaha, "Matsuura Rieko," 131.

oneself with no possibility of hiding behind or under it; in Yonaha's words, "omni-directional eros" (*zen hōi seiai*, for which Yonaha puts *kana* to read as "borderless sex")[98]—involving sensual excitations without reproductive functions. Although the idea of haptic enables sensations traveling beyond space restriction without creating sensory divisions, Matsuura brings the reader's attention yet again to the skin by way of widening the possibility of eroticism. The sensations are felt through the skin in the continuous process of building gestures, personality, and relationship: skin as a site of infinitely variable intimate, interpersonal, and erotic interactions.

Matsuura tries to overcome the gender binarism, by calling for an escape from or "undressing" of the sexual organ (*seiki wo nugu*) in a form of "gentle castration," and shifting the focus of pleasure from the genitals to the skin. When Matsuura uses the term "castration" (*kyosei*) in her essay in 1988, "Sekkusu Gyangu Chairudo no Uta" ["The Song of the Sex-Gang-Child"], collected as a part of "For a Gentle Castration," it is metaphorical; what she has in mind is a gentle form of castration aimed at the male organ as marker of sexual difference:

> Even in our castrated bodies, the genitals remain, but as mere organs. When they are at peace, they are not an obstruction. They have no particular value, they don't speak for anything, they aren't a symbol, and they suggest nothing. Perhaps they don't even show sexual difference. You and I stop using genitals as an "expression."
>
> You and I enjoy a pleasure that doesn't depend on genitals.
>
> We call it "sex-gang-child": sex that belongs to us.[99]

Matsuura aims to rid the (male) fantasy, meaning, and norms that she sees as based on the central role played by the genitals and tries to see the body free from societal expectations. As I have discussed elsewhere, this reminds us of the concept of the "Body without Organs," a body that is without judgment and values, a bare body that is free from the fantasy and

---

98. Yonaha, "Matsuura Rieko,"

99. Matsuura Rieko, "For a Gentle Castration," in *Woman Critiqued: Translated Essays on Japanese Women's Writing*, ed. Rebecca L. Copeland, and trans. Amanda Seaman (Honolulu: University of Hawai'i Press, 2006), 205. Matsuura, "Yasashii Kyosei no tameni," in *Yasashii Kyosei no tameni*, 261–262. The essay "The Song of the Sex-Gang-Child" was originally published in *GS* in September 1988.

meaning attached to the body. Deleuze and Guattari designate a body that is the site of an event as, coined with Antonin Artaud's term, the "Body without Organ," as "what remains when you take everything away,"[100] dismantling the phantasy prevalent in psychoanalysis, while being "a becoming, the opposite of a childhood memory."[101] When Artaud wrote in 1947 about his concept of the Body without Organs, he conceived it as a way for man to restore his liberty.[102] Matsuura's method to do so—for getting rid of the meaning attached to organs and "becoming" being (sexually) undefinable—seeks a development in the form of continued puberty.

In her essay on Genet in 1986, which is indeed titled, "Jean Genet, Seiki naki Nikutai" ["Jean Genet: the Body without Genitals"] Matsuura offers her accounts on Genet and her reading of Genet's sensual depictions to detail psychological progress arising from one's interactions with the object to yearn (*shibo no taishō*) rather than to detail sexual descriptions. Here, Matsuura recognizes orgasm in Genet as a sensation that does not necessarily converge on the genitals but rather that involves a "shivering of the senses" (*seiki ni shūren sarenai kannō no furue*).[103] Such attention crystallizes Matsuura's standpoint, neither to prioritize genitals over other parts of the body nor to divide bodily and psychological developments: physical sensuality and emotional sensuality thrive together.

Characters in Matsuura relate to others through what is felt with their body, through the skin, expanding the stimulation of instinct from the genitals to the skin. In her essay, "Bettina Rheims Toraburu" ["Bettina Rheims Trouble"], on Bettina Rheims's 2001 collection of nude photography, *FEMALE TROUBLE*, which avoids an obsessive focus on the genitals, Matsuura writes:

---

100. Deleuze and Guattari, *A Thousand Plateaus*, 151.

101. Deleuze and Guattari, *A Thousand Plateaus*, 164.

102. Artaud writes:

For you can tie me up if you wish,

but there is nothing more useless than an organ.

When you will have made him a body without organs,

then you will have delivered him from all his automatic reactions

and restored him to his true freedom.

Antonin Artaud, "To Have Done with the Judgement of God, a radio play," in *Antonin Artaud: Selected Writings*, trans. Helen Weaver, and ed. Susan Sontag (Berkeley and Los Angeles: University of California Press, 1988), 571.

103. Matsuura, "Jean Genet, Seiki naki Nikutai," in *Yasashii Kyosei no tameni*, 167. Originally published in *Stajio Boisu* [*Studio Voice*] in August 1986.

What is the thing omnipresent everywhere in the human's body here and there? The skin. What is the thing that exists on the border between the inside and outside of the body and that mingles with the air, and that becomes an outflow of sense of existence? The skin. The reason why Bettina Rheims, who tends to take pictures free from genital lust, reveals by preference her models' skin, is not for the purpose of stimulating the viewer's genital lust but probably because she wants to capture the sensuality of the skin.[104]

Any physiological change triggered by an emotional elevation can be erotic or sensual, including some of the physical and metaphysical sensations that Matsuura describes in her essay, "Seiki no nai Erosu" ["Eros without Genitals"] in 1986: the skin itching, the blood vessels tightening, wet hands pressing the heart, the feeling that the backs of eyeballs are being licked.[105] Air, wind, color, smell, and sound are presented as bearing haptic functions and fulfilling them, and Matsuura employs all senses. Matsuura's eroticism produces sensual conversations through hugging, holding hands, kissing, and other sorts of skin-to-skin relational acts: a non-genital eros. Matsuura describes such interactions as shifting from sexual love to "friendly love" [yūai], and a "deep interaction unmediated via sex."[106]

Skinship is not limited to childhood, but is extended throughout one's life—to the end of life, as indeed suggested by the old man's preoccupation with and need for touch in Kawabata's "House of the Sleeping Beauties." Early on in the postwar period, as Eguchi does and as protagonists in Yoshiyuki do, male characters escaped from public society to the private space with women. This retreat or wandering into private space has, as Noriko Mizuta in her discussion of Hayashi Fumiko's *Drifting Clouds* (1949–1950) suggests, gendered difference often involving "the rejection of a conventional marriage and an escape with men of their own

---

104. Matsuura, "Bettina Rheims Toraburu," in *Poketto Fetisshu*, 119–120.

105. Matsuura, "Seiki no nai Erosu," in *Yasashii Kyosei no tameni*, 79. "Seiki no nai Erosu" was originally published in *Shineasuto* in July 1986. This is similar to Freud's discussion of instinctual stimuli that arise from within the organism, not a strong light falling on the eye as an instinctual stimulus, but like a dried mucous membrane of the pharynx or a sense of irritation *making itself felt* in the stomach; Freud terms an instinctual stimulus as a "need." Freud, "Instincts and their Vicissitudes," 118–119.

106. Matsuura, "Seiai kara Yūai he—*Urabājon* wo megutte: Matsuura Rieko Interview," ["From Sexual Love to Friendship—On *Reverse Version:* Matsuura Rieko Interview"], *Bungakukai*, 54: 12 (2000): 256.

choosing": "A woman's wandering thus signified her separation from the culture's definition of 'woman'."[107] Matsuura demonstrates multifaceted nature of relationality, beyond normative or given gender roles. In Matsuura's *The Most Beloved Child*, the collective girl narrators create an imaginary fiction within the story: a first-person narrative by Mashio, in which she talks of Hinatsu patting her cheek lightly with her finger. This "sign of affection"—written as "sign of affection," the narrator referring to the English definition of "affection" (as love and gentle feeling, *aijō/yasashii omoi*, though rather more specific than "love," more like the feeling one might have toward a wife and child)—makes Mashio feel soft, comfortable, and shy.[108] This nameless shape of skinship, or indeed sign of affection, between high school girls replaces that of the real family, forming the home to turn to (yet again to leave eventually)—to the extent that it makes Itsuko, the real mother of her daughter Utsuho, feel jealous of Hinatsu. The affective interaction through the skin displaces the locus and widens the space where sensations are exchanged.

As discussed in this chapter, although the discussion of Matsuura's works tends to focus on her preoccupation with lesbianism, eroticism, and sexual acts, the "erotic" in her work in fact entails wider connotations than the sexual. Likewise, the extended idea of skinship brings a wider circuit to the relational construction through the skin that is focused on the infant–mother/parent dyad. It may also neutralize the infantilization of haptic experience in existing research. Especially in the context where there is a divide between socially accepted infant skinship, which normally ends by the time a child enters preschool,[109] and privately conducted sexual touch in adults as well as promiscuous public contact as in packed trains, feeling "sensual" may involve a variety of ways of being relational to others in time and space, through interaction, verbal communication, skinship, and thought.

Matsuura has consistently tried to write about sensuality through touch; touch as a way of interacting with the other as well as conceiving of the self. By shifting the sensual focus from the genitals to the skin, she

---

107. Noriko Mizuta, "In Search of a Lost Paradise: The Wandering Woman in Hayashi Fumiko's *Drifting Clouds*," in *The Woman's Hand: Gender and Theory in Japanese Women's Writing*, ed. Paul Gordon Schalow and Janet A. Walker (Stanford, CA: Stanford University Press, 1996), 332.

108. Matsuura, *Saiai no Kodomo*, 139–140.

109. Takie Lebra, *The Japanese Self in Cultural Logic* (Honolulu: University of Hawai'i Press, 2004), 75.

constructs characters who have a floating, undefinable sexuality, neither heterosexual, nor homosexual, nor, for that matter, simply and uncomplicatedly bisexual, who then become aware of their own sexuality, desires, and needs. Matsuura's writing effectively presents skin sensuality as a way of conveying sensualities and "touching" the reader, the writing itself forming a relationship through them as a matter of everyday practice. The moment of repudiation or negation of the mother, in repressing the mother's influence, shapes a new subject. It is such a negation of the primary otherness that allows skinship to be a continually self-reforming system beyond the mother in search of loving the other and loving the self. In this regard, touch not only affects the construction of self-awareness, but also gives rise to an affective language that lies partly in an interpersonal realm beyond the symbolic. The symbolic is not completely independent from the sensual, as touch can affect the formation of statements and their use in interactions with others. Touch is a form of bodily "doing," bringing various sensations and affects and raising one's awareness of the self and of the other, while shaping and reshaping relationality.

Touch is not only represented but is enacted in Matsuura's texts. Hasumi Shigehiko discusses the possibility of an *écriture* in Matsuura that does not let sex come into vision and that is not centered on the genitals: with something like kissing (*seppun-teki*) or "intercourse without the genitals" (*seikinaki seikō*).[110] Matsuura's language also evokes in readers sensations narrated in the story, in a manner that, in contrast with the distanced depictions of protagonists' felt sensations in Yoshiyuki, is inviting and seductive. Naitō Chizuko articulates, in her discussion of *Natural Woman*, the erotic/tactile aspects of the novel to verbalize what cannot be verbalized, thus tactility resisting any conclusion of meaning.[111] The fissure between the moment of sensing the other as well as the self and becoming aware of it through language with its pressure, texture, and temperature situates the reader in a given environment and shapes them as a subject. Skinship thrives in between the body and language, bringing preverbal bodily affects to relation-building, stimulating the emergence of linguistic expressions in capturing not-yet or never-completely verbalized expressions.

---

110. Hasumi, "Hajirai no Secushuaritī," 87.
111. Naitō Chizuko, *Shōsetsu no Ren'ai Kanshoku*, 22–23.

Conclusion

Touching through Language

I began my study on touch with questions regarding the unreachability in touching, or the unknowability of the other in touching. Despite the widely accepted practice of skinship in Japanese childhood, and indeed promiscuous contact in urban life, "touch" with the other beyond the context of childhood and family has been treated either as tenuous or extreme: literary descriptions of touch, such as kissing and hugging, are generally nuanced, leaving adolescent touch ample space to develop beyond the construct of the family. I have argued that touch, and the longings and fears that surround it, in writer, characters, and reader, and in the relationships between them, is a crucial concept to bear in mind when we engage with literature—and when we are talking about modern Japanese writing represented by the authors I discussed, perhaps, something to pay careful attention to, due to the strong social mores and inhibitions that surround touch in adult life. In particular, my readings have elucidated: heightened yearning for the loved object due to its unreachability; the subtle and incomplete forms of communication that possess haptic functions via distance, shadow, and light; membranes formed via past contact traces that mediate touch; and forms of skinship that replace familial relationships and regenerate lost or absent touch. Writers let their literary characters perform touch, with the fundamental contradiction that physical touch between authors, characters, and readers is unrealizable; sometimes, as we have seen, touch is barely possible even between characters in the texts. Writers write about touch because they cannot quite reach their yearned-for objects, including their literary characters; being a writer is solitary.

Touch as portrayed in these texts often communicates pre-verbal inter-personal/objectal affects; the characters do not utter, "I touch you," or "Please touch me," but their irresistible surging sensations mobilize the relationship, letting them move in such a way that they almost reach the other. Thus, the written, with its necessarily disembodied aspect, conveys imagination rather than actual touch. Layers of sensations, affects, and memories may not be quite recognized by literary characters but are present in the texts written by authors; the authors show phenomena that the characters themselves may not articulate into language. Touch regulates the reachability of the other, by reflexively raising the awareness of the self, such that it contributes to reconceiving the narrative "I" of the character who tries to reach the other and of the author who tries to reach his or her characters and readers.

As I have read touch in Japanese texts in dialogue with both phenom-enology and psychoanalysis in this book, these theoretical perspectives on touch do not necessarily need to be used to interpret the texts in cer-tain manners, almost as if this book was offering a psychoanalytical or phenomenological "reading" of the Japanese texts. Needless to say, I have not used these theoretical frameworks to subject Japanese texts to analyses and I have not necessarily treated these frameworks as exclusively Western; rather it is a continuous process to engage with them. Moreover, touch examined through certain perspectives presented by respective authors rather question such cultural categories, as well as theoretical categories. They do have respective processes of development, but they also engage with and inform one another to revise themselves. More precisely, how touch is examined through Japanese texts suggests in this book that pre-verbal elements written in the texts (lived by characters but not yet or not always verbally registered as such, but captured by the authors' language) illuminate the moment when embodied elements of touch (such as past traces and memories of touch) connect or react to new contact to be made through the body in language. This is precisely the intervention that lit-erary touch makes: to join the lived experiences with incoming unnamed sensations by negotiating with otherness and to bring this process of bodily knowing to some extent to verbal recognition. Once verbalized, these lived elements are, in a sense, disembodied. Yet, some disembodied parts could be revitalized by making new contact with others, through touch. These are the subtle but infinitely dynamic interactions that literary touch can achieve at the intersection of these theoretical perspectives through the continuous translation between the bodily experience and language, and this is the everyday practice of the body by way of language to mediate one's relationality to the other.

The depictions and imagination surrounding touch in literary texts expand our understanding of interpersonal communication related to touch. This includes the psychological turmoil that happens before the attempt to touch, the physiological responses occurring at the moment of contact and encounter with the other, layers of mediation relevant to touch, and gestures and responses. Touch is already mediated through the skin, an imaginary membrane, a page and language when written. In addition, the consciousness of the self itself is mediated by the consciousness of the others and culture, and by the translation between the conscious and the unconscious, and between language and the body. This means that the attempt to write about touch as well as to touch others is necessarily a process of attempting to relate to others, which then brings failure, realization, or collapse. In other words, touch, something that we usually assume to be a simple physical act, consists of a fragile combination of distance, time, pressure, feeling, among other elements. Although touch and contact have been often discussed via the lens of distance, I hope that my study has showed that touch is not a simple act of closing the distance, and is surrounded by a plethora of possible memories, fears, longings, and other kinds of feeling.

Touch in Kawabata's texts demonstrates his protagonists' psychological investments in "human" communication, with withdrawal from it, which yet affirms the otherness of the desired object which is shaped by this interaction even though it may stay unreachable. Tanizaki vitalizes touch through an incomplete reach: the characters in his stories are prevented from being able to touch the other fully, and are invited to interact with each other through alternative modes such as the combination of multiple senses and imagination. Yoshiyuki's autobiographical fiction presents a combination of the physiological and psychological effects at work on his characters when contact traces and imaginary membranes mediate touch between them. Yoshiyuki's descriptions of the skin, the body, and intimate relationships encourage us to reflect on how impossible it is to assume that we understand another. Finally, Matsuura, in boldly and freely depicting heterosexual, homosexual, and even interspecies tactile encounters marked by acute physicality, consciously writes against male-centred descriptions of intimate relationships. Such descriptions of touch not only challenge existing female–male/infant–mother power relationships, but also open the possibility for reconceiving relationality through the skin beyond the family construct by renewable skinship. It is therefore not that Japanese literature does not present touch, or literary characters do not touch others. The texts indeed demonstrate a breadth of tactile experiences ranging from deferred, mediated, or imagined touch, to touch that is wholly reconceived, by approaching while distancing with the loved objects. Indeed, the literary touch effectively translates what is embodied into language, which is now disembodied by being written, by revitalizing those disembodied affects via language. Literary touch itself is an attempt to touch something that is fundamentally difficult to reach.

This book has problematized the different meanings and categories of touch arising out of the transition from childhood to adults, the gap witnessed in Japanese culture wherein adolescents experience varied uncategorized modes of touch that fall in between homosocial, homosexual, and heterosexual, intimate friendship and romantic love. Despite the close (or potentially closed) tie between parents and children, in Japan parents and children often do not maintain the same sort of skinship throughout life. There is a transitional period from the familial skinship to the sexual skinship where intimate friendship marks a way to recognize one's sexuality and the sexual imagery of touch. The portrayals of touch in Kawabata's fiction are of a hesitant nature due to the protagonist's self-consciousness and excessive anxiety about disturbing the loved object's purity and virginity. Portrayals in Yoshiyuki that often sexually objectify the young female body including that of virginal girls represent middle-aged male perspectives, but his attentiveness to the senses simultaneously reflects the search for the body not as a knowable mass, but rather as something that is not-fully-knowable. This is related to characters' psychological and physiological effects responding to the elements external to their bodies, such as air, humidity, and ambience; this is a way beyond compensating the lack of his own skinship with the mother in childhood. Matsuura depicts various examples of skinship that provide an intimate, occasionally shy, experience of touch, one that does not rely on a dichotomy between sexual and non-sexual. Tanizaki, in contrast, continuously suspends complete touch (mostly but not solely heterosexual), through a particular duality or multiplicity of the senses. The examples provided by these writers demonstrate the intricacy of touch, with one sensory modality compensating for another, and one relation replaced by or generating another. While tactile communication seems to disappear in the adolescent transitional stage, (the desire for) it is precisely what these authors write about in their texts. Subjects in the texts construct, shape, and develop relationality to the other as well as to the self by touching others. Such an awareness keeps rising as new relationality emerges, so that the relationality through the skin is never fixed—it is rewritable.

This regenerative aspect of skinship features another set of interventions offered by my analyses of touch in modern and contemporary Japanese literature in conversation with phenomenology and psychoanalysis toward affect theory. As discussed in this book, the concept of skinship has been discussed in the anthropological and psychological or pediatric literature related to Japan, with a strong emphasis on childhood: skinship in the mother–child relationship. However, the literary texts I have examined in this book, on the one hand, tell us about skinship in a transitional state between childhood and adulthood as an undefinable relationality, having a sensual aspect and yet not exclusively being either sexual or non-sexual. On the other, they go beyond the views of skinship offered by the studies thus far that either identify the split between childhood and adulthood and recognize the disappearance of skinship in adolescents or attribute the lack or shortage of skinship, which is to be yearned for, as a cause of later psychological disorders. My analyses of literary touch have demonstrated the perspectives of skinship that are not chronologically defined modes of development or cause–effect relationships; touch does bridge and mediate these assumed gaps and bring them together in conversation. This book has offered the new aspect of skinship, or relationality through the skin, that extends throughout one's life as a bodily process of knowing the self as well as the other. Put in the context of literary texts, especially those of Yoshiyuki and Matsuura, we are shown that their characters might already be practicing the body as phenomenon in everyday life, even when the authors are not intending or registering as such.

In the relative absence of prevailing Christian practices in Japan, writers describe touching the invisible beyond the physical body, not through the presence of the absolute body as the source of love, care, and benediction. This excludes the war-time context where the national polity might have been considered as the absolute. But touch is conceived through the uncertainty of the other, via sensory perceptions. Such uncertainty regarding the tangible heightens the desire to reach it, which conversely shapes the otherness of the intended objects. My reading of these literary expressions suggests that, even in a moment in which such a desired object becomes available, one does not always reach it. It is as if the not-realizing might rather allow for an alternative way of grasping the other, and indeed of the self, suspending the direct "friction" involved in encountering that otherness, and intensifying the longing. In this sense, it is not that delayed, incomplete, or mediated touch are not effective: mediated touch might suspend the actual moment of completion, but those who are involved are nevertheless transformed, possibly more profoundly than if immediate touch had occurred. At the same time, it is clear that Matsuura makes intimacy especially among adolescents visible, without objectifying the girls, or without limiting the potentiality of touch to any categories. For this reason, relationality developed through the skin, or skinship, is interpersonal/objectual, intersensorial, and transitional. Touch written in the text furthermore makes characters' feelings visible, by translating and mobilizing the relationship between the embodied and disembodied.   —

In conclusion, contrary to the assumption that indirect modes of communication in Japan involve little touch, my reading of literary touch exhibits unbound bodily relations through touch. The emotional and bodily sensations arising from touch reshape the awareness of the body as well as of the self. Skinship is largely considered to be conducted in childhood, and to gradually disappear in adolescence, reappearing in adulthood, when touch becomes more sexual. This does not mean that Japanese literary characters do not touch others even in adolescence; but rather only that literary characters demonstrate a variety of touch and corresponding response throughout life. Yet, when they touch others in literary texts, they necessarily do so in variously mediated manners, between the touchable and the untouchable, the tangible and visible, and what can be verbalized and not. Under these circumstances, touch may not necessarily engage with the full body; in Kawabata's fiction, it might be through one arm or with a body that sleeps. The repressed desire for touch results in detailed observations of the loved object as if narrators' language and characters' gaze touch and caress the other. In this sense, overt descriptions of touch and sexuality do not necessarily possess any more impact or profundity than those that are subtle and marked by hesitation and repression. Repressed desire may exhibit a greater richness of tactile sensibility due to its inability to complete. A desired object is seductive due to its unreachability, almost touchable but never fully reachable, thereby creating a dynamic potentiality that involves the possibility of reaching the intended. Characters' desire for touching the loved object is represented via repression or withdrawal not only of gesture but also of the written. The writers and subsequently the readers attend to and gradually discover what touch is, although the gap between the felt and the written also underlines the always-only-partial understanding of what the body really tells. The body necessarily engages with whatever elements surround it and press on it, which include moisture, pressure, and temperature.

This study of touch shows that writers I examined do not simply suppose that one can touch and reach others. Their extensive and detailed attention to the moments before, during, and after touch is rather ethical in that they do not assume that their characters are entitled to be able to touch others in the first instance; they are also aware of the risky encounter with the other through touch that may threaten their (characters') comfortable degree of distance from the other. Touch, even motherly touch, is not always safe: it does not always only offer warmth and comfort. Rather, touch is a site of encounter that allows those who come into contact with an other to push, to give, and to pull, with friction. William Haver writes of the (fatally) erotic relation: "The incorporation of the radically other becomes the very mortality of the proper identity of the self: the other *is* my finitude."[1] Through touch and encounter with the other, one comes to reflexively find and reform the self. In this sense, it could be said that in their preoccupation with touch the writers respect the otherness of others. The realization that one barely or hardly ever reaches the other itself means that one recognizes the otherness of the other to a large extent. At the same time, the simple conduction of touch is not the only way to reach the other and accept otherness; touch can be conducted in innumerable ways. And writing about touch is also one way to reach the intended other.

Can we touch the other, or do we reach something else by touching it? One may reach others, but the process of touch is more complex than it appears, involving layers of mediation and affect. It often happens that

---

1. Haver, *The Body of This Death*, 12.

the protagonist attends to another thing or another figure, one that exists beyond the here and now, by touching the other's body; touch necessarily invites others that are not physically there, including those of past contact traces or memories, and those of future contact in a form of projection. Touch has been much more philosophically addressed in France, but literature is an effective, or possibly the most productive, venue for exploring touch at least in the Japanese context, as literary texts depict what the characters may be concerned with but may not necessarily say out loud. Such a moment of capturing the gap between the felt and the said—the interaction between the body and language—can be effectively analyzed only by paying attention to layers of verbalization, or indeed translation, by characters' utterances, authors' depictions, and readers' interpretations. As touch affects the awareness of the self, it is a bodily way to reconceive and constantly reshape the self as well as the other—and, when it is written about, it provides a way to know what one might have physically recognized but might not have yet linguistically registered.

The modes of touch described in the texts that I have discussed in this book extend their forces to contact the readers. As the characters in the text are "touched," we are touched through the act of reading the sensibility behind variously convoluted moments of attempted touch in texts. Moreover, in the same way as Tanizaki elucidates how imagination fills the gap of what is visible and invisible, reachable and unreachable, or visible and tangible, aesthetically and literally, language not only marks the absence, but also prompts the imaginative use of absence. Patrick C. Hogan writes that because the human mind is "modular" and organized into numerous systems, the collection of memories is continuously altered, the personal memories of the readers contributing to the imagination of the literary work. "Fragmentary memories complete or fill in our imagination of a work and simultaneously give rise to our emotional response … our imagination of these literary events incorporates elements from the actual, biographical source of our emotions."[2] In reading gaps, the readers supply their own memories in the act of reading. The texts convey sensations of characters, or of authors represented through characters, complemented by the readers.

---

2. Patrick Colm Hogan, *Cognitive Science, Literature, and the Arts: A Guide for Humanists* (Routledge: London and New York, 2003), 162.

Barthes writes, "A certain pleasure is derived from a way of imagining oneself as *individual*, of inventing a final, rarest fiction: the fictive identity."[3] As much as the fictive texts themselves are interwoven beyond the texts themselves through narrative, interpretation, and readers' responses, fictive touch is also invitational. The way in which characters sense, embody, or imagine touch is depicted by authors, and readers work with and act upon such written sensations. Touch written in the texts is not merely represented, but evokes responses in readers—concern, disgust, pleasure, surprise, among other feelings. Even in its suspension and deferral, the act of reading touch in texts is for the reader an attempt to reach the unreachable (characters, experiences, and sensations within the texts), in correlation to the extent that characters try to reach their intended objects, and the extent that writers try not to depict but to bring about sensations in us. This is performative: affecting others as well as the self and forming a dynamic relationality between them through "doing," at the moment of touching the unreachable. Writing and reading sensations—or, more precisely, trying to reach the intended no matter how far and how difficult this may be—is precisely what touch is about; that is, touching the not always fully reachable or not readily available. Yet, that attempt, even if imaginary, consists of the body, continuously translating the embodied and disembodied while reforming the awareness of those who are in contact. The reader is ceaselessly attempting to reach the writer's meaning and, in that process, ceaselessly re-emerging through this attempt to touch through language. The body emerges through that attempt at touching.

---

3. Barthes, *The Pleasure of the Texts*, 62.

Bibliography

Ahmed, Sara. *Queer Phenomenology: Orientations, Objects, Others.* Durham, NC and London: Duke University Press, 2006.

Akari, Chiaki. "Kyū Dōtoku wo koete: 'Kagi' no Konnichi sei." In *Tanizaki Ju'ichirō: Kyōkai wo koete.* Edited by Chiba Shunji and Anne-Bayard Sakai, 55–72. Tokyo: Kasama Shoin, 2009.

Akutagawa, Ryūnosuke. "Bungeiteki na, Amarini Bungeiteki na." In *Akutagawa Ryūnosuke Zenshū.* Vol. 9, 3–80. Tokyo: Iwanami Shoten, 1978.

Akutagawa, Ryūnosuke. "The Faint Smiles of the Gods." Translated by Tomoyoshi Genkawa and Bernard Susser. In *The Essential Akutagawa: Rashomon, Hell Screen, Cogwheels, A Fool's Life and Other Short Fiction.* Edited by Seiji Lippit, 115–128. New York: Marsilio, 1999.

Alexy, Allison. "Introduction: The Stakes of Intimacy in Contemporary Japan." In *Intimate Japan: Ethnographies of Closeness and Conflict.* Edited by Allison Alexy and Emma E. Cook, 1–34. Honolulu: University of Hawai'i Press, 2019.

Allison, Anne. *Nightwork: Sexuality, Pleasure, and Corporate Masculinity in a Tokyo Hostess Club.* Chicago, IL & London: University of Chicago Press, 1994.

Allison, Anne. *Permitted and Prohibited Desires: Mothers, Comics, and Censorship in Japan.* Boulder, CO: Westview Press, 1996.

Angles, Jeffrey. "Translator's Introduction." In *Killing Kanoko / Wild Grass on the Riverbank* by Itō Hiromi. Translated by Jeffrey Angles, 3–18. Sheffield: Tilted Axis Press, 2020.

Angles, Jeffrey. *Writing the Love of Boys: Origins of Bishonen Culture in Modernist Japanese Literature.* Minneapolis: University of Minnesota Press, 2011.

Anzieu, Didier. *The Skin-Ego.* Translated by Naomi Segal. London: Karnac, 2016.

Artaud, Antonin. "To Have Done with the Judgement of God, a radio play." In *Antonin Artaud: Selected Writings.* Edited by Susan Sontag. Translated by Helen Weaver, 555–571. Berkeley and Los Angeles: University of California Press, 1988.

Austin, J. L. *How to Do Things with Words.* Cambridge, MA: Harvard University Press, 1975.

Ayame, Hiroharu. *Hankotsu to Henkaku: Nihon Kindai Bungaku to Josei, Oi, Kakusa.* Tokyo: Ochanomizu Shobō, 2012.

Bal, Mieke. *Quoting Caravaggio: Contemporary Arts, Preposterous History*. Chicago, IL and London: The University of Chicago Press, 1999.

Balint, Michael. *Primary Love, Psycho-analytic Technique*. London: Hogarth Press, 1952.

Barthes, Roland. *Camera Lucida: Reflections on Photography*. Translated by Richard Howard. New York: Hill and Wang, 1981.

Barthes, Roland. *Image Music Text*. Translated by Stephen Heath. London: Fontana Press, 1977.

Barthes, Roland. *The Neutral: Lecture Course at the Collège de France (1977–1978)*. Translated by Rosalind E. Krauss and Denis Hollier, text established, annotated, presented by Thomas Clerc, directed by Eric Marty. New York: Columbia University Press, 2005.

Barthes, Roland. *The Pleasure of the Text*. Translated by Richard Miller. New York: Hill and Wang, 1975.

Bataille, Georges. *Eroticism: Death and Sensuality*. Translated by Mary Dalwood. San Francisco, CA: City Lights Books, 1986.

Baxandall, Michael. *Shadows and Enlightenment*. New Haven, NJ and London: Yale University Press, 1997.

Ben-Ari, Eyal. *Body Projects in Japanese Childcare: Culture, Organization and Emotions in a Preschool*. Richmond: Curzon Press, 1997.

Benjamin, Walter. *Illuminations*. Edited by Hannah Arendt. Translated by Harry Zohn. London: Jonathan Cape, 1970.

Bersani, Leo. "The Power of Evil and the Power of Love." In *Intimacies* by Leo Bersani and Adam Phillips, 57–87. Chicago, IL: The University of Chicago Press, 2008.

Bigō Gashū. Commented by Sakai Tadayasu. Tokyo: Iwasaki Bijyutsusha, 1982 [1973].

Bion, Wilfred Ruprecht. *Experiences in Groups and Other Papers*. London: Routledge, 1989.

Bourdaghs, Michael K. *The Dawn that Never Comes: Shimazaki Tōson and Japanese Nationalism*. New York: Columbia University Press, 2003.

Bourdaghs, Michael K. "Editor's Introduction: Buried Modernities—The Phenomenological Criticism of Kamei Hideo." In *Transformations of Sensibility: The Phenomenology of Meiji Literature*. Translation edited by Michael Bourdaghs, vii–xxviii. Ann Arbor: Center for Japanese Studies, the University of Michigan, 2002.

Bowen-Struyk, Heather. "Sexing Class: 'The Prostitute' in Japanese Proletarian Literature." In *Gender and Labour in Korea and Japan: Sexing Class*. Edited by Ruth Barraclough and Elyssa Faison, 10–26. Abingdon: Routledge, 2009.

Brinton, Mary C. *Women and the Economic Miracle: Gender and Work in Postwar Japan*. Berkeley: University of California Press, 1993.

Bullock, Julia C. *The Other Women's Lib: Gender and Body in Japanese Women's Fiction*. Honolulu: University of Hawai'i Press, 2010.

Butler, Judith. *Gender Trouble: Feminism and the Subversion of Identity*. New York: Routledge, 2007.

Chiba, Shunji. "Fukusei Gijyutsu no Jidai ni okeru 'In'ei Raisan'." In *Tanizaki Jun'ichirō: Kyōkai wo koete*, 7–25.

Chiba, Shunji. *Tanizaki Jun'ichirō: Kitsune to Mazohizumu*. Tokyo: Ozawa Shoten, 1994.

Cixous, Hélène. "Difficult Joys." In *The Body and the Text: Hélène Cixous, Reading and Teaching*. Edited by Helen Wilcox, Keith McWatters, Ann Thompson and Linda R. Williams, 5–30. New York: St Martin's Press, 1990.

Cixous, Hélène. "Grace and Innocence: Heinrich von Kleist." In *Readings: The Poetics of Blanchot, Joyce, Kafka, Kleist, Lispector, and Tsvetayeva*. Edited and translated by Verena A. Conley, 28–73. Minneapolis, University of Minnesota Press, 1991 [1984].

Classen, Constance, ed. *The Book of Touch*. Oxford; New York: Berg, 2005.

Connor, Steven. *The Book of Skin*. London: Reaktion Books, 2004.

Cornyetz, Nina. *The Ethics of Aesthetics in Japanese Cinema and Literature: Polygraphic Desire*. Abingdon; New York: Routledge, 2007.

Crary, Jonathan. "Modernizing Vision." In *Vision and Visuality*. Edited by Hal Foster, 29–44. New York: New Press, 1999.

Crowley, Martin. "Contact!." *L'Esprit Créateur* 47: 3 (2007): 1–6. http://doi.org/10.1353/esp.2007.0053.

Csordas, T. J. "Introduction." In *Embodiment and Experience: The Existential Ground of Culture and Self*. Edited by T. J. Csordas, 1–24. Cambridge: Cambridge University Press, 1994.

Deleuze, Gilles. *Cinema 1: The Movement-Image*. Translated by Hugh Tomlinson and Barbara Habberjam. Minneapolis: University of Minnesota Press, 2013.

Deleuze, Gilles. "Coldness and Cruelty." In *Masochism*, 9–138. Translated by Jean McNeil. New York: Zone Books, 1991.

Deleuze, Gilles, and Felix Guattari. *A Thousand Plateaus: Capitalism and Schizophrenia*. Translated by Brian Massumi. Minneapolis: University of Minnesota Press, 1987.

Derrida, Jacques. "Aletheia." Translated by Pleshette De Armitt and Kas Saghafi. *The Oxford Literary Review* 32: 2 (2010): 169–188. https://www.jstor.org/stable/44030777.

Derrida, Jacques. *On Touching—Jean-Luc Nancy*. Translated by Christine Irizarry. Stanford, CA: Stanford University Press, 2005.

Dodd, Stephen. "History in the Making: The Negotiation of History and Fiction in Tanizaki Jun'ichirō's 'Shunkinshō." *Japan Review* 24 (2012): 151–168. https://www.jstor.org/stable/41592692.

Dodd, Stephen. "An Outstanding Storyteller." In *Shunkin* performance catalogue, 10–11. London: The Barbican, 2010.

Doi, Takeo. *Amae no Kōzō*. Tokyo: Kōbundō, 2007.

Dollase, Hiromi Tsuchiya. "Mad Girls in the Attic: Louisa May Alcott, Yoshiya Nobuko, and the Development of *Shōjo* Culture." PhD Diss., Purdue University (2003).

Eco, Umberto. *On Beauty*. Translated by Alastair MacEwen. London: Secker & Warburg, 2004.

Edogawa, Rampo. "The Horrors of Film." In *The Edogawa Rampo Reader*. Edited and translated by Seth Jacobowitz, 137–142. Fukuoka: Kurodahan Press, 2008.

Etō, Jun. *Seijuku to Sōshitsu: Haha no Hōkai*. Tokyo: Kōdansha, 1993.

Fairbairn, W. R. D. *Psychoanalytic Studies of the Personality*. London: Routledge, 2001.

Felman, Shoshana. *The Scandal of the Speaking Body: Don Juan with J. L. Austin, or Seduction in Two Languages*. Translated by Catherine Porter. Stanford, CA: Stanford University Press, 2003.

Ferenczi, Sándor. *Final Contributions to the Problems and Methods of Psycho-analysis.* Edited by Michael Balint. Translated by Eric Mosbacher et al. New York: Brunner/Mazel, 1980.

Ferenczi, Sándor. *First Contributions to Psycho-analysis.* Translated by Ernest Jones. London and New York: Karnac, 1994.

Ferguson, Harvie. *Modernity and Subjectivity: Body, Soul, Spirit.* Charlottesville: University Press of Virginia, 2000.

Field, Tiffany. *Touch.* Cambridge, MA: MIT Press, 2001.

Freud, Sigmund. "The Economic Problem of Masochism." In *The Standard Edition of the Complete Psychological Works of Sigmund Freud* [*SE*]. Translated by James Strachey, Anna Freud, Alix Strachey and Alan Tyson. Vol. 19, 159–170. London: Hogarth Press, 1964.

Freud, Sigmund. "Fetishism." In *SE.* Vol. 21, 152–157. London: the Hogarth Press, 1961.

Freud, Sigmund. "Instincts and their Vicissitudes." In *SE.* Vol. 14, 117–140. London: Hogarth Press, 1962 [1957].

Freud, Sigmund. "A Note upon the 'Mystic Writing-Pad'." *SE.* Vol. 19, 227–232. London: Hogarth Press, 1964

Freud, Sigmund. "The Psychogenesis of a Case of Homosexuality in a Woman." In *SE.* Vol. 18, 147–172. London: Hogarth Press, 1955.

Freud, Sigmund. "Resistance and Repression." In *SE.* Vol. 16, 286–302. London: Hogarth Press, 1964.

Freud, Sigmund. "Studies on Hysteria." *SE.* Vol. 2. London: Hogarth Press, 1962.

Frühstück, Sabine. "Male Anxieties: Nerve Force, Nation, and the Power of Sexual Knowledge." *Journal of the Royal Asiatic Society of Great Britain & Ireland* 15: 1 (April 2005): 71–88. http://doi.org/10.1017/S1356186304004717.

Fujii, Takashi. "'Dokushin-sha no Kikai' to 'Ikei no Shintai' Hyōshō: 'Tanin no Kao,' 'Kataude,' 'Ningyō zuka' no Dōjidai sei." *Nihon Kindai Bungaku* 91 (2014): 95–110. https://doi.org/10.19018/nihonkindaibungaku.91.0_95.

Fukuda, Junko. "Kawabata Yasunari to Shōsetsu 'Nemureru Bijo'." In performance program *Opera Nemureru Bijo.* Tokyo: Tokyo Bunka Kaikan, 2016.

Funabashi, Seiichi. "Gamō." In *Funabashi Seiichi Senshū.* Vol. 2, 231–277. Tokyo: Shinchōsha, 1969.

Gessel van, C. *Three Modern Novelists: Sōseki, Tanizaki, Kawabata.* Tokyo: Kōdansha International, 1993.

Green, André. "To Love or Not to Love: Eros and Eris." In André Green and Gregorio Kohon. *Love and its Vicissitudes,* 1–39. London and New York: Routledge, 2005.

Green, André. "The Intuition of the Negative in *Playing and Reality*." In *The Dead Mother: The Work of André Green.* Edited by Gregorio Kohon, 205–221. London: Routledge, 2005 [1999].

Green, André. *On Private Madness.* London and New York: Karnac, 2005.

Grosz, Elizabeth. *Volatile Bodies: Toward a Corporeal Feminism.* Bloomington: Indiana University Press, 1994.

Hall, Edward T. *The Silent Language.* New York: Doubleday & Company, 1959.

Harootunian, Harry. "Japan's Postwar and After, 1945–1989: An Overview." *From Postwar to Postmodern: Art in Japan 1945–1989.* Edited by Doryun Chong,

Michio Hayashi, Kenji Kajiya, and Fumihiko Sumitomo, 17–21. New York: The Museum of Modern Art, 2012.

Hartley, Barbara. "The Ambivalent Object of Desire: Contesting Gender Hegemonies in Kawabata Yasunari's Shônen." *Asian Studies Review* 30: 2 (2006): 123–140. https://doi.org/10.1080/10357820600714223.

Hasegawa, Kei. "Feminizumu/Jendā Hihyō de Yomu <Kazoku> Hyōshō—Nihon no Kingendai Bungaku, Media ni Miru Kindai Kazoku no Hensen to Gendai Kazoku." *Jōsai Tanki Daigaku Kiyō* 29: 1 (2012): 1–9.

Hasegawa, Kei. "Sekushuaritī Hyōgen no Kaika—Feminizumu no jidai to Mori Yoko, Tsushima Yuko, Yamada Eimi." In *Ribu toiu Kakumei: Kindai no Yami wo Hiraku, Bungaku shi wo Yomikaeru*. Vol. 7. Edited by Kanō Mikiyo, 102–118. Tokyo: Impact Shuppankai, 2003.

Hashizume, Keiko. "Shokkaku wo Chūshin toshita Bachelard Shintai ron heno Ichi shiza: Busshitsu teki Sōzōryoku wo chūshin ni." *Bigaku Geijutsugaku Kenkyū* 31 (2012): 41–67.

Hasumi, Shigehiko, "[Shōtokushū Intabyū] Hajirai no Secushuaritī." *Bungei* 32: 4 (1993): 77–91.

Hasumi, Shigehiko, "Toritomenonai Namamekashisa ni tsuite: Matsuura Rieko, 'Saiai no Kodomo'." *Bungakukai* 71: 6 (2017): 164–173.

Hatashita, Kazuo. "Sakka ron kara no Rinshō Shindan: Yoshiyuki Junnosuke." *Kokubungaku: Kaishaku to Kanshō* 39: 14 (1974): 134–135.

Haver, William. *The Body of This Death: Historicity and Sociality in the Time of AIDS.* Stanford, CA: Stanford University Press, 1996.

Higashi, Masao. "Kaisetsu: Shinrei to Seiai to." In *Bungō Kaidan Kessaku Sen, Kawabata Yasunari Shū: Kataude.* Edited by Higashi Masao, 369–380. Tokyo: Chikuma Shobō, 2006.

Hijiya-Kirschnereit, Irmela. "Body and Experiment—Reflecting Kawabata Yasunari's Counter-aesthetics." *Japan Forum* 30: 1 (2018): 42–59. https://doi.org/10.1080/09555803.2017.1307250.

Hillenbrand, Margaret. *Literature, Modernity, and the Practice of Resistance: Japanese and Taiwanese Fiction, 1960–1990.* Leiden and Boston, MA: Brill, 2007.

Hirai, Nobuyoshi. *Sukinshippu de Kokoro ga Sodatsu.* Tokyo: Kikakushitsu, 1999.

Hirai, Nobuyoshi. *Ushinawareta Boseiai: Kosodate wo Tanoshimu tame ni.* Nagoya: Reimei Shobō, 1981.

Hirata, Hosea. *Discourses of Seduction: History, Evil, Desire, and Modern Japanese Literature.* Cambridge, MA: Harvard University Press, 2005.

Hobson, John Allan. *Dreaming: An Introduction to the Science of Sleep.* Oxford and New York: Oxford University Press, 2002.

Hogan, Patrick Colm. *Cognitive Science, Literature, and the Arts: A Guide for Humanists.* Routledge: London and New York, 2003.

Ichikawa, Hiroshi. *Mi no Kōzō.* Tokyo: Kōdansha, 2007.

Ichimura, Takako. "Judith Butler to Matsuura Rieko: Shisen no Kōsa." *Artes Liberales* 66 (2000): 23–37.

Igarashi, Yoshikuni. *Bodies of Memory: Narratives of War in Postwar Japanese Culture, 1945–1970.* Princeton, NJ: Princeton University Press, 2000.

Iida, Yuko. *Kanojo tachi no Bungaku: Katarinikusa to Yomareru koto*. Nagoya: Nagoya Daigaku Shuppankai, 2016.

Ikezawa, Natsuki. "Yoshiyuki Junnosuke wo Yomu: 'Suna no Ue no Shokubutsu gun' to Seiteki Jikken." In *YJZ*. Vol. 6, 448–457. Tokyo: Shinchōsha, 1998.

Ikoma, Natsumi. *Yokubō suru Bungaku: Odoru Kyōjo de Yomitoku Nichiei Gendā Hihyō*. Tokyo: Eihōsha, 2007.

Innami, Fusako. "Co-sleeping: Engaging with the Commodified Dozing Body in Kawabata, Yoshimoto, and Yamazaki." *Contemporary Japan* 27: 1 (2015): 33–52. https://doi.org/10.1515/cj-2015-0003.

Innami, Fusako. "Gendered High and Low Culture in Japan: The Transgressing Flesh in Kawabata's Dance Writing." In *The Routledge Companion to Gender and Japanese Culture*. Edited by Jennifer Coates, Lucy Fraser, and Mark Pendleton, 373–381. Abingdon; New York: 2020.

Innami, Fusako. "The Touchable and the Untouchable: An Investigation of Touch in Modern Japanese Literature." PhD diss., University of Oxford, 2014.

Irigaray, Luce. *An Ethics of Sexual Difference*. Translated by Carolyn Burke and Gillian C. Gill. London: Continuum, 2004.

Irigaray, Luce. "Perhaps Cultivating Touch Can Still Save Us." *SubStance* 40: 3 (2011): 130–140. https://doi.org/10.1353/sub.2011.0035.

Isoda, Kōichi. *Sajō no Kyōen*. Tokyo: Shinchōsha, 1972.

Itō, Hiromi. *Teritori-ron I*. Tokyo: Shichōsha, 1987.

Itō, Hiromi. *Teritori-ron II*. Tokyo: Shichōsha, 1985.

Itō, Hiromi. *Yoi Oppai Warui Oppai*. Tokyo: Tōjusha, 1985.

Izumi, Keishun. "'Kako no Otoko' no Konseki wo Aibu suru Watashi: Yoshiyuki Junnosuke 'Chōjūchūgyo' ron." *Rikkyō Daigaku Nihon Bungaku* 116 (2016): 66–79.

Izutani, Shun. "Hōi sareru/Shōtotsu suru Josei Dōseiai—Matsuura Rieko 'Nachuraru Ūman' ni okeru Yokubō to Kankeisei." *Ronkyū Nihon Bungaku* 99 (2013): 37–52.

Izutani, Shun. "Jikai suru Teikoku, Sekai ni Nosabaru Shintai: Matsuura Rieko, 'Himantai Kyōfushō' ron." *Ritsumeikan Bungaku* 652 (2017), 106–118.

Jolivet, Muriel. *Japan: The Childless Society? The Crisis of Motherhood*. London: Routledge, 1997.

Kamei, Hideo. "Shintai ron teki ni mita Tanizaki Jun'ichirō: Nyotai to Meikyū." *Kokubungaku: Kaishaku to Kyōzai no Kenkyū* 30: 9 (1985): 36–42.

Karatani, Kōjin. *Nihon Seishinbunseki*. Tokyo: Bungei Shunjyū, 2002.

Karatani, Kōjin. *Origins of Modern Japanese Literature*. Translation edited by Brett de Bary. Durham, NC and London: Duke University Press, 1998.

Kawabata, Kaori. "Kaisetsu: Kawabata Yasunari to Shōjo Shōsetsu." In *Shin'yū*. Edited by Yasunari Kawabata, 242–245. Tokyo: Shōgakukan, 2015.

Kawabata, Kaori. "Sekaiteki Kanten kara Kawabata Yasunari wo Miru." *Kokubungaku* 46: 4 (March 2001): 20–24.

Kawabata, Yasunari. "House of the Sleeping Beauties." In *House of the Sleeping Beauties and Other Stories* [*HSB*]. Translated by Edward Seidensticker, 13–99. Tokyo: Kōdansha International, 2004.

Kawabata, Yasunari. "Kataude." In *Kawabata Yasunari Zenshū* [*KYZ*]. Vol. 8, 545–573. Tokyo: Shinchōsha, 1981.

Kawabata, Yasunari. "Koji no Kanjō." In *KYZ*. Vol. 2, 153–172. Tokyo: Shinchōsha, 1980.

Kawabata, Yasunari. "Nemureru Bijo." In *KYZ*. Vol. 18, 133–228. Tokyo: Shinchōsha, 1980.

Kawabata, Yasunari. "One Arm." In *HSB*. Translated by Edward Seidensticker, 103–124. Tokyo: Kōdansha International, 2004.

Kawabata, Yasunari. "Otome no Minato." In *KYZ*. Vol. 20, 7–183. Tokyo: Shinchōsha, 1981.

Kawabata, Yasunari. "Shinshin Sakka no Shinkeikō Kaisetsu." In *KYZ*. Vol. 30, 172–183. Tokyo: Shinchōsha, 1982.

Kawabata, Yasunari. *Shin'yū*. Tokyo: Shōgakukan, 2015.

Kawabata, Yasunari. "Shōnen." In *KYZ*. Vol. 10, 141–255. Tokyo: Shinchōsha, 1980.

Kawabata, Yasunari. *Snow Country*. Translated by Edward G. Seidensticker. London: Penguin Books, 2011.

Kawabata, Yasunari. "Sobo." In *KYZ*. Vol. 2, 437–444.

Kawabata, Yasunari. "Thousand Cranes." In *Snow Country and Thousand Cranes*. Translated by Edward G. Seidensticker, 115–204. London: Penguin Books, 1986.

Kawabata, Yasunari. "Yama no Oto." In *KYZ*. Vol. 12, 241–541. Tokyo: Shinchōsha, 1980.

Kawabata, Yasunari. "Yūgeshiki no Kagami." In "Yukiguni (pure-orijinaru)." In *KYZ*. Vol. 24, 73–86. Tokyo: Shinchōsha, 1982.

Kawabata, Yasunari. "Yukiguni." In *KYZ*. Vol. 10, 7–140.

Kawamoto, Saburō. "'Ren'ai Shōsetsu' no Fukanōsei: Yoshiyuki Junnosuke, Yūgure made." *Kaie* (November 1978): 15–23.

Kawamura, Jirō. "'Anshitsu' ni tsuite." In *Yoshiyuki Junnosuke no Kenkyū*. Edited by Yamamoto Yōrō, 38–46. Tokyo: Jitsugyō no Nihonsha, 1979.

Kawamura, Jirō. *Kankaku no Kagami: Yoshiyuki Junnosuke ron*. Tokyo: Kōdansha, 1979.

Kawamura, Jirō, Takahashi, Takako, and Ōhashi Kenzaburō. "Dai 37 kai Sōsaku Gappyō." *Gunzō* 34: 1 (1979): 337–356.

Kawashima, Itaru. "Sei no Genfūkei." In *Yoshiyuki Junnosuke no Kenkyū*, 98–109.

Kimura, Bin. *Bunretsubyō to Tasha*. Tokyo: Chikuma Shobō, 2007.

Kishimoto, Sachiko. "*Hen'ai Shōsetsu: Hen'ai Zadan*." *Gunzō* 69: 10 (2014): 53–68.

Kitamura, Tōkoku. "Iki wo Ronjite Kyara-makura ni Oyobu." In *Gendai Nihon Bungaku Zenshū*. Vol. 9 *Higuchi Ichiyō shū Kitamura Tōkoku shū*, 151–154. Tokyo: Kaizōsha, 1931.

Kitayama, Osamu. *Prohibition of Don't Look: Living through Psychoanalysis and Culture in Japan*. Tokyo: Iwasaki Gakujutsu Shuppansha, 2010.

Klein, Melanie. "A Contribution to the Psychogenesis of Manic-Depressive States." *The Selected Melanie Klein*. Edited by Juliet Mitchell, 115–145. New York: The Free Press, 1987.

Klein, Melanie. "Notes on Some Schizoid Mehcanisms." In *SMK*, 175–200.

Klein, Melanie. "The Psychological Principles of Infant Analysis." In *SMK*, 57–68.

Klein, Melanie. "A Study of Envy and Gratitude." In *SMK*, 211–229.

Kleist, Heinrich von. "On the Marionette Theater." Translated by Christian-Albrecht Gollub. In *German Romantic Criticism*. Edited by A. Leslie Wilson, 238–244. New York: Continuum, 1982.

Kohon, Gregorio. "The Greening of Psychoanalysis: André Green in Dialogue with Gregorio Kohon." In *The Dead Mother*, 10–58.

Koide, Hiroshi. "'Kagi' to Furansu Eiga: Tanizaki Jun'ichirō no Sakuhin Seisakujō no Hitotsu no Patān." *Kokubungaku Kenkyū* 30 (1964): 78–84.

Koikari, Mire. "Gender, Power, and U.S. Imperialism: The Occupation of Japan, 1945–1952." In *Bodies in Contact: Rethinking Colonial Encounters in World History.* Edited by Tony Ballantyne and Antoinette Burton, 342–362. Durham, NC: Duke University Press, 2005.

Kōno, Taeko. *Tanizaki Bungaku to Kōtei no Yokubō*. Tokyo: Chūoh Kōronsha, 1980.

Kōno, Taeko. "Yōji gari." In *Kōno Taeko Zenshū*. Vol. 1, 7–23. Tokyo: Shinchōsha, 1994.

Kōno, Taeko. "Yoshiyuki Bungaku ni okeru Nenrei no Imi." In *Yoshiyuki Junnosuke no Kenkyū*, 133–140.

Kōno, Taeko, and Saeki, Shōichi. "Joryū Shinjin no Genzai: Taidan Jihyō." *Bungakukai* 35: 3 (1981): 194–207.

Kōno Taeko, *Toddler-Hunting: And Other Stories*. Translated by Lucy North. New York: New Directions, 2018, 45–68.

Kristeva, Julia. *Powers of Horror: An Essay on Abjection*. Translated by Leon S. Roudiez. New York: Columbia University Press, 1982.

Kuki, Shūzō. *Iki no Kōzō*. Tokyo: Iwanami Shoten, 1971.

Kumin, Ivri. *Pre-Object Relatedness: Early Attachment and the Psychoanalytic Situation.* New York and London: The Guilford Press, 1996.

Kuriyama, Shigehisa. *The Expressiveness of the Body and the Divergence of Greek and Chinese Medicine*. New York: Zone Books, 1999.

Lacan, Jacques. *The Four Fundamental Concepts of Psycho-analysis*. Edited by Jacques-Alain Miller. Translated by Alan Sheridan. Harmondsworth: Penguin Books, 1986.

Lacan, Jacques. "Nihon no Dokusha ni Yosete." In *Ecuri*. Translated by Miyamoto Tadao, Takeuchi Michiya, Takahashi Tohru, and Sasaki Takatsugu, i–v. Tokyo: Kōbundō, 1972.

LaFleur, William R. *Liquid Life: Abortion and Buddhism in Japan*. Princeton, NJ: Princeton University Press, 1992.

LaMarre, Thomas. *Shadows on the Screen: Tanizaki Jun'ichirō on Cinema and "Oriental" Aesthetics.* Ann Arbor: The Center for Japanese Studies, the University of Michigan, 2005.

Laplanche, Jean, and Pontalis, Jean-Bertrand. *The Language of Psychoanalysis.* Translated by Donald Nicholson-Smith. London: Kanarc Books, 2006.

Lebra, Takie S. *The Japanese Self in Cultural Logic*. Honolulu: University of Hawai'i Press, 2004.

Levinas, Emmanuel. *Time and the Other*. Translated by Richard A. Cohen. Pittsburgh, PA: Duquesne University Press, 1987.

Levinas, Emmanuel. *Totality and Infinity: An Essay on Exteriority*. Translated by Alphonso Lingis. Pittsburgh, PA: Duquesne University Press, 1969.

Long, Margherita. "Tanizaki and the Enjoyment of Japanese Culturalism." *Positions: East Asia Cultures Critique* 10: 2 (2002): 431–469.

Long, Margherita. *This Perversion Called Love: Reading Tanizaki, Feminist Theory, and Freud*. Stanford, CA: Stanford University Press, 2009.

Mackenzie, Iain M. *The "Obscurism" of Light: A Theological Study into the Nature of Light*. Norwich: The Canterbury Press, 1996.

Maeda, Rui. "Hyakunen no Kōdoku: Matsuura Rieko, 'Kenshin' wo megutte." *Gunzō* 63: 2 (2008): 206–229.

Marinetti, F. T. "Tactilism." In *Marinetti: Selected Writings*. Edited by R. W. Flint. Translated by R. W. Flint and Arthur A. Coppotelli, 109–112. London: Secker & Warburg, 1971.

Marks, Laura. *Touch: Sensuous Theory and Multisensory Media*. Minneapolis: University of Minnesota Press, 2002.

Marran, Christine. "From Pathography to Pulp: Popular Expressions of Female Deviancy, 1930–1950." In *A Century of Popular Culture in Japan*. Edited by Douglas Slaymaker, 45–69. Lewiston, NY: The Edwin Mellen Press, 2000.

Maruya, Saiichi. "Yoshiyuki Junnosuke wo Yomu: Kōshoku to Taikutsu." In *YJZ*. Vol. 7, 461–479. Tokyo: Shinchōsha, 1998.

Marx, Karl. *Capital: A Critique of Political Economy*. Vol. 1. Translated by Ben Fowkes. London: Penguin Books, 1990.

Mathy, Jean-Philippe. "From Sign to Thing: The French Literary Avant-Garde and the Japanese Difference." In *Confluences: Postwar Japan and France*. Edited by Douglas Slaymaker, 34–48. Ann Arbor: Center for Japanese Studies, the University of Michigan, 2002.

Matsuda, Matt. "EAST OF NO WEST: The *Posthistoire* of Postwar France and Japan." In *Confluences: Postwar Japan and France*, 15–33. Ann Arbor: Center for Japanese Studies, The University of Michigan, 2002.

Matsuura, Rieko. *The Apprenticeship of Big Toe P*. Translated by Michael Emmerich. Tokyo: Kōdansha International, 2009.

Matsuura, Rieko. "Asobareru Kodomo tachi." In *Poketto Fetisshu*, 20–25. Tokyo: Hakusuisha, 2000.

Matsuura, Rieko. "Bettina Rheims Toraburu." In *Poketto Fetisshu*, 113–120. Tokyo: Hakusuisha, 2000.

Matsuura, Rieko. "<Bosei> Shinwa wa Tsumi tsukuri: Nishi Masahiko, Itō Hiromi 'Papa wa Gokigen Naname.'" In *Yasashii Kyosei no tameni*, 201–202. Tokyo: Chikuma Shobō, 1997.

Matsuura, Rieko. "For a Gentle Castration." Translated by Amanda Seaman. In *Woman Critiqued: Translated Essays on Japanese Women's Writing*. Edited by Rebecca Copeland, 194–205. Honolulu: University of Hawai'i Press, 2006.

Matsuura, Rieko. "Himantai Kyōfushō." In *Sōgi no Hi*, 155–235. Tokyo: Kawade Shobō Shinsha, 1993.

Matsuura, Rieko. "Intabyū Matsuura Rieko: Sekushuaritī no Jiko Jitsugen no tameni." *Subaru* 37: 10 (2015): 193–199.

Matsuura, Rieko. "Jean Genet, Seiki naki Nikutai." In *Yasashii Kyosei no tameni*, 163–169. Tokyo: Chikuma Shobō, 1997.

Matsuura, Rieko. "Kawaku Natsu." In *Sōgi no Hi*, 73–153. Tokyo: Kawade Shobō Shinsha, 1993.

Matsuura, Rieko. *Kenshin*. Tokyo: Asahi Shimbun Shuppan, 2010.

Matsuura, Rieko. *Kika*. Tokyo: Shinchōsha, 2012.

Matsuura, Rieko. "Kore ga Nihon no Homosōsharu." *Gunzō* 61: 5 (2006): 234–237.

Matsuura, Rieko. *Nachuraru Ūman*. Tokyo: Kawade Shobō Shinsha, 2007.

Matsuura, Rieko. *Oyayubi P no Shugyō Jidai*. Tokyo: Kawade Shobō Shinsha, 1993.
Matsuura, Rieko. "Oyayubi Penisu toha Nanika?" In *Oyayubi P no Shugyō Jidai*. Vol. 2, 325 –333.
Matsuura, Rieko. *Saiai no Kodomo*. Tokyo: Bungei Shunjū, 2017.
Matsuura, Rieko. "Seiai kara Yūai he—*Urabājon* wo megutte: Matsuura Rieko Interview." *Bungakukai* 54: 12 (2000): 250–257.
Matsuura, Rieko. "Seiki kara no Kaihō wo." In *Yasashii Kyosei no tameni*, 82–86. Tokyo: Chikuma Shobō, 1997.
Matsuura, Rieko. "Sōgi no Hi." In *Sōgi no Hi*, 7–71. Tokyo: Kawade Shobō Shinsha, 1993.
Matsuura, Rieko. "Yasashii Kyosei no tameni." In *Yasashii Kyosei no tameni*, 213–262. Tokyo: Chikuma Shobō, 1997.
Matsuura, Rieko, and Kawakami, Mieko. "Taidan Matsuura Rieko and Kawakami Mieko: Sei no Jubaku wo koete." *Bungakukai* 62: 5 (2008): 164–177.
Matsuura, Rieko, and Shōno, Yoriko. *Okaruto Odokumi Teishoku*. Tokyo: Kawade Shobō Shinsha, 1997.
Matsuura, Rieko, and Tomioka, Kōichirō. "Kikei kara no Manazashi" ["The Gaze from Deformity"]. In Matsuura Rieko, *Sebasuchan*, 187–214. Tokyo: Kawade Shobō Shinsha, 2007.
Matsuura, Rieko, and Tsumura, Kikuko. "Taidan: Mainā na Kyōdōtai no Romansu." *Bungakukai* 71: 6 (2017): 146–162.
Mauss, Marcel. "Techniques of the Body." *Economy and Society* 2: 1 (1973): 70–88.
Maynard, Patrick. *The Engine of Visualization: Thinking through Photography*. Ithaca, NY and London: Cornell University Press, 1997.
Mebed, Sharif Ramsey. "Kawabata Bungaku ni okeru Furoito Shisō no Eikyō wo meguru Ichi Kōsatsu: Jiyū Rensō kara 'Bukimi ma Mono' made." PhD Diss., Nagoya University, 2015.
Merleau-Ponty, Maurice. "The Child's Relations with Others." Translated by William Cobb. In *Primacy of Perception: And Other Essays on Phenomenological Psychology, the Philosophy of Art, History and Politics*. Edited by James M. Edie, 96–155. Evanston, IL: Northwestern University Press, 1964.
Merleau-Ponty, Maurice. "Man and Adversity." In *The Merleau-Ponty Reader*. Edited by Ted Toadvine and Leonard Lawlor, 189–240. Evanston, IL: Northwestern University Press, 2007.
Merleau-Ponty, Maurice. *Phenomenology of Perception*. Translated by Donald A. Landes. Abingdon, Oxon; New York: Routledge, 2014.
Merleau-Ponty, Maurice. *Signs*. Translated by Richard C. McCleary. Evanston, IL: Northwestern University Press, 1964.
Merleau-Ponty, Maurice. *The Structure of Behavior*. Translated by Alden L. Fisher. Pittsburgh, PA: Duquesne University Press, 2015.
Merleau-Ponty, Maurice. *The Visible and the Invisible*. Translated by Alphonso Lingis. Evanston, IL: Northwestern University Press, 1968.
Miki, Yoshiko, Hohashi, Naohiro, and Maekawa, Atsuko. "Wagakuni no Hoken Iryō Ryōiki ni okeru Sekushuaritī no Gainen Bunseki." *Nihon Kangokagaku kaishi* 33: 2 (2013): 70–79.

Mishima, Yukio. "Eien no Tabibito: Kawabata Yasunari shi no Hito to Sakuhin." In *Kindai Bungaku Kanshō Kōza: Vol. 13 Kawabata Yasunari*. Edited by Yamamoto Kenkichi, 259–269. Tokyo: Kadokawa Shoten, 1958.

Mishima, Yukio. "Introduction." In *House of the Sleeping Beauties and Other Stories*, by Kawabata Yasunari, 7–10. Tokyo: Kōdansha International, 1969.

Mishima, Yukio. "Kaisetsu." In *Nemureru Bijo* by Kawabata Yasunari, 241–248. Tokyo: Shinchōsha, 2011.

Mitchell, Juliet. "Introduction." In *SMK*, 9–32.

Mitchell, Stephen A. *Relationality: From Attachment to Intersubjectivity*. New York: Psychology Press, 2014.

Miura, Masashi. *Merankorī no Suimyaku*. Tokyo: Fukutake Shoten, 1984.

Miyao, Daisuke. *The Aesthetics of Shadow: Lighting and Japanese Cinema*. Durham, NC: Duke University Press, 2013.

Miyoshi, Yukio. *Nihon Bungaku Zenshi*. Vol. 6. Tokyo: Gakutōsha, 1978.

Mizuta, Miya Elise. "Luminous Environment: Light, Architecture and Decoration in Modern Japan." *Japan Forum* 18: 3 (2006): 339–360. https://doi.org/10.1080/09555800600947223.

Mizuta, Noriko. "In Search of a Lost Paradise: The Wandering Woman in Hayashi Fumiko's *Drifting Clouds*." In *The Woman's Hand: Gender and Theory in Japanese Women's Writing*. Edited by Paul Gordon Schalow and Janet A. Walker, 329–351 Stanford, CA: Stanford University Press, 1996.

Momose, Natsumi. "'Kenshin'-ron 1: Senkō Sakuhin Kōsatsu." *Gesuto Hausu* 4 (2012): 28–37.

Momose, Natsumi. "'Kenshin'-ron 2: Seiai-kan to Ningen-kankei no Tōtatsuten." *Gesuto Hausu*, additional volume, 4 (2012): 34–42.

Mori, Ōgai. "Kanoyōni." In *Ōgai Zenshū*. Vol. 10, 43–78. Tokyo: Iwanami Shoten, 1972.

Muñoz, José Esteban. *Disidentifications: Queers of Color and the Performance of Politics*. Minneapolis: University of Minnesota Press, 1999.

Muñoz, José Esteban. "Feeling Brown, Feeling Down: Latina Affect, the Performativity of Race, and the Depressive Position." *Signs* 31: 3 (2006), 675–688.

Murakami, Haruki. *Wakai Dokusha no tame no Tanpen Shōsetsu Annai*. Tokyo: Bungei Shunjū, 2004.

Murayama, Noriaki. "'Mise en abyme' ni kansuru Ichi Kōsatsu: Proust, Kafū, Yoshiyuki." *Senshū Daigaku Hokkaidō Tanki Daigaku Kiyō* 37 (2004): 49–62.

Nagai, Yoshikazu. *Shakō Dansu to Nihonjin*. Tokyo: Shōbunsha, 1991.

Nagaike, Kazumi. "Matsuura Rieko's *The Reverse Version*: The Theme of 'Girl-Addressing-Girl' and Male Homosexual Fantasies. In *Girl Reading Girl in Japan*. Edited by Tomoko Aoyama and Barbara Hartley, 107–118. Abingdon: Oxon, 2010.

Naitō, Chizuko. *Shōsetsu no Ren'ai Kanshoku*. Tokyo: Misuzu Shobō, 2010.

Nancy, Jean-Luc. *Corpus*. Translated by Richard A. Rand. New York: Fordham University Press, 2008.

Nancy, Jean-Luc. *The Fall of Sleep*. Translated by Charlotte Mandell. New York: Fordham University Press, 2009.

Nancy, Jean-Luc. *Noli Me Tangere: On the Raising of the Body*. Translated by Sarah Clift, Pascale-Anne Brault, and Michael Naas. New York: Fordham University Press, 2008.

Nancy, Jean-Luc. *The Sense of the World*. Translated by Jeffrey S. Librett. Minneapolis: University of Minnesota Press, 1997.

Napier, Susan J. *The Fantastic in Modern Japanese Literature: The Subversion of Modernity*. London: Routledge, 1996.

Ngai, Sianne. *Ugly Feelings*. Cambridge, MA: Harvard University Press, 2005.

Nihon Daijiten Kankōkai. *Nihon Kokugo Daijiten*. Vol. 11. Tokyo: Shōgakukan, 1972.

Nishihara, Daisuke. "Said, Orientalism, and Japan." *Alif: Journal of Comparative Poetics* 25 (2005): 241–253. www.jstor.org/stable/4047459.

Nishizono, Masahisa. "Culture, Psychopathology, and Psychotherapy: Changes Observed in Japan." In *Asian Culture and Psyhchotherapy: Implications for East and West*. Edited by Wen-Shing Tseng, Suk Choo Chang, and Masahisa Nishizono, 40–54. Honolulu: University of Hawai'i Press, 2005.

Noe, Keiichi. "Phenomenology in Japan: Its Inception and Blossoming." *The Bloomsbury Research Handbook of Contemporary Japanese Philosophy*. Edited by Michiko Yusa, 23–39. London: Bloomsbury Publishing, 2019.

Nosaka, Akiyuki. "Shunkinshō." In *Kokubungaku: Kaishaku to Kyōzai no Kenkyū* 23: 10 (1978), 90–91.

Ochiai, Emiko. *The Japanese Family System in Transition: A Sociological Analysis of Family Change in Postwar Japan*. Tokyo: LTCB International Library Foundation, 1997.

Ōe, Kenzaburō. *Japan, the Ambiguous, and Myself: The Nobel Prize Speech and Other Lectures*. New York: Kōdansha International, 1995.

Ogawa, Yōko. *Mīna no Kōshin*. Tokyo: Chūoh Kōron Shinsha, 2009.

Ogura, Chikako. "Neotenī no Fukushū." *Bungei* 32: 4 (1993): 95–98.

Ohno, Ryōji. "Tanizaki Jun'ichirō 'Kagi' ni okeru 'Dokusha' no Yōsō (<Tokushū> Henyō suru Dokusha ron, Dokusho ron)." *Nihon Bungaku* 52: 1 (2003): 30–39.

Ohtaki, Kazuo. "Yoshiyuki Junnosuke no Byōseki: Utsu no Imi ni tsuite." *Byōseki shi* 37 (1989): 49–55.

Oka, Fukuko. "Katoki no Dorama." In *Yoshiyuki Junnosuke no Kenkyū*, 180–187.

Okonogi, Keigo. "Psychoanalysis in Japan." In *Freud and the Far East: Psychoanalytic Perspectives on the People and Culture of China, Japan, and Korea*. Edited by Salman Akhtar, 9–25. Lanham, MD: Jason Aronson, 2009.

Ōkubo, Takaki. "Kōki Kawabata Yasunari Sakuhin no Nisō (2) 'Kataude.'" *Tokyo Jyoshi Daigaku Kiyō Ronshū* 34: 1 (1983): 73–88.

Ozawa, Takeshi. *Bakumatsu, Meiji no Shashin*. Tokyo: Chikuma Shobō, 2010.

Paterson, Mark. *The Sense of Touch: Haptics, Affects and Technologies*. Oxford, New York: Berg, 2007.

Paulhan, Jean. "A Slave's Revolt: An Essay on *The Story of O*." In Pauline Réage, *Story of O*, 265–287. London: Corgi Book, 1972.

Proust, Marcel. *The Way by Swann's. In Search of Lost Time*. Vol. 1. Translated by Lydia Davis. London: Penguin Books, 2002.

Réage, Pauline. *Story of O*. London: Corgi Book, 1972 [1970].

Rimer, J. Thomas. *Modern Japanese Fiction and its Traditions: An Introduction*. Princeton, NJ: Princeton University Press, 1978.

Roach, Joseph. *Cities of the Dead: Circum-Atlantic Performance*. New York: Columbia University Press, 1996.

Roquet, Paul. *Ambient Media: Japanese Atmospheres of Self*. Minneapolis: University of Minnesota Press, 2016.

Saeki, Junko. Iro *to* Ai *no Hikaku Bunkashi*. Tokyo: Iwanami Shoten, 2000.

Saeki, Shōichi. "Katari no Miwaku." In Tanizaki Jun'ichirō, *Mōmoku Monogatari, Shunkinshō*, 211–220. Tokyo: Iwanami Shoten, 1986.

Saitō, Shinnosuke. "Yoshiyuki Junnosuke no Yūutsu: Utsu byō ni yoru Sōzō to Sōshitsu ni tsuite." *Byōseki shi* 91 (2016): 7–19.

Saitō, Shinnosuke, and Kobayashi, Toshiyuki. "Yoshiyuki Junnosuke no Byōseki: Schizoid Pāsonaritī no Chiryō no Ba toshite no Bungaku." *Byōseki shi* 89 (2015): 35–45.

Saitō, Tamaki. *Hikikomori Bunkaron*. Tokyo: Kinokuniya Shoten, 2003.

Sakaguchi, Ango. "Discourse on Decadence. Translated by Seiji Lippit. *Review of Japanese Culture and Society* 1: 1 (October 1986): 1–5.

Sakaguchi, Ango. "Nikutai Jitai ga Shikō suru." In *Sakaguchi Ango Zenshū*. Vol. 4, 268–269. Tokyo: Chikuma Shobō, 1998.

Sakaki, Atsuko. "Tanizaki Jun'ichirō, or Photography as Violence." *Japan Forum* 22: 3–4 (2010): 381–404. https://doi.org/10.1080/09555803.2010.534839.

Samuel, Yoshiko Yokochi. "The Apprenticeship of Big Toe P." *World Literature Today* 84: 4 (2010): 64–65. www.jstor.org/stable/27871146.

Sartre, Jean-Paul. *Being and Nothingness: An Essay on Phenomenological Ontology*. Translated by Hazel E. Barnes. Abingdon: Routledge, 2003.

Sas, Miryam. *Experimental Arts in Postwar Japan: Moments of Encounter, Engagement, and Imagined Return*. Cambridge, MA: Harvard University Asia Center, 2011.

Satō, Mioko. "Tanizaki Jun'ichirō 'Aozuka shi no Hanashi' ni okeru Eiga no Isō: Eiga Seisaku/Juyō wo meguru Yokubō no Arika." *Nihon Kindai Bungaku* 91 (2014): 49–62. https://doi.org/10.19018/nihonkindaibungaku.91.0_49.

Schechner, Richard. *The Future of Ritual: Writings on Culture and Performance*. London: Routledge, 1993.

Segal, Naomi. *Consensuality: Didier Anzieu, Gender and the Sense of Touch*. Amsterdam and New York: Rodopi, 2009.

Seigworth, Gregory J, and Gregg, Melissa. "An Inventory of Shimmers." In *The Affect Theory Reader*. Edited by Melissa Gregg and Gregory J. Seigworth, 1–25. Durham, NC: Duke UP, 2010.

Sekine, Eiji. *"Tasha" no Shōkyo: Yoshiyuki Junnosuke to Kindai Bungaku*. Tokyo: Keisō Shobō, 1993.

Sekine, Eiji. "Tekusuto no Kōzō Bunseki III: Yoshiyuki Junnosuke 'The Dark Room' – sono Shūkyōsei." *Baikō Jogakuin Daigaku Ronshū* 16 (1983): 17–36.

Seremetakis, C. Nadia. "The Memory of the Senses, Part I: Marks of the Transitory." In *The Senses Still: Perception and Memory as Material Culture in Modernity*. Edited by C. Nadia Seremetakis, 1–18. Chicago, IL and London: The University of Chicago Press, 1994.

Shibusawa, Tatsuhiko. *Homo Erotikusu*. Tokyo: Gendai Shichōsha, 1967.

Shibusawa, Tatsuhiko. "Tanizaki Jun'ichirō to Mazohizumu." *Kokubungaku: Kaishaku to Kyōzai no Kenkyū* 23: 10 (1978), 6–12.

Shingū, Kazushige. "Freud, Lacan and Japan." In *Perversion and Modern Japan: Psychoanalysis, Literature, Culture.* Edited by Nina Cornyetz and J. Keith Vincent, 261–271. London: Routledge, 2010.

The Shin Kokinshū: The 13th-century Anthology Edited by Imperial Edict. Translated by Honda Heihachirō. Tokyo: Hokuseidō Press, 1970.

Shirakawa, Masayoshi. "Yoshiyuki Junnosuke: Sei no Dandism." *Kokubungaku* 39: 14 (1974): 126–133.

Siebers, Tobin. *Disability Theory.* Ann Arbor: University of Michigan Press, 2008.

Silverberg, Miriam. *Erotic, Grotesque, Nonsense: The Mass Culture of Japanese Modern Times.* Berkeley: University of California Press, 2006.

Slaymaker, Douglas N. *The Body in Postwar Japanese Fiction.* London: Routledge Curzon, 2004.

Slaymaker, Douglas. "Sartre's Fiction in Postwar Japan." In *Confluences: Postwar Japan and France,* 86–109. Ann Arbor: Center for Japanese Studies, The University of Michigan, 2002.

Sone, Hiroyoshi. "Furoito no Shōkai to Eikyō: Shin Shinrishugi Seiritsu no Haikei." In *Shōwa Bungakushi no Shomondai.* Edited by Shōwa Bungaku Kenkyūkai, 77–100. Tokyo: Kasama Shoin, 1979.

Starrs, Roy. *Soundings in Time: The Fictive Art of Kawabata Yasunari.* Richmond: Japan Library, 1998.

Stewart, Harold. *Michael Balint: Object Relations Pure and Applied.* London: Routledge, 1996.

Suzuki, Tomi. "Jendā Ekkyō no Miwaku to Mazohizumu Bigaku: Tanizaki Shokisakuhin ni okeru Engekiteki, Eigateki Kairaku." In *Tanizaki Jun'ichirō: Kyōkai wo koete,* 26–54.

Suzuki, Tomi. *Narrating the Self: Fictions of Japanese Modernity.* Stanford, CA: Stanford University Press, 1996.

Tahhan, Diana Adis. "Blurring the Boundaries between Bodies: Skinship and Bodily Intimacy in Japan." Japanese Studies 30: 2 (2010): 215–230.

Tahhan, Diana Adis. *The Japanese Family: Touch, Intimacy and Feeling.* Abingdon: Routledge, 2014.

Takahara, Eiri. "Kawabata Yasunari no Shōnen Ryōiki." *Kokubungaku* 46: 4 (2001): 104–114.

Takahashi, Takako. "Ningyō Ai." In *Takahashi Takako Jisen Shōsetsu shū.* Vol. 4, 387–427. Tokyo: Kōdansha, 1994.

Takahashi, Takako. *Sora no Hate made.* Tokyo: Shinchōsha, 1973.

Takahashi, Takako, Kawamura, Jirō, and Ōhashi, Kenzaburō. "Dai 37kai Sōsaku Gappyō." *Gunzō* 34: 1 (1979): 337–356.

Takayama, Hiroshi. "'Bukimi na Monoga…' Kawabata Gensō Bungaku no Atarashisa: 'Kataude' 'Nemureru Bijo' ni Furete." *Kokubungaku* 46: 4 (March 2001): 78–85.

Tamura, Taijirō. "Nikutai ga Ningen de aru." In *Tamura Taijirō Senshū.* Edited by Hata Masahiro and Onishi Yasumitsu. Vol. 5, 187–191. Tokyo: Nihon Tosho Sentā, 2005.

Tanaka, Kazuo. "Kazoku Shōsetsu no Genzai." *Gunzō* 61: 5 (2006): 190–232.

Tanizaki, Jun'ichirō. "Aozuka shi no Hanashi." In *Tanizaki Jun'ichirō Zenshū.* Vol. 14, 9–50. Tokyo: Chūoh Kōronsha, 2016.

Tanizaki, Jun'ichirō. "'Caligari Hakase' wo miru." In *TJZ*. Vol. 8, 452–456. Tokyo: Chūoh Kōronsha, 2017.

Tanizaki, Jun'ichirō. "The Children." Translated by Anthony H. Chambers. In *The Gourmet Club: A Sextet*. Translated by Anthony H. Chambers and Paul McCarthy, 7–37. Ann Arbor: University of Michigan Press, 2017.

Tanizaki, Jun'ichirō. *Diary of a Mad Old Man*. Translated by Howard Hibbett. London: Vintage Books, 2000.

Tanizaki, Jun'ichirō. "Eiga no Tekunikku." In *TJZ*. Vol. 8, 460–466. Tokyo: Chūoh Kōronsha.

Tanizaki, Jun'ichirō. "Fumiko no Ashi." In *TJZ*. Vol. 6, 235–268. Tokyo: Chūoh Kōronsha, 2015.

Tanizaki, Jun'ichirō. "Jōzetsuroku." In *TJZ*. Vol. 12, 287–372. Tokyo: Chūoh Kōronsha, 2017.

Tanizaki, Jun'ichirō. "Kagi." In *TJZ*. Vol. 22, 91–207. Tokyo: Chūoh Kōronsha, 2017.

Tanizaki, Jun'ichirō. *The Key*. Translated by Howard Hibbett. London: Vintage Books, 2004.

Tanizaki, Jun'ichirō. "Mr. Bluemound." Translated by Paul McCarthy. In *The Gourmet Club*, 123–160.

Tanizaki, Jun'ichirō. *Naomi*. Translated by Anthony H. Chambers. New York: Vintage International, 2001 [1985].

Tanizaki, Jun'ichirō. "Nihon ni okeru Kurippun Jiken." In *TJZ*. Vol. 13, 9–21. Tokyo: Chūoh Kōronsha, 2015.

Tanizaki, Jun'ichirō. *In Praise of Shadows*. Translated by Thomas J. Harper and Edward G. Seidensticker. London: Vintage Books, 2001.

Tanizaki, Jun'ichirō. "A Portrait of Shunkin." In *Seven Japanese Tales*. Translated by Howard Hibbett, 3–84. New York: Vintage International, 2001.

Tanizaki, Jun'ichirō. "Shisei." In *TJZ*. Vol. 1, 9–17. Tokyo: Chūoh Kōronsha, 2015.

Tanizaki, Jun'ichirō. "Shōnen." In *TJZ*. Vol. 1, 35–70. Tokyo: Chūoh Kōronsha, 2015.

Tanizaki, Jun'ichirō. *Some Prefer Nettles*. Translated by E. G. Seidensticker. London: Vintage Books, 2001.

Tanizaki, Jun'ichirō. "Tadekuu Mushi." In *TJZ*. Vol. 14, 53–217. Tokyo: Chūoh Kōronsha.

Tanizaki, Jun'ichirō. "The Tattooer." In *Seven Japanese Tales*. Translated by Howard Hibbett, 160–169. New York: Vintage International, 2001.

Tayama, Katai. "The Quilt." In *The Quilt and Other Stories by Tayama Katai*. Translated by Kenneth G. Henshall, 35–96. Tokyo: University of Tokyo Press, 1981.

Tomkins, Silvan. *Shame and its Sisters: A Silvan Tomkins Reader*. Edited by Eve Kosofsky Sedgwick and Adam Frank. Durham, NC: Duke University Press, 1995.

Traina, Cristina L. H. *Erotic Attunement: Parenthood and the Ethics of Sensuality between Unequals*. Chicago, IL and London: University of Chicago Press, 2013 [2011]. https://doi.org/10.7208/chicago/9780226811376.001.0001.

Treat, John Whittier. "Yoshimoto Banana Writes Home: Shojo Culture and the Nostalgic Subject." *Journal of Japanese Studies* 19: 2 (1993), 353–387.

Tsuboi, Hideto. "Itō Hiromi ron (ge)." *Nihon Bungaku* 39: 4 (1990), 22–33.

Tsuboi, Hideto. "Odoru Shōjo, Kaku Shōjo: Dōyō Buyō, Tsudurikata, Sonota." *Nihon Kindai Bungaku* 72 (2005): 87–102.

Tsuboi, Hideto. *Sei ga Kataru: 20 Seiki Nihon Bungaku no Sei to Shintai*. Nagoya: Nagoya Daigaku Shuppankai, 2012.

Tsujimoto, Chizu. "*Nachuraru Ūman* Shiron." *Gengobunka Ronsō* 6 (2012): 77–87.

Tsujimoto, Chizu. "Yama no Oto ron: Sono Ai no Yōsō." *Ronkyū Nihon Bungaku* 50 (1987): 57–67.

Ueno, Chizuko. "In the Feminine Guise: A Trap of Reverse Orientalism." In *Contemporary Japanese Thought*. Edited by Richard F. Calichman, 225–245. New York: Columbia University Press, 2005.

Ueno, Chizuko, Ogura, Chikako, and Tomioka, Taeko. *Danryū Bungakuron*. Tokyo: Chikuma Shobō, 1992.

Vasseleu, Cathryn. *Textures of Light: Vision and Touch in Irigaray, Levinas and Merleau-Ponty*. London: Routledge, 1998.

Vincent, J. Keith. *Two-Timing Modernity: Homosocial Narrative in Modern Japanese Fiction*. Cambridge, MA: Harvard University Asia Center, 2012.

Vlastos, Stephen. "Tradition: Past/Present Culture and Modern Japanese History." In *Mirror of Modernity: Invented Traditions of Modern Japan*. Edited by Stephen Vlastos, 1–16. Berkeley and London: University of California Press, 1998.

Watanabe, Naomi. "Byōsha to Yokubō: Mazohisto (Shōsetsuka) Tanizani Jun'ichirō." *Shinchō* 87: 6 (1990): 191–211.

Watanabe, Naomi. *Tanizaki Jun'ichirō: Gitai no Yūwaku*. Tokyo: Shinchōsha, 1992.

Watkin, Christopher. *Phenomenology or Deconstruction? The Question of Ontology in Maurice Merleau-Ponty, Paul Ricœur and Jean-Luc Nancy*. Edinburgh: Edinburgh University Press, 2009.

Wei, Chen. "Kawabata Yasunari to *Tsudurikata*: Senjichū no Teikokushugi to Tsunagaru Kairo." *JunCture: Chōikiteki Nihon Bunka Kenkyū* 5 (2014): 104–113.

Williams, Raymond. *Marxism and Literature*. Oxford: Oxford University Press, 1989.

Williams, Simon J. *Sleep and Society: Sociological Ventures into the (Un)known ….* Abingdon: Routledge, 2005.

Winnicott, Donald. W. *Playing and Reality*. London: Routledge, 2005.

Wright, M. R, ed. *Empedocles: The Extant Fragments*. New Haven, NJ and London: Yale University Press, 1981.

Yamaguchi, Hajime. *Hifu Kankaku no Fushigi: "Hifu" to "Kokoro" no Shintai Shinri gaku*. Tokyo: Kōdansha, 2016.

Yamamoto, Kenkichi. "Kinjū" (112–141), "Kawabata Yasunari: 'Hito to Sakuhin' Josetsu" (5–22), and "Yama no Oto" (202–238). In *Kindai Bungaku Kanshō Kōza*. Edited by Yamamoto Kenkichi. Vol. 13. Tokyo: Kadokawa Shoten, 1958.

Yamazaki, Masakazu. "Kōritsuita Waisetsu: Rekishi no Kiretsu II." *Shinchō* 76: 9 (1979): 174–194.

Yashiro, Masako. "Shīkuretto Rabu." In *Yashiro Masako Meisaku Shirīzu 3 Shikuretto Rabu*, 5–33. Tokyo: Asahi Sonorama, 1978.

Yoda, Tomiko. "The Rise and Fall of Maternal Society: Gender, Labor, and Capital in Contemporary Japan." *The South Atlantic Quarterly* 99: 4 (Fall 2000): 865–902.

Yonaha, Keiko. "Matsuura Rieko: Ekkyō suru Sei." *Kokubungaku: Kaishaku to Kyōzai no Kenkyū* 37: 13 (1992): 129–131.

Yonaha, Keiko. "Sakka Gaido: Matsuura Rieko." In *Josei Sakka Sirīzu 21 Yamada Eimi, Masuda Mizuko, Matsuura Rieko, Shōno Yoriko*. Edited by Kōno Taeko, Ōba Minako, Satō Aiko, and Tsumura Setsuko, 460–462. Tokyo: Kadokawa Shoten, 1999.

Yosano, Akiko. "Pari yori." In *Teihon Yosano Akiko Zenshū*. Vol. 20, 529–612. Tokyo: Kōdansha, 1981.

Yoshiyuki, Junnosuke. "Anshitsu." In *YJZ*. Vol. 7, 136–342. Tokyo: Shinchōsha, 1998.

Yoshiyuki, Junnosuke. "Bara Hanbai nin." In *YJZ*. Vol. 1, 7–34. Tokyo: Shinchōsha, 1997.

Yoshiyuki, Junnosuke. "Birds, Beasts, Insects and Fish." Translated by Maryellen Toman Mori. *Japan Quarterly* 28: 1 (1981): 91–102.

Yoshiyuki, Junnosuke. "Chōjūchūgyo." In *YJZ*. Vol. 2, 60–89. Tokyo: Shinchōsha, 1997.

Yoshiyuki, Junnosuke. *The Dark Room*. Translated by John Bester. New York: Kōdansha International, 1979 [1975].

Yoshiyuki, Junnosuke. "Funabashi Seiichi Shōron." In *YJZ*. Vol. 12, 233–241. Tokyo: Shinchōsha, 1998.

Yoshiyuki, Junnosuke. "Genshoku no Machi." In *YJZ*. Vol. 5, 7–101. Tokyo: Shinchōsha, 1998.

Yoshiyuki, Junnosuke. "Hoshi to Tsuki ha Ten no Ana." In *YJZ*. Vol. 7, 7–135.

Yoshiyuki, Junnosuke. "In Akiko's Room." Translated by Howard Hibbett. *Contemporary Japanese Literature: An Anthology of Fiction, Film, and Other Writing since 1945*. Edited by Howard Hibbett, 401–411. Boston, MA: Cheng & Tsui Company, 2005 [1977].

Yoshiyuki, Junnosuke. "Katsushika." In *YJZ*. Vol. 4, 254–274. Tokyo: Shinchōsha, 1998.

Yoshiyuki, Junnosuke. "Katsushika Ward." Translated by Lawrence Rogers. In *Fair Dalliance: Fifteen Stories by Yoshiyuki Junnosuke*. Edited by Lawrence Rogers, 155–171. Kumamoto: Kurodahan Press, 2011.

Yoshiyuki, Junnosuke. "Kawabata Yasunari den Danpen." In *YJZ*. Vol. 12, 347–377.

Yoshiyuki, Junnosuke. "My Bed is a Boat." Translated by Lawrence Rogers. In *Fair Dalliance*, 1–13.

Yoshiyuki, Junnosuke. "Nedai no Fune." In *YJZ*. Vol. 2, 31–45.

Yoshiyuki, Junnosuke. "Otoko to Onna no Ko." In *YJZ*. Vol. 5, 235–348.

Yoshiyuki, Junnosuke. "Sasai na Koto." In *YJZ*. Vol. 8, 242–252. Tokyo: Kōdansha, 1971.

Yoshiyuki, Junnosuke. "Shimetta Sora, Kawaita Sora." In *YJZ*. Vol. 8, 115–236. Tokyo: Shinchōsha, 1998.

Yoshiyuki, Junnosuke. "Shōfu no Heya." In *YJZ*. Vol. 2, 7–30.

Yoshiyuki, Junnosuke. "Shūu." In *YJZ*. Vol. 1, 93–118.

Yoshiyuki, Junnosuke. "Sudden Shower." Translated by Geoffrey Bownas. *Japan Quarterly* 19: 4 (1972): 446–457.

Yoshiyuki, Junnosuke. "Suna no Ue no Shokubutsu gun." In *YJZ*. Vol. 6, 105–285. Tokyo: Shinchōsha, 1998.

Yoshiyuki, Junnosuke. "Watashi ha Naze Kakuka?" In *YJZ*. Vol. 8, 252–258. Tokyo: Kōdansha, 1971.

Yoshiyuki, Junnosuke. "Watashi no Bungaku Hōrō." In *YJZ*. Vol. 8, 7–114.

Yoshiyuki, Junnosuke. "Yami no Naka no Shukusai." In *YJZ*. Vol. 6, 7–104.

Yoshiyuki, Junnosuke. "Yūgure made." In *YJZ*. Vol. 7, 343–460.

Film

Air Doll. Directed by Kore'eda Hirokazu. 2009. Tokyo: Bandai Visual, 2010. DVD.

Blind Beast. Directed by Matsuura Yasuzō. 1969. Tokyo: Kadokawa Herald Pictures. DVD.

In the Realm of the Senses. Directed by Ōshima Nagisa. 1976. Tokyo: Tōhō, 2000. DVD.

A Woman Called Abe Sada. Directed by Tanaka Noboru. 1975. Tokyo: Nikkatsu. DVD.

Seishin. Directed by Sōda Kazuhiro. 2008. Tokyo: Kinokuniya Shoten, 2010. DVD.

Performance

Shōnen. The Yasunari Kawabata Trilogy. Produced by Mirei Yamagata. Directed by Liang Yen Liu and performed by Kawaguchi Takao. Tokyo, Taipei, and Shanghai in 2012–2014.

Shun'kin. A Complicité co-production with Setagaya Public Theatre and barbican-bite09. Directed by Simon MacBurney. Premiere at Setagaya Public Theatre, 2008.

Index